# The Crime Scene
## Criminalistics, Science, and Common Sense

**Malcolm R. Greenshields**
*University of Lethbridge*

**Gordon D. Scheurman**
*Lethbridge Community College*

Prentice
Hall

Toronto

**Canadian Cataloguing in Publication Data**

Greenshields, Malcolm
    The crime scene : criminalistics, science, and common sense

Includes bibliographical references and index.
ISBN 0-13-085116-7

1. Crime scene searches – Canada. 2. Forensic sciences – Canada. I. Scheurman, Gordon, 1950- . II. Title.

HV8073.G73 2001                 363.25                 C00-931822-4

ISBN 0-13-085116-7

Vice President, Editorial Director: Michael Young
Editor-in-Chief: David Stover
Senior Marketing Manager: Sophia Fortier
Developmental Editor: Madhu Ranadive
Associate Editor: Susan Ratkaj
Production Editor: David Peebles
Copy Editor: Rodney Rawlings
Production Coordinator: Wendy Moran
Page Layout: Nelson Gonzalez
Art Director: Julia Hall
Cover Design: Amy Harnden
Cover Image: PhotoDisc

17 18 19 DPC 09 08 07


Printed and bound in Canada.

# Contents

## Chapter 5:  The Forensic Laboratory and Forensic Science   48

## Chapter 6:  Fingerprints   73

## Chapter 7:  Impressions    100

## Chapter 8:  Firearms and Ammunition  143

# Preface

This book is designed to fulfill the need for a concise, practical manual in criminalistics for those involved in law enforcement, whether they are students of the subject or professionals in the field. We have tried to avoid overly theoretical discussion in favour of clear explanations. Rather than attempting to provide extensive information on every aspect of forensic science, the book concentrates on the detection, gathering, preservation, and presentation of physical evidence. It is a guide to the management of crime scenes.

Laboratory analysis is also described insofar as it is instructive to the officer who must gather and prepare evidence for submission and interpret the results of analysis as they pertain to particular offences. It is important that officers understand the analytical possibilities of the evidence collected and hence the necessity for preventing its contamination and destruction.

It is hoped that this book will help to ensure a more professional approach to problems of evidence and proof so crucial to the administration of justice.

# Acknowledgments

The persons from every province in Canada and from the United States, the United Kingdom, and elsewhere who contributed their expertise to this book are too numerous to mention individually. We can only name some major contributors and give our heartfelt thanks to the rest. Alberta Crown Prosecutor Vaughan Hartigan generously contributed what essentially became the last chapter. Police services, police officers, forensic specialists, and related persons and groups across Canada were ready to assist with information and materials.

Among organizations, we must particularly thank the RCMP and its Forensic Services for permission to use manuals and other materials; the police and fire services from Calgary, Saskatoon, and Lethbridge for numerous photographs; and the Canadian Firearms Centre for its illustrations. The Canadian Police College and the University of Lethbridge gave us assistance and information, as did the police services from a number of cities and provinces—Ottawa, Toronto, Halifax, and Quebec to name but a few of the most prominent.

The individuals who have been particularly helpful include B. Yamashita of the RCMP Forensic Identification Research Section, Lee Fraser from RCMP headquarters, Glenn Carroll of the Canadian Police Research Centre, Larry Fender of Lethbridge Community College, and David Greenshields. Among the many helpful members of city police services, W. Basso of Lethbridge, J. Edwards of Calgary, and J. Penney of Saskatoon gave us assistance far beyond the call of duty. Deb Beaton gave invaluable research assistance, and the editorial staff at Pearson Education provided sound advice. Finally, we must thank Mrs. Charlene Sawatsky, who deciphered hundreds of manuscript pages without complaint.

Despite all this generous expert assistance, there may be errors or omissions in this book, and those are entirely our own.

M. Greenshields
G. Scheurman

# INTRODUCTION: JUSTICE SYSTEMS, PROFESSIONALISM, AND COMMON SENSE

**Criminalistics** is an applied science for the analysis of physical evidence. The term **forensic science** is also sometimes used to describe the activities of criminalists. Although many police departments and other enforcement services usually have personnel extensively trained in forensic identification, almost all police officers and many others will at some time deal with physical evidence. It is crucial therefore that all investigative personnel be able to recognize and understand the importance of physical or "real" evidence, which is often regarded as having more weight in criminal procedure than testimony. Memories may fade, after all, but physical evidence, for the most part, does not. Officers dealing with evidence must be aware of the necessity of preserving a crime scene intact and may require a basic knowledge of how to gather and present physical evidence. It is hoped that readers will learn the fundamental principles of criminalistics.

If you remember only one principle, it should be the first and most important idea concerning a crime scene, the **Principle of Alteration**: *Everyone who enters a crime scene changes it and is changed by it.*

While the changes may not always be detected, they can affect the outcome of an investigation. This idea was first clearly expressed in the early twentieth century by the French scientist Edmond Locard and is often called **Locard's Exchange Principle**. Locard's theory was basically that every time a person enters a place or makes contact with another individual or thing, he or she leaves something behind and also takes something away from the point of contact. The criminalist today can detect trace evidence and transient evidence that would have remained invisible

1

only a few years ago; the steadily developing technology of detection may soon enable us to detect what is now unimaginable. This constant evolution of techniques in criminalistics makes the principle of crime-scene alteration more important with every passing year.

The following chapters will first take you to a crime scene, discuss the problem of recognizing it as such, and recommend the best method of safely approaching and managing it. The second and third chapters will discuss what to look for at the scene and how to look for it, introducing you to the types of evidence, some basic investigative equipment, and the recognition, collection, presentation, continuity, and legal admissibility of evidence. In Chapter 4 you will learn about processing the crime scene and the principle of identification, as well as methods of handling and recording the scene. Chapter 5 will provide you with information on laboratory submissions and an introduction to the way in which a variety of sciences contribute to the analysis of physical evidence. Subsequent chapters will examine in more detail the types of physical evidence as they relate to the crime scene. The successful conclusion to an investigation often occurs in a court of law, and the presentation of evidence in court will be the subject of the final chapter.

# THE EVOLUTION OF MODERN POLICING AND POLICE ETHICS

Police officers in a democracy are citizens empowered by their fellow citizens to help preserve the peace, order, liberty, and security that we consider essential. As officers of the courts, they must be devoted to the cause of truth. Unlike judges and juries, however, they are not "triers of fact," but rather they gather and present the evidence that may help to establish innocence or guilt. No matter how often the police may be viewed as partisan in difficult situations, it is their professional duty to remain objective, unbiased, and truthful in their work. There is a human tendency in most endeavours to select the evidence that confirms a prejudice or theory. But in police science the goal must always be to gather all the evidence, rather than to convict or to exonerate. Otherwise police investigations could not be considered scientific.

In addition to the necessity of seeking objective truth, police officers are upholders of the rule of law; they must practise within the law themselves when acquiring and presenting evidence. Police services are of necessity constantly in the public eye. They are observed minutely in all their activities. The popular culture of films, television, and books provides a steady critique of police practices and personnel. It is important therefore not only that officers act with professional objectivity but also that they are seen to do so.

Visible professionalism in law enforcement is essential. This means that all your conduct, down to what may seem inconsequential details, is important. You may later be judged on attitudes and actions of which you were scarcely conscious in the heat of the moment. So it is best to develop habits of honesty, objectivity, human empathy, and an imaginative and creative approach to the job at hand. The character and behaviour of a law enforcement officer can critically affect the outcome of a case. This is particularly true when presenting evidence, a duty for which honesty and clarity are absolute necessities. It is important, for example, that an officer gather and present all of the evidence, whether it "hurts" or "helps" the accused. The honest presentation, by an officer with a reputation for professional integrity, of evidence that seems to favour the accused will often increase the weight of negative evidence which follows it, and vice versa. It is also essential to present evidence for which you may have no explanation; others sitting in judgement may find it important and in fact understandable. The truth is therefore practical as well as ethical; its constant use will make you a more effective, credible law enforcement officer, and enhance the reputation of your profession generally.

## The Law Enforcement Officer's Code of Ethics

The reputation of police services has been won gradually over time. The desired character of the law enforcement professional is extensively described in the following code of ethics from the International Association of Chiefs of Police:

All Members shall abide by the following Law Enforcement Officers' Code of Ethics:

As a Law Enforcement Officer I recognize that my primary obligation is to service the public effectively and efficiently by protecting lives and property, preventing and detecting offences, and preserving peace and order. I will faithfully administer the law in a just, impartial, and responsible manner, preserving the equality, rights and privileges of citizens as afforded by law.

I accept that all persons rich or poor, old or young, learned or illiterate, are equally entitled to courtesy, understanding, and compassion. I will not be disparaging of any race, creed or class of people.

In the performance of my duties I acknowledge the limits of my authority and promise not to use it for my personal advantage. I vow never to accept gratuities or favours or compromise myself or the Department in any way. I will conduct my public and private life as an example of stability, fidelity, morality, and without equivocation adhere to the same standards of conduct which I am bound by duty to enforce.

I will exercise self-discipline at all times. I will act with propriety toward my associates in law enforcement and the criminal justice system. With self-confidence, decisiveness, and courage I will accept all the challenges, hardships, and vicissitudes of my profession. In relationships with my colleagues I will endeavour to develop an "esprit de corps."

I will preserve the dignity of all persons and subordinate my own self-interests for the common good. I will be faithful in my allegiance to Queen and Country. I will honour the obligations of my office and strive to attain excellence in the performance of my duties.

## The Development of Police Services

To understand the position of police officers today, it is useful to look at the evolution of professional police investigation. Police services as we know them now are of relatively recent origin. In both Canada and the United States the formation of police forces was influenced by British traditions. In Britain, while villages often had constables, and towns and cities the night watch, before the nineteenth century in most places there were no unified police organizations above the level of the church parish. In fact, the idea of a larger organized police was widely regarded as a dangerous one. While the British wanted to protect their lives and property, it was commonly thought that a unified, permanent force of policemen would threaten the privacy and liberty of individuals. The prevention and investigation of crimes and the apprehension of offenders were consequently dependent on the watchfulness of local people and investigations by magistrates and their employees. In cases of serious disorder, the army could be called in.

France, whose royal government had formed a national mounted police force in the early 1500s, was used by the British as an example of the oppression that could result from police forces that were too extensive. But the reality was probably that most investigations in France were also carried out by judges and subordinate officers of the court. Many people in France seldom if ever saw a police officer and, as it was elsewhere, the vigilance of local people was the main preventer and detector of crime. In order for organized police services such as those of today to become acceptable it was necessary for officers to establish a reputation for fairness, honesty, and professional competence. And despite the current acceptance of the police, the historic tendencies towards the fear of police oppression and the dependence of police officers on the help of fellow citizens are still with us today in the constant examination of police actions and the emphasis on community policing.

Worries over the growth of crime and the political skill of Sir Robert Peel finally overcame British fears of oppression in 1829 and the London Metropolitan Police was formed. Peel's new police service became a model for other countries, including Canada and the United States. The growing cities in both of these countries formed bodies of officers to prevent and investigate crime. There were, however, crucial differences between the two countries. While in Canada the criminal law became a federal responsibility, in the United States individual states controlled the nature of their criminal codes. Moreover, the establishment of the Northwest Mounted Police, who headed west in 1874, not only gave Canada a celebrated and distinctive symbol, but also established order in advance of settlement, whereas in the United States a descendant of the medieval English office of sheriff had often become the most important local authority after or during the establishment of frontier communities.

Police services have grown and changed with the communities they serve, and nowhere is this truer than in the field of forensic science. With the centralization and professionalization of police services and the advancement of science in general came new methods of detecting and analyzing evidence. Interestingly, the scientific approach to police investigations was often anticipated in the imaginative work of writers such as Sir Arthur Conan Doyle, the author of the Sherlock Holmes stories, and Edgar Allan Poe, whose detective in *The Murders in the Rue Morgue* was a model of logical, scientific detection. In two novels by the American author Mark Twain in the 1880s and 1890s, fingerprints were used by the characters to solve problems of proof and identification. Fiction and fact were very close in the 1880s, for it was at about the same time that **Francis Galton**, a brilliant English amateur of science, was experimenting with the same idea. In 1892, Galton published his book *Finger Prints*, and a new era of forensic science was about to begin. By the early twentieth century, fingerprint identification was being adopted by police forces, first in Britain and then in North America. This new means of identification, and Locard's Exchange Principle, are the two essential bases on which criminalistics is founded. Most further developments of investigative technique, which shall be discussed in later chapters, are in some way refinements of these basic discoveries.

Like the physical evidence of crime, the conduct of police is often put under a microscope, whether in court or in the public eye. In small cities or towns where officials quickly become known in the legal community and by the public at large, the credibility of officers can disappear quickly and this loss can follow them through their entire careers, just as a reputation for reliability can enhance both the pleasure and the prospects of a career in law enforcement. The issues of **credibility** and **honesty** are particularly important in criminalistics. One shred of evidence thrown out of court due to a question of credibility could affect the outcome of the whole investigation. The notebook drawing or memory of transient evidence of an officer who lacks credibility is unlikely to be as acceptable as that of someone with a reputation for professionalism. The practice of honesty establishes credibility. *In the handling of physical evidence in particular the objective of finding and presenting the entire truth must always come first.*

# ARRIVAL AT THE CRIME SCENE

In many cases, a routine call for service can in fact make you the first officer at a crime scene. The dispatch information may be detailed enough to allow you to plan approaching the scene; but often the first call will only give you an initial indication of the circumstances you are entering. Remember that this may be a drastically changing situation. The victim of an assault, for example, may have become a murder victim by the time you arrive. You must be prepared to react to the worst-case scenario in a constantly changing environment.

## ENSURING OFFICER AND VICTIM SAFETY

Officers who are injured, or worse, cannot render service to victims and others; in fact, they are compounding the problem of crime. It is essential therefore that you get all the information possible from support staff and approach the scene with the necessary caution. A furtive crime such as a burglary might require the officer not to enter with sirens and emergency lights activated. Not only are you going to scare away the perpetrators; you may also be allowing a dangerous person to plan an attack.

Two officers in a small western city knocked loudly on the door of a house named in a complaint of domestic violence. The complainant opened the door in front of which the officers were standing to inform them calmly and quietly that her husband was behind the door with a gun. The two officers immediately pulled the woman to safety, at the time jumping out of the possible line of fire while the husband moved into the open doorway and began shooting.

As often happens, the domestic violence complaint had turned suddenly into an armed confrontation. The officers had their wits about them and managed to stop what could have become a hostage situation. The initial dispatch information had told them nothing about the presence of a suspect, let alone an armed one. The victim, under a steady assault, had had the chance to make one brief call, but could not warn the officers with a second call. The officers had faced a dilemma common in domestic disputes, which are among the most frequently called-in complaints of violence. Most police departments advise standing to the side of a doorway on such a call; but at some point the necessity of making contact with the victim will put an officer in danger. Every call for service is unique, with new and unexpected circumstances. You must therefore be constantly prepared for the unexpected by the professional training you have received, the equipment you carry, and above all by alertness and common sense.

You have entered a dangerous profession and there can never be a guarantee of officer safety; but alertness to the possibility of danger can reduce risks. In some circumstances officers may have to choose between the safety of a victim and their own.

The other priority of the first officers at the scene is the safety of fellow citizens, both victims and onlookers. The scene could be either quiet or chaotic. Any planned response that you formulate en route may have to change. People's lives depend on the decisions you make in moments, and other people may later sit in judgement on those decisions. This is particularly true with decisions about living victims in need of immediate assistance; emergency medical services must take precedence over other considerations, even if this means damaging the evidence at a crime scene.

## Attitude

You must take into consideration several possibilities that demand your professional detachment and attention to the job at hand. First of all, in many cases you are the help that many people have been awaiting, the solution to their worst problem, the calm eye of the storm. Although you may feel it, you are not permitted to show obviously the excitement, grief, or shock of those who surround you. For citizens, you should be the antidote to those emotions. Secondly, you may be about to see some of the worst things you will ever see, things most other citizens may never see. Moreover, you may, depending on your duties, see these things several times in your career, or in some cases frequently. Some scenes may evoke your most unpleasant memories or excite your deepest anxieties. Officers investigating a sudden infant death, for example, may in fact have infant children of their own at home. At times like these, your strongest memory must be that of your professional duty, which

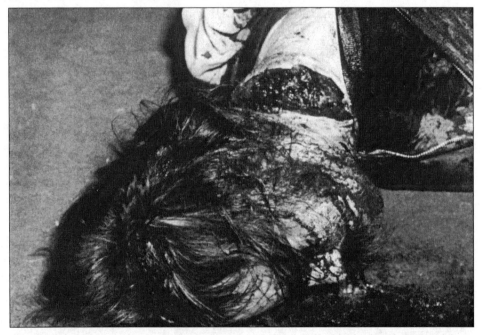

**Illustrations 2-1 and 2-2.** This homicide scene gave a considerable shock to the responding officer, who only discovered the seriousness of the crime upon close inspection of the victim.

calls on your inner strength, and whose highest purpose is to bring the perpetrator of crime to justice. It would be a falsehood to claim that any amount of professional training can enable everyone to face the atrocities that some human beings suffer, but experience and professional detachment offer the greatest likelihood of success.

## Making Sure It *Is* a Crime Scene

But wait! Is the scene to which you have been called even a crime scene? Let us examine the criteria that lead you to decide. *A crime is an act in violation of the criminal law.* To prove a crime, you must prove the elements of an offence (facts in issue). You may, on the other hand, be gathering proof that actually no crime has been committed. In the event that all elements required are not satisfied you will not be able to "prefer an information" and support a criminal charge.

*The elements of crime common to all charges are time, date, place, identity of the accused, and all actions specific to the crime in question.* As one of the first persons on a crime scene, practically speaking, it is up to you to decide whether you are investigating a criminal offence. Initially, during what may be a brief time at the scene, you must justify in your own mind that the elements are there to prove a specific offence.

This situation calls for an observant, commonsensical, and informed approach. You must not, for example, leave behind physical evidence that may support a charge of assault with a weapon when your first impression is that assault alone has occurred. The weapon used may be so minor or inconspicuous in nature as to go unnoticed at first, and your witness may make no mention of it, but it is a crucial piece of evidence in your charge. Your professionalism and investigative integrity are therefore crucial to the recognition of crime. On the same note, you are not necessarily at a crime scene; but your professional approach is still required because the scene must be investigated to a proper conclusion.

If not approached correctly the scene may become one of embarrassment. In Canada all sudden deaths are investigated to rule out foul play, or to establish non-criminal causes of death. Two officers of our acquaintance were investigating a report of a possible sudden death called in by someone who had not seen an elderly neighbour for several days. The officers responding undertook a perimeter search of the house and looked through a window. An elderly woman was lying on a couch, and repeated knocking and bell-ringing failed to get a response. The two officers, expecting the worst, forced the door open, approached the couch, and began to remove a medic alert bracelet from the woman's body. The "corpse" immediately awoke from her nap, frightened by the two intruders, who held a large pair of bolt cutters, and greatly annoyed at the destruction of her front door. Remember, things are not always what they seem. When in doubt, take a pulse!

# ENTERING AND SECURING THE CRIME SCENE

Let us assume for the moment that you have been called to the scene of a break-and-enter. Having taken into consideration the most important matter, that of safety, it is now time for you to consider the management of the crime scene. If you are alone, *you must immediately take charge.* If more than one responding unit is present, more than likely the senior officer will take charge. In any event, this must be a rapid decision and only one person should take charge to avoid confusion and make the most effective use of personnel and resources. Whoever takes charge should delegate the duties of other officers on the scene.

You must decide at this point how to contain the crime scene and therefore think carefully about the likely **outer perimeter of the crime scene**. How large is your outer perimeter? Judgement and common sense are invaluable in this decision, for the perimeter may vary a great deal according to the nature of the crime. Remember that you can expand the perimeter if necessary, but a crime scene perimeter that is initially too small quickly runs the risk of contamination by onlookers and even by other officers. Where do you draw the line? The scene of a break-and-enter from which the suspect has fled, for example, is naturally the building that has been burglarized, but may also theoretically include the escape route of the culprit(s) for a considerable distance. While evidence may be encountered along such a route, common sense demands a realistic assessment of what is possible.

# PRELIMINARY INVESTIGATION

Keeping in mind that in this case the suspect has fled, you are beginning a preliminary investigation. At this point you may do a **perimeter search** to identify a possible point of entry. If you do find an obvious point of entry, you must *identify any possible physical evidence and attempt to protect it*, bearing in mind factors such as weather. If the point of entry is not obvious, remember that you are often likely to use it yourself when entering the building.

*Touch things as little as possible.* Try not to touch surfaces that may yield fingerprint evidence. Wear gloves when touching a doorknob, for example, and turn it lightly. At this point, be alert and aware of possible evidence such as tool marks, fibres, and footwear impressions. Once inside, take a quick overview. An easy way to identify footwear impressions, for example, is to lay a flashlight on the floor and let its beam reveal footwear impressions. If you have seen such impressions outside, compare them with those inside. *When entering, you should also be careful to avoid the likely path of the suspect.* It is best to walk around the edge of a room in which the culprit's path was probably through the centre. If the point of entry is obvious, for example the broken glass door of a business, either use another entrance with the help of someone who has the key, or enter only after a thorough visual examination for footwear impressions on the glass at the point of entry.

The next step is to walk through the interior of the building to identify things that may have been affected by the suspect. Good note-taking and sketching are important at this point. If a supporting unit such as the identification section is not available, you may later be the investigating officer who processes the physical evidence at this crime scene. Processing the crime scene will be discussed in Chapter 4. For the moment, if you have secured the scene, it is under control, and you should proceed to interview the complainant, who can inform you about the condition of the scene before the crime and identify possible suspects. You must also try to identify and interview witnesses before they leave the area.

## Dealing with People

Depending on the time and location of the incident, you may immediately be faced with the problem of onlookers, drawn by the appearance of a police car. Do your best in this case to move everyone as far back as possible from the burglarized building. If you are alone, this may be difficult; in this case, try to get some responsible citizens to help you control the crowd. Every call will be different.

In some instances, there will already be people inside the crime scene, perhaps the occupants of the building and/or the complainants. If so, there is a risk that they may contaminate it—for example, by removing broken glass or otherwise "cleaning up." While this risk may be unavoidable, you must control further action by these persons, and if possible ask them to leave. A hysterical person, for example, might be best made to sit in an area that on initial examination looks relatively free of physical evidence.

## Barricades, Reporters, and Serious Crimes

While we have examined a simple break-and-enter, crime scenes can vary a great deal, and no description can cover every possibility. In the case of serious violent crimes, for example, the matter of officer and victim safety may be more crucial and the approach more cautious. Such crimes will probably attract much more attention from both onlookers and others, such as reporters for various news media. Again, one officer will need to take charge. Crowd control will be more difficult and support more urgently needed. As soon as you have dealt with the important issues of health and safety, it will probably be necessary to secure an outer perimeter with use of crime-scene tape, ropes, barricades, or, temporarily, police cars. Ideally, there will be officers to stand guard on that perimeter. The officer in charge must control the crime scene inside the perimeter to avoid contamination by other officers as well as onlookers, victims and suspects. Again, remember that in an emergency living victims must receive medical attention, and be evacuated if necessary, as soon as possible. If suspects are present, they should be removed to avoid further interference with the scene, whether it be contamination or the attempt to build alibi evidence from their observations of your investigation. If the suspect has left the scene, any information acquired by this point should be communicated to dispatch to enable the capture of the suspect.

It is extremely important that you establish a route or pathway through which all investigative traffic can pass. This can be done quickly and efficiently with crime-scene tape. Any authorized officer can then enter the scene and avoid contaminating it. Outside the perimeter, representatives of the news media will be seeking information as their profession demands. Rather than attempting vainly to exclude them totally, it is a sound practice to move them to a controlled area within the perimeter, normally at the outer edge. There you can control their movement by establishing a command post ideally with an officer assigned to them for liaison. This practice will be more likely to satisfy reporters by a recognition of their distinctive task. They should all be treated equally and enabled to do their work. Don't try to hide all fundamental facts of the case, but do not release information that could jeopardize an investigation.

Generally speaking, provided that discipline, common sense, and organization are sound, the more personnel you bring to a crime scene, the more control you will be able to establish. If you are able to assign different tasks to different persons, one can be interviewing witnesses while others are establishing a perimeter, and fellow officers are taking care of the remaining steps in the preliminary investigation. While the various tasks are under way it is important always to keep taking notes and remain alert to the essentials of the job at hand.

*Your ultimate goal should always be to preserve physical evidence at the scene.* This principle is the basis of the next chapter, on crime scene coverage.

# 3

# CRIME SCENE COVERAGE

## EVIDENCE

*To the investigator, evidence is anything that helps to prove the facts of an incident or crime.*

While the above definition may seem general to you, it must be remembered that evidence could lead you to believe that no crime has been committed. Authorities identify a variety of categories of evidence. Generally, however, in Canada and the United States evidence falls into three categories: *testimonial evidence, documentary or written evidence,* and *physical or real evidence.* While written documents could be considered a subcategory of physical evidence or simply a record of testimony, you should note that the courts and hence most police services consider them to be a separate type of evidence. In any case, they have an independent physical existence and, practically speaking, can at times be considered and analyzed as a type of physical evidence. Testimonial evidence is evidence given orally by a witness.

Here our concern is with physical evidence. **Physical or real evidence** can be defined as evidence that has substance; it is composed of matter. **Trace evidence** is physical evidence that has been deposited at or carried away from the scene of a crime or incident. It is usually found in the form of minute particles transferred from one thing to another. The fibres from a carpet on which an accused murderer struggled with his victim, for example, may later be found on the suspect's clothing, and would be called trace evidence. There is also **transient evidence**, that is to say, evidence "of short duration." In a sense, any physical evidence that can be destroyed could be considered transient; but the term is more usually applied to evidence that is in danger of destruction by natural forces or human error. Tire impressions in snow, for example, are transient in nature, as are bloodstains at an outdoor crime scene or insects feeding on a corpse. Blowfly larvae (maggots) containing human DNA from a murder victim will eventually grow up and fly away.

There are many ways of classifying physical evidence. But no matter what system you use, you cannot expect to go to a crime scene with a "shopping list" in hand and work systematically through the categories. It is better that you understand evidence as you encounter it and reconstruct events according to their physical traces, which may help you to build a theory about what occurred. That said, lists are useful to make you aware of the forensic possibilities of evidence.

Physical evidence generally falls into several common types, some of which can be the subject of more one type of analysis:

### Types of Evidence

1. ammunition and firearms

2. body organs, body fluids, and DNA

3. documents

4. drugs, legal and illegal

5. explosives: debris, devices, substances

6. fibres, natural or synthetic

7. fingerprints

8. glass

9. hair

10. impressions: tire and snowmobile marks, shoeprints, fabric impressions, bite marks, leather impressions

11. paint and ink

12. petroleum products and other flammable liquids

13. plastic bags

14. powder or gunshot residue

15. serial numbers

16. soil and minerals

17. tools and tool marks

18. vegetative matter: wood and plant materials

19. vehicle lights

20. insects, diatoms, and other organisms

21. wounds and weapons

# RECOGNITION AND IDENTIFICATION OF EVIDENCE

As you can see from the above list, at a crime scene it is possible for even an experienced investigator to miss crucial evidence. You might know the common types of evidence and be able to assess their value, but in many cases a complainant or other informant may be invaluable in pointing out evidence you had not noticed or in telling you about evidence that has been removed from the scene. Common-sense policing demands that even though you may be in charge, you observe and listen.

Imagine yourself for a moment alone at a crime scene. Support staff is unwarranted or unavailable. The accusation alleges assault causing bodily harm. You alone must recognize, collect, and preserve the pertinent physical evidence. What should you collect? How well will you recognize important evidence? An old man is lying unconscious in his kitchen. You call an ambulance and he is removed at your request. There are drops of blood on the floor and what look to be the bloody prints of footwear beside the former location of the body. You notice several clumps of hair of different colours on the floor. Large pieces of what appears to be a liquor bottle are scattered in the kitchen; there doesn't appear to be enough for a complete bottle and the neck seems to be missing. The man's wallet and a considerable number of coins are also on the floor.

It is a dirty house; dishes are in the sink and three beverage glasses are on the kitchen table, along with a loaf of bread, a plate, two knives, and a jar of strawberry jam. The back door was open when you arrived. As you approached the door, you noticed drops of blood on the back step and some on the sidewalk leading to a muddy back alley or lane. The call originated from the victim, who then collapsed. While emergency services have done their work, you must now do yours. Identification technicians are unavailable in this relatively remote location. In contrast to the interior of the house, you have noticed, the yard is well maintained and the lawn adjacent to the alley has recently been mowed. With medical emergencies taken care of, the scene is yours.

You must conclude your investigation at some point and then leave the scene for other work. Think. Rapid and careful decisions are necessary. Once you have left the scene physically, you won't get a second chance. You must mentally process the scene in order to figure out what is of evidential value for an eventual prosecution. What is required to reconstruct this crime scene and take you and perhaps a judge or jury on a journey back in time?

In the above crime scene you should have thought of the following important considerations:

1. Approaching the crime scene, did you park on the tire tracks and other impressions in the back alley?

2. On carefully approaching the house have you noticed the blood on the sidewalk leading to the alley?

3. Did you think, as you noticed the first blood, of the possible extent of the crime scene into and including the alley?

4. Did you look for a point of forced entry? If there seems to be none, perhaps the victim let his assailant(s) in. The door is unlocked, open, and undamaged.

5. When you examined the victim's injuries, did you compare the bloody footwear impressions with the victim's shoes?

6. Have you isolated the indoor portion of the crime scene to the kitchen by a careful walk-through of the house?

7. Have you, as an experienced officer, recognized that the following evidence must be collected?

   • Hair samples for possible matching to victim or culprit.

   • Pieces of glass for fingerprints, physical match, and other trace evidence. The neck of the bottle may be with the culprit or elsewhere on the scene.

   • Separate samples of blood from the victim's location and the outdoors for comparison to a standard sample from the victim for type and DNA.

   • The glasses on the table. Why are there three? Are they moist or dry? They must be seized for fingerprints and possible other analysis.

   • The knives on the table. Why two? They need to be checked for fingerprints.

   • The jam bottle and the bread bag. They may yield fingerprints. There may also have been other transfers of evidence (e.g., jam on the culprit's shirt).

   • Did you carefully examine the wallet to see if it contains money? Keep in mind that it may bear fingerprints.

   • Did you look for tire impressions?

   • Did you look for fingerprints from the doorknob and other likely locations?

Have you formed a theory about what happened here?

How did your theory go? Remember that we are concerned here with physical evidence and not the entire field of criminal investigation. For example, you would no doubt interview neighbours as possible witnesses. Let us reconstruct the scene. The old man had two invited guests with whom he shared a bottle of whiskey (the substance found in the three glasses). An argument erupted and one of the guests struck the householder with the empty bottle. The assailant cut himself with broken glass and left the house with the neck of the bottle, which he threw into the yard. The suspect's prints were on it. The drops of blood on the sidewalk were his; but the blood in which he left his footprints came from the victim's wounds. Tire impressions from the soft soil in the alley and footprints nearby linked the vehicle and the culprit who owned it to the scene, as did grass clippings from the yard found in the vehicles and on the culprits' muddy, bloody shoes. The importance of your skill at recognizing evidence is critical to establishing the facts of a case. In this assault (an assault did in fact occur) the recognition of evidence was the key to a successful investigation and ultimately to the attainment of justice for a friendly senior citizen.

In many cases, you will simply respond to a call and immediately contact others (emergency medical services, coroner or medical examiner, firefighters and investigators, identification specialists, and other, higher-ranking personnel) to deal further with the crime scene. The task of some officers, especially junior officers, will usually involve the protection of evidence on the scene from contamination.

# CONTAMINATION, DESTRUCTION, AND PROTECTION OF EVIDENCE

The crucial principle to remember in any contact with the crime scene is the principle of alteration or exchange defined in Chapter 1 ("Everyone who enters a crime scene changes it and is changed by it" ). If investigation is to rely on the alteration of the scene by a suspect, then any further alteration, whether by responding officers, natural forces, or others at the scene, can alter the evidence and render it questionable or useless (except perhaps to a defence attorney). You must consider then the range of pressures that can affect physical evidence. Like other cases where the perceived behaviour of officers casts their evidence in doubt, behaviour at the crime scene must be seen to be appropriate. The investigation of the celebrated O. J. Simpson case in California (1994), for example, was recorded exhaustively and presented the public with the spectacle of skillful defence attorneys able to question essentially sound evidence, partly on the basis of police behaviour and practices at the crime scene.

The major agent of contamination is human and the contamination is usually accidental. In the search for minute particles whose transfer may indicate the nature of an offence, the investigator should (1) encounter as few accidental contaminants as possible and (2) deposit as few contaminants as possible. Some contamination of the crime scene is inevitable but it must be kept to a minimum. That is why standards of dress and conduct at the crime scene today are stricter than they have ever been. With every advance in our ability to detect, analyze, and match the minutest particles comes a correspondingly greater necessity to avoid the slightest contaminating contacts.

When you consider that today perspiration from a person (secretor) can be detected and analyzed from the handle of a suitcase, it is clear that the bungling officer at the scene has a greater destructive power than ever before. Most investigators, therefore, depending on the nature of the offence, are required to guard against the transfer of trace evidence by wearing protective clothing and footwear that inhibit contamination.

Responding officers who must enter the scene of a major crime must also be aware of this hazard. Amazingly, however, some will occasionally forget the most basic precautions. Eating, drinking, and smoking at a crime scene are out of the question. Officers should never use a telephone that is part of a crime scene until it has been processed and cleared for use by an investigating technician; nor should anyone use a sink or toilet, or run water in a tub. Instinctively, you may move to flush a toilet which could contain evidence. "Naturally neat" persons may be more likely to avoid some kinds of contamination, but their instinct to arrange and clean must be replaced by a newly developed habit of evidence preservation. Turning on a light switch, for example, may be necessary, but you must (1) remember and write down whether the light was on when you arrived and (2) use gloves to avoid contamination.

While avoiding contamination may be impossible to achieve in processing a crime scene, it is well to remember two humorous sayings regarding contamination of evidence at a crime scene:

The perfect piece of evidence is one that is never touched after the crime.

The investigators least likely to contaminate are those with their hands in their pockets.

Both of these sayings refer to the possibilities of crime scene contamination, particularly by police officers. Unfortunately neither of the ideals they express can be applied if you wish to get the job done. But they are useful to remember. In other words: When in doubt, don't touch.

You should also be aware that evidence you are responsible for seizing must be treated with due regard for contamination after it has left the crime scene. Placing two separate pieces of evidence in contact with each other or placing a piece of evidence in direct contact with another contaminating influence can greatly reduce its value. If you follow the compelling urge to place a tool into an impression it probably made, you are in fact making a new impression, and altering or destroying evidence, even if you have only left or lifted a minute particle of paint. Your police car, an essential tool of the profession, can also be highly destructive of evidence. If, for example, you pull up close to the crime scene, you may be destroying valuable tire impressions, in snow, earth and even pavement.

The best intentions sometimes lead to disastrous results. An investigator in one police service had a series of frustrating experiences with enterprising responding officers who contaminated and destroyed evidence. One officer carefully followed the tire impressions of a suspect down a road with several muddy spots on it crisscrossed by tire tracks. Unfortunately the officer also used the same tracks for walking. One impression was later isolated and positively identified (by individual characteristics) as that of a suspect's vehicle. This impression could have told a much more complete crime story had it not been for the large and very clear print of the responding officer's boot in the middle of a very short tire track.

This was not the only "bad impression" the investigator received. Two other officers obligingly decided to protect a footprint in the snow until the identification technician could arrive at the scene of a break-and-enter. They set a cardboard box over the footprint. Meanwhile a warm wind sprang up and the box seemed to act as a conductor of heat. The investigator arrived on the scene to find the perfect rectangular impression of a box under which all the snow had melted and the shoe impression along with it, while all around the box the snow remained intact. In this case, uncontrollable nature combined with human ingenuity to destroy evidence. Nature can destroy most trace evidence if given the opportunity. Physical evidence that is highly transient most often falls victim to natural forces. Rain destroys footwear impressions in soft soil and removes bloodstains from pavement. Wind carries bloodstained leaves away and fills in impressions with soil, snow, or debris. Intense sunlight alters many types of evidence from impressions in snow to bloodstains. Your common sense will be invaluable in protecting evidence in these situations. You might be better advised to protect or collect outdoor evidence first, and then process the indoor crime scene.

# CONTINUITY OF EVIDENCE

For the last and one of the most legally devastating of influences on evidence we must leave the realm of nature and return to that of human error. The notion of continuity of evidence is of paramount importance in police work and we shall consequently return to the subject often throughout this book. All the common sense, professionalism, and diligence in acquiring evidence may be worth nothing if it is neglected.

Continuity of evidence refers to the accounting for the custody of evidence from the time it is seized until its presentation in court. It is also sometimes called the chain of custody of evidence. There must be a clear, dated, and detailed record to show that the evidence seized at the scene is in fact the evidence that appears before the court. If continuity of evidence is broken, if one link in this chain is lost or even weak, the value of the evidence comes into question and it may even be pronounced inadmissible. A responding officer may find it necessary to seize (collect) a weapon that is a piece of evidence, for example, to ensure safety at the scene. That officer has then become part of the chain and has a responsibility to ensure continuity. The RCMP laboratory services manual puts the issue concisely:

> Each exhibit must be accounted for from the time of its discovery or collection until it is tendered in evidence at a trial. (Section 1G)

The issue of neglected continuity of evidence can be one of the most important in police work. It becomes particularly crucial when we begin, in the next chapter, to discuss processing the crime scene.

*C h a p t e r*

# PROCESSING THE CRIME SCENE

So far, we have responded to a call for service; attended emergency needs; performed an initial walkthrough of the scene; and established the perimeter and control of the scene, taking care to avoid contamination and to protect outdoor evidence. It is now time to perform a more intensive examination of the scene, searching carefully and collecting physical evidence. Remember: once you have examined and released this crime scene, you may not return to it to collect any more physical evidence. Any remaining evidence will probably have been destroyed, contaminated, or compromised in some way. You must remember as well that returning to the scene after it has been released may involve legal complications regarding search and seizure as well as questions concerning continuity of evidence.

## THE MATCHING PRINCIPLE: KNOWN TO UNKNOWN

The ultimate purpose in gathering evidence is to find matches between physical substances or impressions left at a crime scene and their original source. For example, a tool mark at a crime scene may be traced to a tool found in a suspect's possession. When you match the tool, a **known** piece of evidence, with the **unknown**, the tool mark found at the crime scene, you have established a vital relationship between the suspect and the crime scene.

How do you know when there is a match between two or more pieces of physical evidence? You do so by finding similarities and explaining or eliminating

21

differences between the two pieces of evidence. The **principle of matching or identification** can be stated this way: *Things that possess too many precisely matching characteristics for their similarity to be coincidental are from the same source, provided that any difference can be accounted for.*

In the case of our tool mark, with sufficient experience and training, you may wish to make a test impression and another mark from the suspect tool, and compare both with the mark at the crime scene. Using the matching principle and comparing "like to like" and "**known to unknown**" (i.e., test impression to crime-scene impression), you can decide whether there are sufficient matching similarities and no unexplainable differences. If these two things can be established, you can be said to have made a **positive identification**. The actual physical identification will often be done by an identification specialist or a forensic scientist. But the initial recognition and seizure of possible evidence may well be performed by the first officer at the scene, and it is important that all officers understand the central role of physical identification in solving crimes. The physical identification, whether it be achieved through the comparison of DNA samples or simply by the physical matching of two pieces torn from the same page, is so important that it will be a constant theme in the remainder of this book.

## Physical Matching

Many authorities in Canada use the phrase "physical matching" to refer to the specific type of comparison in which two pieces of the same physical object can be put back together as in a jigsaw puzzle to recreate the original whole. There are few stronger and more conclusive kinds of evidence than an obvious physical match. Two fragments of glass that fit precisely together with no difficulty can constitute a powerful condemnation of a criminal, and one that requires no particular expertise to achieve.

# CLASS AND INDIVIDUAL CHARACTERISTICS

When comparing items of evidence, you should be aware that the similarities and differences between two physical things can be established with the ideas of class and individual (accidental) characteristics.

**Class characteristics** are characteristics of a piece of evidence that place it with a particular group, but not with a unique source. They establish similarity. For example, a running shoe pattern may identify the source as the shoe of a particular manufacturer. Its size may reduce the breadth of similarity, but you are still, for example, dealing the group or class of all size-11 sneakers from the specific manufacturer. In order to make a complete identification between the impression and a certain object, you must identify individual or accidental characteristics.

**Individual characteristics** are those characteristics that may distinguish the evidence from other evidence of the same group or class. Sometimes, particularly in the case of manufactured objects, these are called **accidental** characteristics, that is, they are induced by "wear and tear" or use. Continuing to examine our shoe impression, we discover an irregular line running across it. When comparing it to the suspect's shoe, we see that the line matches a horizontal cut in the sole of the shoe. This accidental characteristic created by wear is unique to that shoe and allows us to make a positive physical match. The suspect's possession has been linked decisively to the scene of the crime. While matching individual characteristics do not always lead to a positive identification, they add strongly to the probability that known and unknown pieces of evidence are from the same source.

# THE IDENTIFICATION PROCESS

In matching pieces of evidence, you should work systematically from the general to the specific. First identify class characteristics and then proceed toward establishing the individual traits that make your match positive or that eliminate the possibility of a match. In the case of our shoe impression, therefore, we should first make certain if possible of the pattern type, make, manufacturer, year of manufacture, vendor, and so on. Size may remain a class characteristic unless it is unusual. Cuts, wear marks, fractures, and other accidental characteristics can then be used to reduce the possibility of error. Dissimilarities must also be explained. For example, subsequent wear of a shoe may explain the difference between a crime scene impression and accidental characteristics of the shoe not found in the impression.

## Probability

Every set of matching characteristics increases the **probability** of identification. If two independent, separate pieces of evidence or two individual characteristics match two others (with no unexplainable differences), you have raised to the power of two (i.e., squared) the probability of a positive match. Three sets of matching evidence likewise raise the probability to the power of three (i.e., they cube it). Therefore, every match, added to the others, powerfully multiplies the likelihood that you are on the right track.

## Analysis, Comparison, and Evaluation (ACE)

A systematic approach is necessary in order to proceed successfully with the vital task of identification. The Royal Canadian Mounted Police consider three scientific steps in identifying class and individual or accidental characteristics to be **analysis, comparison, and evaluation (ACE)**. In *analyzing* the evidence, you ask and answer questions about it, considering its properties, observing its characteristics, and measuring it. Next you *compare* the unknown evidence from the scene to known evidence, a control sample, or a "test impression." Thirdly, you *evaluate* the evidence you have analyzed and compared, to determine the degree of match and the possible weight of the evidence. The process of evaluation probably requires the most judgement and experience. It is often the kind of judgement required from an expert witness (i.e., someone with the experience, training, and knowledge to be regarded as an expert when testifying). Is it a **positive** match, a **probable** match, or a **possible** match? Such are questions the court may often pose.

## Verification

It is also sound practice to have identifications confirmed, whether by a fellow investigator or someone else with experience in the field. After scientific consideration of the evidence, you may conclude:

- that the dissimilarities in pieces of evidence prevent identification
- that class characteristics match, and while two pieces of evidence are from the same source there are not enough individual or accidental characteristics to distinguish the evidence from other examples of the same class
- that class and accidental characteristics indicate identification with a specific and unique source

# THE CRIME-SCENE SEARCH

## Preparation: The Field Kit

Although you may not be a forensic identification specialist, you ought to be equipped to deal with some basic aspects of the crime scene should you arrive first at a scene that contains extremely transient evidence. You may need to recognize, collect, and preserve physical evidence. Even if you do not touch anything on the scene, you must preserve a clear recollection of it, which can be useful either when specialists arrive at the scene or later on in the investigation or in court. To be ready for whatever scene confronts you, it is wise to keep with you, in addition to whatever equipment is normally issued by your particular service or department, a small,

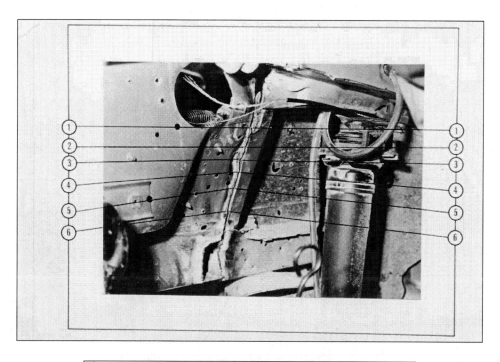

**Illustrations 4-1 and 4-2.** Parts of a stolen automobile cut with a cutting torch were physically matched for similarities. Once a comparison is made, investigators are able to prepare, in chart form, photographs for court presentation.

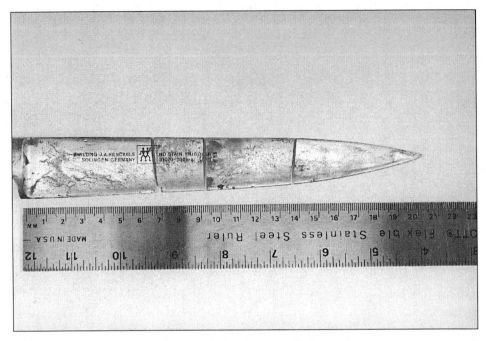

**Illustration 4-3.** Physical matching: Knife from the scene of a homicide. One piece was recovered from the victim's body and matched to the others to show the complete weapon.

portable supply of items routinely used in the field—essentially a field kit. For most officers, it may be practical to designate a section of their satchel or police briefcase and keep their evidence collection field kit there in a suitable container that will keep it clean and separate from other equipment. In some cases the field kit may be as standard to every patrol car as the first-aid kit. If not, you should devise a kit yourself. Here you must use your own common sense to devise the most effective and convenient means of carrying such a kit.

While items such as fingerprint and impression equipment may seem useful, chances are specialists will be called in to use these items. Much depends on the remoteness of your location and the policy and resources of your organization. If you operate in a remote location it may be wise to carry a more complete kit than would an officer with ready and rapid access to well-equipped laboratories and crime scene specialists.

At minimum, your field kit should include:

- paper bags in assorted sizes
- plastic bags in assorted sizes
- some paper in which to fold evidence
- paper envelopes

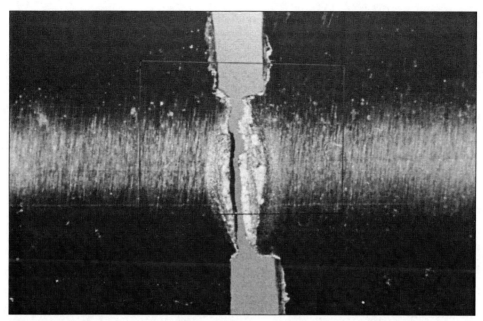

**Illustration 4-4.** Sawed-off rifle used in a robbery. One piece was recovered by a citizen; the other was found in the possession of the suspect. Overall photograph shows the machine markings put on during the manufacturing process as well as cut marks from the hacksaw.

**Illustration 4-5.** Close-up photo showing machine manufacturing marks and the matching characteristics where two sides were snapped apart near the end of the cutting process. Note the match of the parts when viewed microscopically.

- small sealable metal cans (for arson debris etc.)
- small glass jars
- stoppered glass tubes containing swabs
- evidence tape
- an indelible marking pen
- folding pillboxes
- plastic pill containers
- a small amount of distilled water
- a good steel ruler and a steel tape
- a flashlight and spare batteries
- writing paper and report forms
- a clipboard and graph paper
- a metal scribe
- chalk
- cellophane tape and clear bookbinding tape
- scalpels and replacement blades
- various sizes of tweezers and forceps (some rubber-tipped if possible)
- a compass
- protective eyewear
- disposable latex gloves
- small scissors and a pocketknife
- a charcoal-filtering facemask
- an auto-focus camera with built-in flash and extra batteries
- camera films 100 to 800 ASA, black and white and colour (your work with this will not replace the extensive photography done by a specialist, but your initial photograph of a crime scene could be invaluable)
- small 18% greyscale rulers
- small hand-held tape recorder

An extensive collection of crime-scene processing equipment would include many more items, such as fingerprint and impression-casting equipment, photographic supplies, alternative light sources, portable lighting, biohazard kit, blood collection materials, a variety of manual and power tools, a kit for taking prints from corpses, vacuum sweepers, and a host of other items often carried in a mobile crime scene unit. But these are materials carried by well-equipped identification units.

Most officers will not usually be collecting evidence at major crime scenes, except in an authorized assisting role. But let us turn for a moment to the routine of the ordinary officer who is sometimes alone on patrol. Limited resources do not usually allow crime-scene specialists at every break-in or non-injury hit-and-run incident. But resources need not determine the effectiveness of your investigation. The picture you take or the paint chips you gather could be critical to the solution of such an offence. Use your common sense. Should you leave a fabric thread hanging in the broken window because you can't call an identification specialist? Photograph and seize it. Likewise you should be in the habit of taking pictures of other potentially important evidence. Photograph the point of entry, the damaged car, the fire to which you are the first officer, and seize evidence when no one else will be called to do so. When you leave these minor scenes you are releasing them and any uncollected evidence. Remember too that the shred of evidence you collect, even if not immediately submitted to be analyzed by the overburdened labs, may even be useful in a later, major crime investigation. It is not unusual for an offender to become more daring and progress from minor offenses to serious crimes, and earlier evidence could well play a role in the investigation of these later offences.

# PROCESSING THE SCENE

While you have done an initial walk-through and may have identified and noted some prominent evidence, you must now begin to gather carefully the pieces of a puzzle that may later become a court case. Ideally you will make no mistakes and the case can be successfully presented and supported by the evidence you have collected. It is desirable to have with you a person designated as an exhibit clerk to "tag and bag" the evidence, and the scenes of serious crimes will often employ several specialists. Let us look at the tasks essential to a proficient search:

- Determine the point of entry.
- Observe and plan.
- Determine the path of contamination.
- Determine focal points.
- Determine the point of exit.
- Photograph the scene.
- Make notes.
- Develop a search pattern.
- Measure and sketch the scene.
- Gather and catalogue evidence and ensure continuity.
- Do a final overall survey and release the scene.

## Determine the Point of Entry

In your preliminary search you may have located a point of entry. If so you should be sure that you have protected any evidence outside that location if it could be subject to destruction or contamination. The nature of the point of entry may make it necessary for you to process the area first. Depending on weather conditions, for example, you may wish to photograph exterior footwear impressions or other outdoor evidence immediately. But for the moment let us return to the fundamental steps in piecing the puzzle together.

## Observe and Plan

As soon as any extremely transient evidence has been processed, you need to consider thoughtfully the overall scene. Think of the elements of the crime (facts in issue). What are you setting out to prove or disprove? What sort of evidence is such a crime likely to yield? How are you going to proceed with the least contamination possible? What equipment do you need?

## Determine the Path of Contamination

Somehow the suspect entered the scene, committed the crime at a focal point, and then left at a point of exit. Often, for example, an offender will struggle through a difficult point of entry, and then use an easier point of exit, such as a push-bar door that can be opened from the interior of a building. You must use your judgement and alert observation to decide along what path the suspect left evidence. If, for example, with your oblique lighting (flashlight along the floor) or perhaps with the naked eye you are able to see foot impressions, you have probably found the suspect's path. This path may yield valuable evidence and must be protected and processed for physical evidence.

## Determine Focal Points

The focal points are the places where offences were actually committed. These of course will vary widely from crime to crime: the body of a victim would be a focal point in homicide, as will the surface of a table from which a television was stolen or a drawer from which jewelry has been taken. The victim's statement will often guide you to the likely spot. In some cases, focal points are impossible to determine because of extensive damage or vandalism. The focal point is helpful because it is likely to yield a rich harvest of evidence. It is also the core of your search, which you will conduct methodically both to and away from the focal point, being careful to leave no evidence undiscovered.

# Determine the Point of Exit

While the point of entry may indicate some difficulty of access, the point of exit is less likely to do so. It may simply be a push-bar door, locked from the outside, or it may be the point of entry. The focal point and path of contamination, carefully examined, can often provide you with indications of the likely point of exit. Doors, windows, and other openings must be thoroughly examined for evidence if the point of exit is not obvious. Once discovered, the point of exit can give you important evidence, not only of the exit itself, but also of a continued path of contamination and escape. It may lead further to exterior areas of the crime scene.

# Photograph the Scene

The photographic coverage you are able to accomplish will depend on the equipment supplied by your organization. To ensure proper photographic coverage, you must take all of the following:

- overall photographs of the scene at eye level if possible (in some cases overall photos may be aerial shots)
- medium-range photographs of parts of the scene of evidential significance
- close-up photographs of particular pieces of evidence showing as much clear detail as possible

**Illustration 4-6.** Overall crime-scene photograph of a shooting incident. Eye-level photographs are used to depict the unaltered scene as it appeared to the investigator at the time.

**Illustration 4-7.** Medium-range photograph includes markers to show an indication of the evidence important to the investigation and the courts.

**Illustration 4-8.** Close-up photographs show the evidence for visual identification. Further photographs should be taken with a close-up lens from above the object at 90 degrees to it, with a scale ruler.

Photographs after processing the scene should include evidence markers, search grids, and any other investigative devices you are using. But remember that *initial photographs should depict the crime scene unaltered*. Again, the nature of your equipment and the conditions (light or night, etc.; on- or off-camera flash capability, etc.) will determine the quality of the photographs. Trained specialists are often invaluable for successful photographic coverage, given their equipment and training. But if you find yourself without such assistance you must optimize whatever resources you may have. Whatever your expertise, remember that you should take as many photographs as possible. Film is cheap but evidence is precious.

When developing your photographs or having them developed, you are subject to mechanical and human error. If, for example, you have used colour film and your department is not equipped to process it, you must use a commercial processing service and this practice is fraught with dangers to your investigation. The more photographs the better. Be aware that everything you do in processing evidence must be backed up by other methods such as your notes and sketches. Keep a log of all photographs as well as of all evidence observed. Identifying information should also be noted on the backs of photographs and negatives stored securely in order. Never alter the face of a photograph. You may be using photographs as evidence in court and one question that will almost inevitably arise is whether photographs *accurately represent the scene as you saw it at the time*.

Bear in mind that in court you cannot claim to be an expert witness with photographic evidence. For example, the lens, or your automatic camera, may distort the scene. You are simply presenting the best photographic evidence you could acquire.

Always check your equipment. Are the batteries good? Is there old film in the camera? Make a record of the frame on which you started. If your camera has a dating capability, check to be sure that the date is accurate, and always note elsewhere the sequence and date of your photographs.

Persons trained and equipped for proper crime-scene photography will of course accomplish more complete and technically acceptable coverage of scenes and evidence than someone with an automatic camera with built-in flash. First of all, they bring with them an extensive array of equipment. At minimum, besides a range of camera bodies, loaded with various types of film, they will carry:

- a normal lens (i.e., one that views a scene as if through a human eye)
- a wide-angle lens
- a close-up lens
- a telephoto lens
- filters
- an electronic flash with off-camera capability

- a remote or synchronizing cord
- extra batteries
- a locking cable release
- a tripod
- a large supply of film
- 18% grey card or rulers

## Crime-Scene Photography

Having advanced far beyond the "aim and shoot" technology of your automatic camera, knowledgeable photographers are able to take clear photographs in a variety of conditions. They understand how to manipulate several factors in order to admit the right amount of light to any particular film, which is a requirement of a good crime-scene photograph. It must portray clearly the scene as it was found. The elements they must be able to control and adjust are several. The **lens aperture** or **f-stop** controls depth of field and amount of light admitted to the film. The **shutter speed** decides how long the film will be exposed to the amount of light allowed by the f-stop. The films themselves have different degrees of sensitivity to light. They are made for high or low shutter speeds.

In dimly lit scenes, photographers may use added lighting. But if an outdoor scene makes standard flash or other artificial lighting impractical, photographers may rely on a number of other techniques and types of equipment. An open stretch of highway or an extensive hillside cannot be sufficiently lit artificially, nor is there enough ambient light. But a knowledgeable photographer can get acceptable shots even with limited equipment: a solid tripod, a cable release, a manually adjustable 35 mm camera, and a light source. The photographer sets the camera on "B" for bulb and opens the lens aperture completely. When the cable release is activated, the shutter remains wide open, admitting maximum light to the film. Next, the subject of the photograph is "painted" with light. This can be done either with a series of flashes on the subject sufficient to provide even illumination (too many on one spot will cause overexposure) or by moving the beam of a floodlight or flashlight over the subject and evenly "painting" it with light. All this time, with the lens aperture wide open, the film is recording a "light picture" of the subject until the cable release is unlocked. The ideal result is a time exposure of a large area showing fine detail in dark conditions.

There are many more techniques and types of equipment that photographers may use in various lighting conditions. If a photographer using a flash does not want to produce a photograph with overpowering shadows, which distort the scene as it appears to the naked eye, a useful technique is to "bounce" the light off a nearby white or light-coloured surface such as the ceiling or a white card. Usually in this case, sensors on the flash unit will automatically adjust the amount of light used. If this is done using a manual flash, photographers open the aperture to adjust for the dimmer "bounced" light.

Under poor lighting conditions, photographers can compensate by using high-speed films, slower shutter speeds, and more open apertures. However, these techniques are not usually appropriate for crime-scene photographs and are more likely to be found in surveillance work when officers wish to record subjects undetected.

The **depth of field** required for crime scene photographs varies greatly. If you wish to photograph a fingerprint on the hood of a car, you may ignore depth of field entirely, opening the lens aperture as much as necessary to provide a proper exposure. If, however, you wish to show in sharp focus several objects at various depths in one picture, you will need to close the lens aperture and then use a slow shutter speed to admit more light to the film. (Caution: if you are using a flash, you must not set the shutter speed higher than the speed indicated for "flash" on your camera.)

These are only a few of the techniques used by crime-scene photographers. They may have much more extensive equipment, including infrared film, various light filters, and a range of lenses for close-up and wide-angle coverage. In most cases they will also have the expertise to make the necessary adjustments in the darkroom development procedure.

## Make Notes

Notes are the essential tools of all police work. Their importance cannot be exaggerated. Whatever other devices and techniques you will use from time to time, you will always take notes. You and only you are responsible for their condition. Your note-taking must begin with the initial response and continue through the preliminary investigation and all subsequent activities related to the case in chronological order. Notes must be complete, accurate, legible, and carefully compiled with the appropriate times, dates, places, measurements, and sometimes minor sketches.

An incident that happened yesterday may only go to court three years from now. You may have investigated hundreds of cases in the meantime. From your notes you must revive your memory and reconstruct the crime.

Remember that your notes are open to examination and cross-examination. Keep your notebooks professional. The assembled court does not need to see your shopping list, your laundry list, or the phone number of a promising date. Personal information is best kept elsewhere.

Your notes will also form the basis of your report and determine its quality. They must answer the essential questions of who, what, when, where, why, and how. They should accurately describe the scene as you see it, much like a photograph, but with dimensions photography cannot capture. While no list can include all aspects of every crime scene, the following should be found in most investigators' notebooks:

1. time, date, place of the incident

2. the scene as it appeared when you arrived

3. officers and other persons (witnesses)

4. officer in charge of scene

5. detailed crime-scene coverage, for example:

    (a) points of entry and exit—exterior conditions (forced entry, open, locked, etc.)

    (b) lights, on or off

    (c) overall condition of crime scene (e.g., house dirty, clean, damage or no apparent damage, dishes in sink, meals on table, etc.)—signs of staging?

    (d) date and time indicators: mail stacked, condition of foods (rot etc.), entomological evidence (bugs) on food, bodies, etc.

6. description of crime scene structure—house, apartment, number of rooms, common entries, etc.

7. persons with legal access to structure

8. weather and lighting when investigating

9. description of outside location—lighting, street, area, etc., environmental design around structure (e.g., shrubs and bushes, hiding areas, etc.)

10. all evidence, observed, seized, catalogued, etc., and by whom (remember: *continuity*)

11. time and date of release of crime scene and to whom it was released

Many investigators find it convenient and efficient to use a tape recorder or camcorder when conducting crime-scene notation. But nothing can replace proper note-taking as an essential police skill. Whatever recording device is used, remember that the unedited version of your tape can be demanded as evidence in the courts. As with your notes, common sense in recording is important. While these suggestions are useful, experience should ultimately refine your note-taking skills until accurate and complete recording are almost second nature to you.

# Develop a Search Pattern

The only way to conduct a thorough search of the crime scene is to establish a search pattern. The pattern will enable you to optimize your efforts and find more possible evidence more quickly and efficiently than any other method of examining the scene. Your pattern can transform an initially confusing scene into a feasible, systematic task. The number of personnel available, the size and exterior or interior location of the scene, time constraints on the investigator (e.g., the presence of a decomposing body), and other specific circumstances of the scene will affect the type of search pattern you choose. Remember that while your search must be thorough, the passage of time will often be to the advantage of the suspect. You must choose the pattern that fits the circumstances of each case. These patterns can be varied or mixed. The important point is that you plan ahead and be thorough and systematic.

## *Search Patterns*

1. **Zone.** The area is divided into zones or quadrants and an officer is assigned to each. This approach works well for the interior of buildings and the zones can be subdivided depending on how many searchers are available.

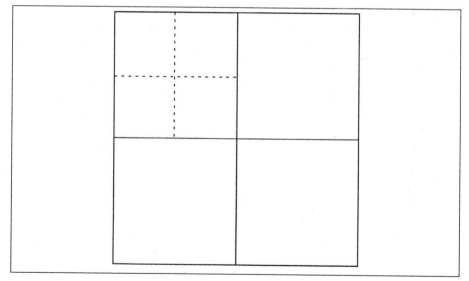

**Illustration 4-9.** Zone or quadrant search.

2. **Grid.** This is a highly regarded pattern, often used for major crime scenes. Searchers pass over each sector twice, choosing any one of a number of approaches to the grid. They can accomplish thorough coverage of large areas,

and chart accurately the precise location of evidence uncovered. Note that the grid search is required in Appendix A.

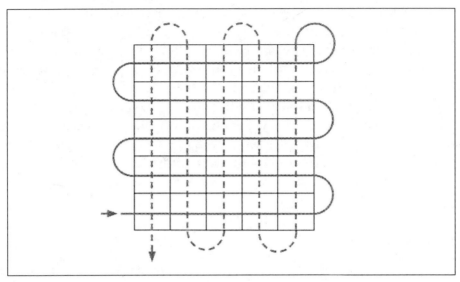

**Illustration 4-10.** Grid search.

3. **Strip, lane, or line.** Various versions of this pattern can be highly effective for both large and small areas, and with a single searcher or numerous personnel. Many searchers, moving shoulder-to-shoulder, can cover a large open area thoroughly. Even a single searcher can also cover an interior crime scene well.

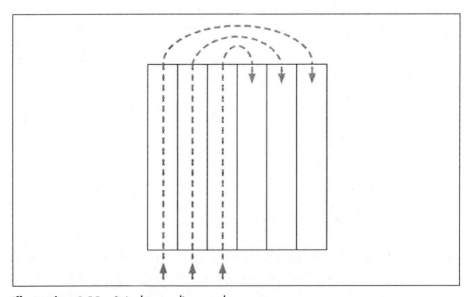

**Illustration 4-11.** Strip, lane, or line search.

4. **Spiral.** With this method, the searcher begins at the centre, or at the outer perimeter, and proceeds in a circular fashion. While the spiral search can work well in a small scene, there is always a danger of missing evidence as the pattern becomes wider.

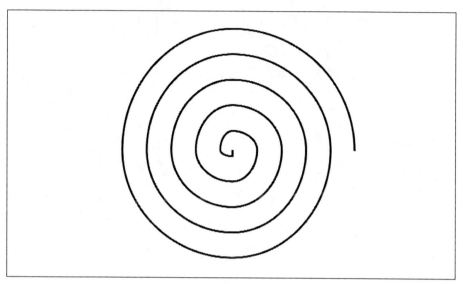

**Illustration 4-12.** Spiral search.

**Illustration 4-13.** Grid search used in the recovery of a homicide victim believed buried in a backyard.

**Illustration 4-14.** Investigators methodically work the grid pattern to recover and record evidence of the homicide.

## Measure and Sketch the Scene

It may seem strange that investigators need to sketch a scene that may also be photographed, but you must always consider making sketches of a crime scene. Sketches are invaluable in refreshing your memory and emphasizing specific evidence and its location. Sketches are selective and neat, in contrast to photographs which may appear cluttered with non-evidential items. You may also find that it takes many photographs to depict a scene and its evidence that could be portrayed in a single sketch. This is especially true if evidence is hidden by other objects. Moreover, when your sketch is done to scale, you can show (or demonstrate later) accurate distances, especially long distances, that may be impossible to depict in a photograph. Ultimately a judge or jury will decide on the significance and value of your sketches for creating their mental picture of a scene they did not witness.

### Rough and Finished Sketches

Not all crime scenes warrant sketches, but in most cases you should at least make a quick, rough sketch in your notebook. You must use your own judgement here. A large or complicated scene will soon outgrow your notebook and you should always have on hand a pencil and plain or graph paper. For measurements always use a steel measuring tape. It is a good idea to include a clipboard and ruler or template in your equipment, along with a compass. Your sketch, though rough, should be neat and accurate; it too can be used as evidence in court. What is more, you may need the information from your rough sketch to prepare a finished sketch some time later.

Crime scene sketches, unlike photos, usually present an "overhead, overall," two-dimensional view of the scene, as if you were, for example, looking at things through the roof of a building or from the sky. If evidence on a vertical plane is important, an elevation drawing is useful. Rough sketches can use a baseline or triangulation method or some combination of them. Many books will refer to various refinements of these two methods but all accurate sketches use either or both.

- **Triangulation.** Can be used with or without a baseline. Reference measurements to the evidence or object to be depicted are taken from two fixed points such as the corners of a room or other immovable objects. If your evidence or other focal point is outside, you may use trees, streetlight standards or the corners of houses from which to measure. An adequate rough sketch will include:

  (a) completion date and time

  (b) address of scene

  (c) points of reference from which the measurement is taken

  (d) proper markings of objects (later to become the legend of a finished sketch)

  (e) compass point indicating north

  (f) any other appropriate information

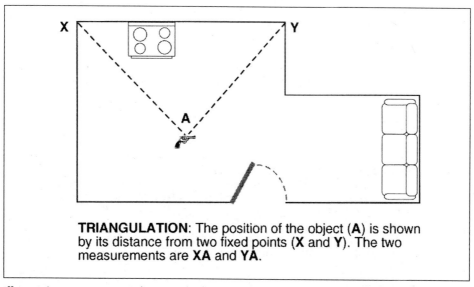

**TRIANGULATION:** The position of the object (**A**) is shown by its distance from two fixed points (**X** and **Y**). The two measurements are **XA** and **YA**.

**Illustration 4-15.** Triangulation method.

- **Baseline.** With this method, you establish a line from which all objects to be sketched are measured. Measurements should usually be made at right angles to the baseline.

***Finished Sketches***   Not everyone has the skill or talent to draft a finished sketch. Check your resources. In some cases, other places can supply the expertise and equipment to prepare a finished sketch. In most cases it will be the job of an identification section or other support unit. Recently, some agencies have turned to the computer programs developed for architects. Some of these are now included in police software programs. The finished sketch is an uncluttered version of the rough sketch completed to a high degree of accuracy and neatness. It will include, in addition to the information of the rough sketch:

- the scale used
- a title block
- the name of person who prepared it
- a legend indicating objects by letter or number
- other significant details

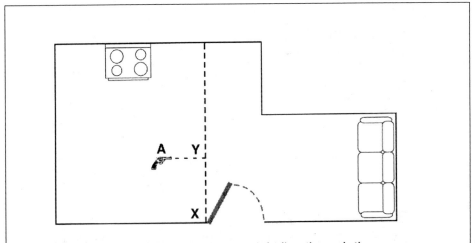

**BASELINE:** The baseline is a straight line through the scene from which all objects are measured at right angles. You may use a measuring tape as a baseline. The two measurements are (1) the distance along the baseline (**XY**) and (2) the perpendicular distance from the baseline to the object (**YA**). You may also measure the location of the objects by triangulation from any two points on the baseline.

**Illustration 4-16.** Baseline method.

If you do not prepare the finished sketch yourself, you should work with the computer or drafting staff member to ensure that the final product is the best possible representation of your crime scene, and both of you should sign off for it.

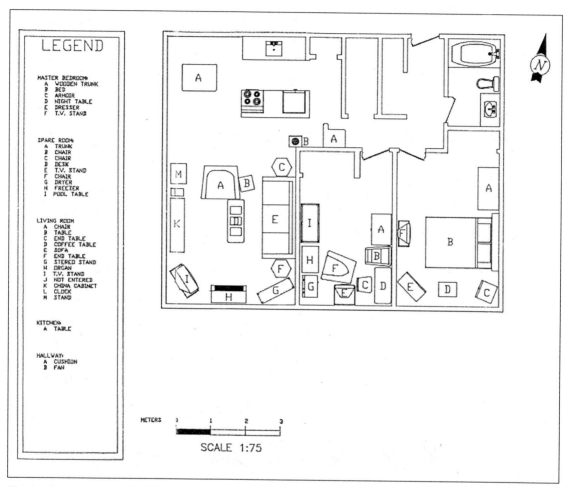

**Illustration 4-17.** Finished sketch. Most finished sketches today are prepared with the aid of a computer program.

# Gather and Catalogue Evidence and Ensure Continuity

A crucial stage of your investigation will be that during which you are actually handling physical evidence. While you must always be conscious of preventing contamination, procedural precautions will vary according to the nature and importance of the investigation. To investigate the scene of a multiple homicide, for example, every precaution is necessary. Specialist investigators and others may wear protective outer clothing, facemasks, footwear, and head coverings as well as the usual rubber gloves. (See Appendix A.) But as a single officer at a crime scene you will often not have occasion or opportunity to thus "suit up." In the day-to-day world of the working officer in a short-staffed department responding to a series of break-and-enters, for example, rubber gloves and your acquired instinct for caution regarding evidence will usually have to suffice.

Ideally the collection of crime-scene evidence is a task requiring more than one investigator, but in many cases you may be collecting and cataloguing the evidence by yourself. In major cases, on the other hand, there is usually a division of labour that ensures efficient and orderly collection, preservation, and storage of exhibits. One officer should be assigned to catalogue the evidence that others are gathering. This exhibit person may set up shop at a desk or table that has already undergone examination, and will receive, number, and describe items of evidence. With serious crimes that involve a considerable amount of evidence, this procedure helps to ensure continuity and order, which will later be essential to accurate and complete reconstruction of the scene. The other investigators bear the responsibility of gathering evidence and placing it in the appropriate containers. They then carry the evidence to the exhibits person, who records all the pertinent information about each item: number of object, name of collecting investigator, description of object, and time, date, and place seized. For example, the record might read:

The means of marking exhibits varies with the nature of the item. A hair or a paint fragment may be placed in a vial that is sealed and marked with the time date and investigator's initials. The vial is then placed in a bag and the same information recorded on the bag. Bags should be sealed with evidence tape, which ensures that the bag cannot be opened and then resealed without detection. A vial of blood seized

---

**EXHIBIT 1**

**Seized by:** Caroline Clewes—Signature _____

**Time of seizure:** 4:00 a.m.

**Date:** 2000/02/02

**Location:** 119 Suspicion Way, northeast bedroom on desktop

**Description:** spent cartridge casing, 9 mm

**Time received:** 4:07 a.m.

**Date:** 2000/02/02

**Signature of receiver (exhibit person):** _____

at an autopsy, for example, can be taped over top of the stopper and then taped around the circumference of the vial's rim so that the tape is covering the stopper and the top part of the vial. The officer sealing the exhibit should sign or initial across intersections of the tape, so that tampering can be noticed.

Your containers and some of your labelling methods will vary as well according to the manufacturers your organization uses as its suppliers. A hair, for example, may be placed in an envelope bearing a label, a stoppered tube, a plastic bag, or a pill bottle, depending on the composition of your investigating kit, or in the case of a sexual assault the containers specified for use by the manufacturers of prepackaged sexual assault kits. Often there is a need to improvise the suitable containers because of the size and nature of exhibits. Improvised containers should be clean and as little likely as possible to contaminate or destroy evidence. To seize an accelerant from the scene of an arson, for example, an investigator should use a clean paint can, available from a hardware or paint store.

Plastic bags may often seem the most convenient and protective containers, and they have the added feature of making evidence visible. But they must be used with caution. A bloodstained piece of clothing, if packaged moist, will turn mouldy and deteriorate, its evidential value destroyed. Bloodstains that cannot be submitted immediately or at least quickly to a forensic laboratory should be air-dried before packaging and submission or storage. Even when air-dried, however, in many moist climates blood samples will go mouldy in sealed plastic bags and are better preserved in paper wrapping. Plastic bags also tend to acquire static electricity. Small particles of paint excited by static electricity have been known to jump from the opening of a plastic bag, never to be seen again!

It is important, even in minor break-and-enter investigations, to remember the need for professionalism. This is an especially crucial point if you are alone. There is no one there with whom you can compare notes; nobody will remind you of evidence left behind, or of the necessity to observe careful and systematic procedures of evidence collection. The courts, the forensic labs, and the public in general are relying on you. What you do in these "solo" situations will often be taken as an indication of your capacity for leadership in serious cases. Every case is important.

Let us suppose all physical evidence has been seized, put into suitable containers, properly marked, and catalogued. If it is not immediately taken to a forensic laboratory, it must be transported to a proper evidence lockup. It should never be left in a briefcase, patrol car, or your personal locker. Be careful of the sightseers, usually other officers, who may be fascinated enough to handle the crime scene exhibit you have placed on your desk while writing your report. In a police service that shall remain unnamed, an identification specialist was able recently to lift two separate fingerprints from a piece of evidence only to find that the prints didn't match the "criminal" collection, but were positively identified from the employee records

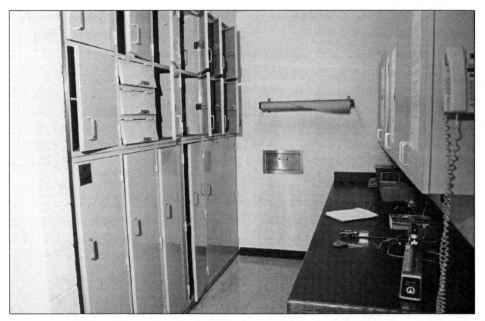

**Illustration 4-18.** Exhibit packaging area. Exhibits should be tagged, packaged, sealed, and stored to ensure proper continuity at all times.

as belonging to two sergeants from the station! The incident is now used in that city police service as a training illustration.

Transportation of evidence to the storage room is sometimes the cause of cross-contamination (contamination of one piece of evidence by another). Avoid contamination between pieces of evidence, or between evidence and the means of transporting it. Remember the **Principle of Alteration or Exchange.** Fibres from your patrol-car trunk should not be found on the bloodstained weapon you have seized and moved to storage.

The evidence lockup facilities will vary from one police service to another. In large urban departments, there may be full-time staff members in charge of all exhibits. Once the evidence is signed over to them, they are part of the vital chain of evidence and responsible for the maintenance of continuity. In a smaller organization, individual officers may be responsible for lockup and storage. They may select a certain "bin" for the deposit of evidence and lock it up. Continuity in these situations remains primarily the concern of the officer who placed the evidence in storage.

Continuity of evidence is particularly problematic in those smaller police services where all officers have access to one exhibit room, and if you are serving in a small department you must be aware of the dangers. In such departments, it is sometimes a sound idea to designate one person as the receiver of exhibits so that only the necessary personnel will ever touch evidence. The fewer the persons who handle

**Illustration 4-19.** Once in the custody of an exhibit clerk, items can be stored inside the exhibit room in a secure gun storage area, a drug storage area, or a vault.

an exhibit, the better. When you need to sign out an exhibit for a court appearance, you want to be sure continuity of evidence is intact.

## Do a Final Overall Survey and Release the Scene

Once you have processed the crime scene, it is useful to reexamine it overall. Your collection of evidence may have changed the way you think of the scene now; you may even wish to take additional photographs from new angles. Review your notes briefly to be sure that you have processed the scene thoroughly. Reconsider the basic steps presented earlier in this chapter under "Processing the Scene" and the body of observations and physical evidence you have compiled.

If, and only if, you are satisfied that your work is complete, the area can be "released"—returned to its normal uses. It will no longer be protected, so you must be sure to have done your forensic work. Should you find that you need to examine or seize further evidence, two problems will immediately arise: (1) continuity of evidence has been broken, the scene will be considered contaminated, and the value of evidence greatly diminished if not lost; (2) you may have to secure further permission in the form of a warrant.

# THE FORENSIC LABORATORY AND FORENSIC SCIENCE

*Chapter* 5

The forensic laboratory is the destination of much of the evidence you have gathered at the crime scene. There scientists and technicians will analyze the evidence and apply to it knowledge from a wide variety of sciences to discover its properties and assess its meaning. Most members of a police department will have little direct contact with forensic laboratory work, other than to package collected evidence appropriately for conveyance to the laboratory and to use laboratory results to develop or support a case. For some kinds of evidence the in-house services of a police department may be sufficient. Many police services can not only collect but also complete the comparison of fingerprints and various other things such as tire tracks, tool impressions, footwear impressions, and glass fragments. This is usually the work of identification units whose members are trained specialists. For analyses of ballistics, blood, or bodily fluids or for DNA matching, however, the more complete facilities and highly trained personnel of the forensic laboratory are required. With the increasing sophistication and complexity of analysis, laboratory scientists and technicians have become vital supports to the investigator in the field.

Forensic scientists, technicians, and investigators are also often required to give "expert" testimony in court. In order to speak with authority in this capacity, witnesses must be considered by the courts to be "expert," that is, having knowledge of the subject of testimony in some combination of (1) **education**, (2) **experience**, and (3) **training**. In other words, experts are persons whose opinions on a subject are valuable because of some combination of study and experience in that subject. In court they may offer opinions once they have been designated "expert" by the court. For

48

any officer or forensic practitioner who wishes to excel at police work, it is wise therefore to take advantage of educational or training opportunities that may arise in the
course of one's career. To maintain and enhance their status of "expert," forensic
professionals constantly attempt to stay current in their field, through awareness of
new techniques and research, study programs, and further training. A person trained
in fingerprinting, for example, is often required to work for a year under the guidance of a highly experienced identification technician so that initial court submissions are sound. The same principle is applied in laboratory training.

The field and the laboratory are two arms of police investigation essential to
the solution of many crimes. It is necessary that investigators at the crime scene
understand and take into account the needs of the forensic laboratory. The first and
most important steps to successful laboratory analysis of evidence are the recognition, collection, preservation, and packaging of evidence which are responsibili-
ties of the investigating officers.

# PACKAGING EVIDENCE FOR SUBMISSION TO THE LABORATORY

While you have collected and packaged evidence at the crime scene in Chapter 4, you
must now consider the task of packaging evidence for submission to the laboratory
for analysis. As we encounter the many types of evidence found at crime scenes,
we will discuss the specific collection and packaging requirements of each substance. But it is well at this stage to establish some general guidelines.

The two major factors you must keep in mind when packing evidence for submission to the laboratory are continuity and preservation of evidence. The chain of
custody of evidence must not be broken, nor should evidence be allowed to break,
leak, spoil, or be otherwise damaged. Evidence packaged and tagged at the scene of
the crime must now be packed in appropriate outer containers for shipping, mailing,
or transportation. The search for appropriate containers sometimes requires imagination, effort, and ingenuity. A rifle to be sent for ballistics examination is best
packed in a container designed for its original shipment to a retailer. The hardware
store or gun shop owner is a good resource for such packages. A map tube was
found to be an ideal container for shipping an arrow from a poaching incident; the
vital trace evidence on the arrowhead was protected with a paper bag taped well
up the shaft of the arrow (which had been examined for fingerprints) and the arrow
shaft packed tightly in the tube. Fragments of broken glass sent to a laboratory for
a physical matching after having been examined for fingerprints should not simply be thrown together into a box. Any further breakage could ruin the evidence.
If the goal is to reconstruct the single piece from which the fragments came, the

fragments can be placed between layers of tissue and packed firmly to prevent movement during shipping.

Evidence from pathologists or coroners is usually shipped in containers seized after an autopsy with the cooperation of the scientist. The containers must be sealed with tape and marked with signatures as outlined in Chapter 4. Remember the problems of leakage, continuity of evidence, and cross-contamination. Pick a suitable outer container for the shipment of exhibits with these dangers in mind. The RCMP laboratory services manual is clear on this point:

> Ensure there is a sufficient amount of packing to impede movement of the exhibit [evidence] container and that the outer container is strong enough to withstand the effects of transportation and handling. The outer container should be wrapped in paper and taped across all openings of the wrapping. The person wrapping and sealing it should initial it across all joints of tape and paper so that it cannot be opened and resealed without detection. Continuity of evidence must be preserved. Avoid brightly colored evidence tape on the exterior of your package; it could draw attention to your package in the mail. (Chapter 4, F.4.b)

The evidence shipment must be accompanied by the appropriate correspondence. While the demands of various laboratories and police services may vary, generally there will be a multi-copy form available from the laboratory, much similar to RCMP form C-414, which is shown in Illustration 5-1. There is usually a requirement that copies of the form be placed inside the outer container and also in a separate sealed enveloped affixed to the outside of the outer container. This practice ensures that when the exhibit arrives at the lab, it can be directed to a specific department or person without compromising the integrity of the outer container.

The method of shipment will depend partly on the nature and importance of the evidence. Never use ordinary mail; you cannot ensure continuity of evidence. In Canada, you should at least use a courier service that requires a signature at the point of departure and another at the point of arrival; confirmation is then sent to you by the laboratory.

The surest method of delivery is by hand. This can be costly, especially if you are using a distant laboratory, but in serious violent crimes such as homicide it is often essential. In other cases, delivery by courier will be sufficient.

## FORENSIC LABORATORIES IN CANADA

In Canada there is a system of regional forensic laboratories supported by the federal government and under the management of the Royal Canadian Mounted Police. There is also a Centre of Forensic Science in Toronto and a central laboratory in Montreal. For any assistance beyond the expertise of your local services, these laboratories can be contacted at the following locations and telephone numbers given in Table 5-1.

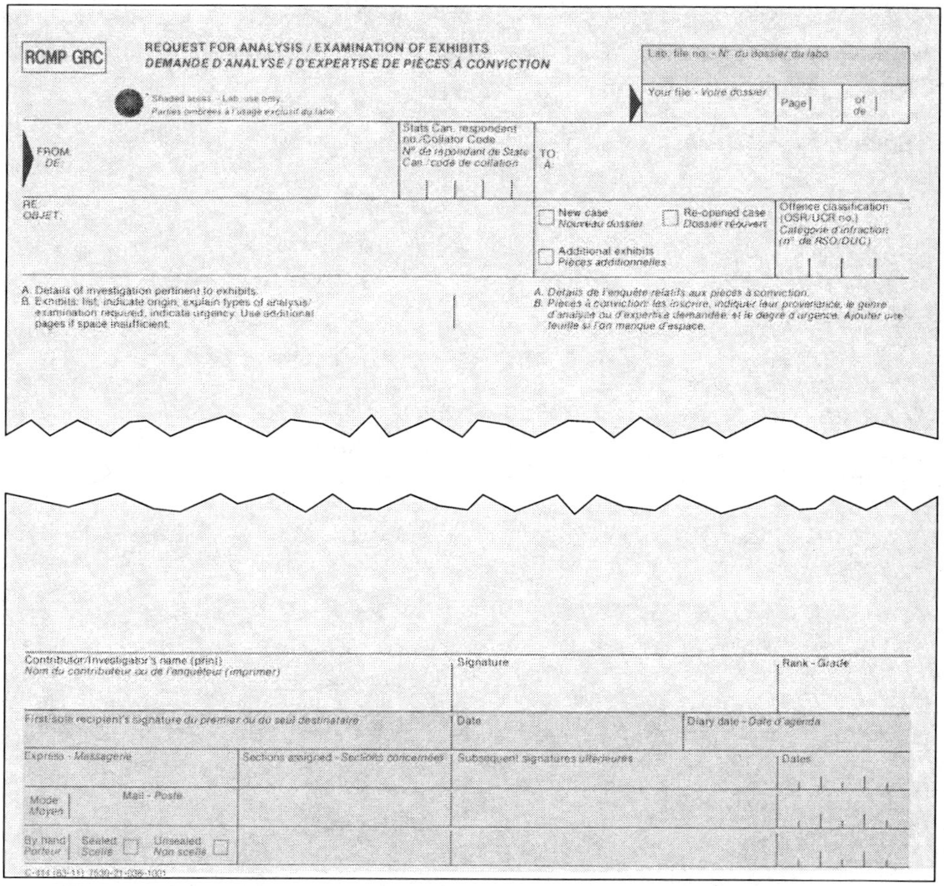
RCMP GRC
REQUEST FOR ANALYSIS / EXAMINATION OF EXHIBITS
DEMANDE D'ANALYSE / D'EXPERTISE DE PIÈCES À CONVICTION
Shaded areas - Lab. use only
Parties ombrées à l'usage exclusif du labo
Lab. file no. - N° du dossier du labo
Your file - Votre dossier
Page
of
de
FROM
DE:
Stats Can. respondent no./Collator Code
N° de répondant de Stats Can./code de collation
TO
A:
RE
OBJET:
New case
Nouveau dossier
Re-opened case
Dossier réouvert
Additional exhibits
Pièces additionnelles
Offence classification (OSR/UCR no.)
Catégorie d'infraction (n° de RSO/DUC)
A. Details of investigation pertinent to exhibits.
B. Exhibits: list, indicate origin, explain types of analysis/examination required, indicate urgency. Use additional pages if space insufficient.
A. Détails de l'enquête relatifs aux pièces à conviction.
B. Pièces à conviction: les inscrire, indiquer leur provenance, le genre d'analyse ou d'expertise demandée et le degré d'urgence. Ajouter une feuille si l'on manque d'espace.
Contributor/Investigator's name (print)
Nom du contributeur ou de l'enquêteur (imprimer)
Signature
Rank - Grade
First/sole recipient's signature du premier ou du seul destinataire
Date
Diary date - Date d'agenda
Express - Messagerie
Sections assigned - Sections concernées
Subsequent signatures ultérieures
Dates
Mode
Moyen
Mail - Poste
By hand
Porteur
Sealed
Scellé
Unsealed
Non scellé
C-414 (83-11) 7530-21-038-1001

**Illustration 5-1.** RCMP laboratory Request for Analysis, Form C-414.

As far as possible, you should direct your packaged samples to the appropriate section of the laboratory and also state on the accompanying form, along with your list of exhibits, the analysis requested. The major sections of RCMP Forensic Laboratory services are Alcohol, Biology, Chemistry, Documents, Firearms, Toxicology, and Counterfeits. With the changes in forensic science, these sections may change.

The RCMP Forensic Laboratory services will assist in investigations by any accredited law enforcement agency in Canada. They provide the full range of laboratory analyses of the evidence you provide. While these laboratories will not conduct your investigation for you, they supply invaluable technical and scientific assistance. After analyzing physical evidence for probable matching, for example, RCMP technicians and scientists will usually tell the submitting officer whether the match is "positive," "probable," "possible," or not a match at all. These three

| TABLE 5-1 | Regional Forensic Laboratories and Centres in Canada |
|---|---|

| RCMP Laboratories | Provincial Laboratories |
|---|---|
| **Halifax, Nova Scotia:** | **Montreal, Quebec:** |
| 3151 Oxford Street | Laboratoire de sciences judiciaires et de médecine légale |
| Halifax, Nova Scotia, B3K 5L9 | Édifice Wilfrid Derome |
| (902) 426-8886 | 1701, rue Parthenais, 12e étage |
| | Montréal, Québec, H2K 3S7 |
| **Regina, Saskatchewan:** | (514) 873-2704 Fax: (514) 873-4847 |
| Box 6500 | |
| Regina, Saskatchewan, S4P 3J7 | **Toronto, Ontario:** |
| (306) 780-5807 | Centre of Forensic Sciences |
| | 25 Grosvenor Street |
| **Ottawa, Ontario:** | Toronto, Ontario, M7A 2G8 |
| 1200 Vanier Parkway | (416) 314-3224 Fax: (416) 314-3225 |
| Ottawa, Ontario, K1A 0R2 | |
| (613) 993-0986 | **Sault Ste. Marie, Ontario:** |
| | Northern Regional Forensic Laboratory |
| **Winnipeg, Manitoba:** | 70 Foster Drive |
| 621 Academy Road | Sault Ste. Marie, Ontario P6A 6V3 |
| Winnipeg, Manitoba, R3N 0E7 | (705) 945-6552 Fax: (705) 945-6569 |
| (204) 983-5906 | |
| **Edmonton, Alberta:** | |
| 15707—118 Avenue | |
| Edmonton, Alberta, T5J 1B7 | |
| (403) 451-7400 | |
| **Vancouver, British Columbia:** | |
| 5201 Heather Street | |
| Vancouver, British Columbia, V5Z 3L7 | |
| (604) 264-3400 | |

findings fit all types of identification analysis. **Positive** is the highest degree of correlation; in a firearms report, a positive match would allow the statement "this shell casing and bullet were fired from this weapon." **Probable** matches in a laboratory report usually indicate a strong likelihood of correlation between "known" and "unknown" samples, but the issue is uncertain; a probable match can nonetheless be crucial to building the weight of evidence in a case or perhaps refuting alibi evidence. It may be that some laboratory examinations are valuable to your investigation but will not be necessary for presentation in court. **Possible** matches indicate that while the correlation may not be strong, it cannot be eliminated. The further away from a positive identification the report stands, the more it is open to the interpretation of the courts.

Matching is only one example of the services forensic laboratories provide. You may wish them to identify a chemical, a soil, or some other substance to determine the presence of gunshot residue, analyze handwriting samples, or provide any one of a host of other analyses from blood typing to identification of explosives. Forensic laboratory reports can be highly influential in a court case. In some instances, usually serious crimes, the personnel of forensic laboratories will appear in court to present their findings as expert witnesses. Investigators seeking expert advice or analysis should also compile a list of other sources of support, such as provincial and commercial laboratories, university departments, hospital laboratories, and agriculture research stations. And don't forget persons in the community who may have extensive training or experience in a particular area, even if it is just long acquaintanceship gained through a hobby or private study such as coin collecting or the examination of historical documents.

# SCIENCES ASSOCIATED WITH FORENSIC SCIENCE

As should gradually become clear, forensic science, and therefore investigators, may make use of many widely differing branches of science in dealing with physical evidence. It is useful to be aware of these disciplines and what they offer in the way of forensic analysis. The following will give you a general idea of the range of sciences and their application to crime.

The word "science" originally came from the Latin word meaning "to know." For a long time afterward, it meant simply a body of knowledge, and "sciences" were various fields of knowledge and scholarship. While the word is still sometimes used in the same way, sciences have increasingly come to refer to systematic studies in particular fields where data are analyzed to develop and test hypotheses or theories that may explain them. The scientific method involves the collection, observation, and interpretation of data in a systematic, logical, and objective fashion. With these definitions in mind, you can see how much police work can also be considered scientific. The police discover a phenomenon, incident, or crime. They conduct an investigation in which they gather facts (data) about the nature and possible causes of the event. Finally, they also develop hypotheses, theories, and reconstructions that may explain a crime.

A major feature distinguishing police work from other sciences is that it is always performed with reference to the law. It is **forensic** work. ("Forensic" once referred to the use of the skill or ability to argue or debate and is now commonly used to apply to law.) Forensic scientists are therefore practitioners of various scientific disciplines in support of law enforcement. Their laboratories exist to examine the nature of evidence gathered and submitted by investigators and technicians. Their analyses are then used to build, confirm, or disprove the theories about a crime that have been developed by police and other members of the justice system.

Virtually any field of knowledge could conceivably be applied to the problems of evidence. Language specialists or historians might be called upon to help with the interpretation of documents, or the identification of evidence, for example, or scholars of religion to explain the thought patterns of religiously inspired offenders. But in the analysis and evaluation of physical evidence, the most commonly applied techniques rely on discoveries related to the physical, natural, and medical sciences, and on specific specializations that have developed in response to the needs of criminal investigation.

Principles, research, and equipment from chemistry, physics, geology, biology, medicine, dentistry or odontology, physical anthropology, engineering, pharmacy, and psychology have been invaluable to the development of forensic sciences and laboratories. In addition to the development of particular forensic areas, such as the examination of questioned documents, basic sciences have given birth to a variety of subfields and areas of specialization that are especially useful in forensic analysis. Recently developed studies, such as those in computer science and biological "fingerprinting," are quickly becoming precious to forensic science. It is therefore useful for law enforcement personnel to acquaint themselves with some of the sciences and techniques that provide critical support to their investigations.

## Life Sciences

**Biology** is the study of all living things: plant and animal life, pollen, cells, insects, and diatoms, among others. **Forensic biologists** use their knowledge to identify and analyze these things in the course of an investigation. Their analyses of biological evidence on a body could locate the unknown scene of a homicide, for example.

**Entomology** is branch of biology devoted to the study of insects. **Forensic entomologists** use their knowledge of insect life cycles in the investigation of crimes. Perhaps the most frequent employment of entomological experts is in estimating time of death. When a body begins to decompose, insects usually lay eggs on it. These hatch into larvae or maggots which feed on the body. Eventually, the larvae mature, becoming adult insects such as blowflies. The speed of their life cycle is well known to entomologists, although it may vary depending on the climate to which they are exposed (lower temperatures, for example, may slow down some insects' development). The forensic entomologist can take environmental and other factors into consideration, and use the degree of insect development to establish the length of time a body has been subject to insect infestation. This in turn can be used to estimate the time of death.

Experts in the various studies related to basic biological inquiries give more frequent forensic support than biologists themselves. This is especially true of various specialties related to medicine and human life, such as **forensic pathology**, **forensic odontology**, **forensic psychiatry and psychology**, and **forensic serology**. There is, however, one area of biological research in particular that has made a contribution that is nothing short of amazing in its implications for forensic science: DNA typing or "fingerprinting."

## DNA Typing and Serology

The biological field of **genetics** specializes in the study of heredity. In the late twentieth century, it provided the most exciting and significant discovery for forensic science since the development of fingerprinting. It has been closely associated with serology. This new "fingerprint" is provided by the analysis of **deoxyribonucleic acid** or **DNA**. It requires only minute amounts of tissue, blood, or other biological matter to link a sample to its source. In many cases, the evidence may be old or quite degraded, but a match is still possible. (Complications do still arise in the case of identical twins, who share basically the same DNA.) With the discovery of the individual distinctiveness of some parts of each person's DNA, a new era in the science of identification began. "Cold squads," using evidence from unsolved or mistakenly identified major crimes of the past, immediately began to reexamine the conclusions of trials and investigations. In some cases, suspects who thought they had committed "the perfect crime" found themselves convicted on old physical evidence submitted to new analysis. In others, perhaps even more vexing and dramatic, persons who had been wrongfully convicted were exonerated and freed from prison through the same process of DNA analysis. Among these was Guy Paul Morin, a Canadian wrongfully convicted of sexually assaulting and murdering a child. His release in 1996 from a long confinement was followed by an inquiry, resulting in the report given in Appendix A of this book ("Major Crime Scene Protocols: Judical Instructions to Police"). (Details on the collection, preservation, and packaging of DNA evidence are also presented in Chapter 9.)

You will notice that most of the recommendations following the Morin case are recommendations for investigators concerning the care they must take in the collection, handling, storage, and preservation of evidence. This emphasis serves to reinforce a point we make continually in this book: *As the techniques for analyzing and comparing evidence become more precise, complex, and accurate, the possi-*

*bilities of contamination and the necessity for care in recognizing, collecting, and storing evidence increase.*

This is both a scientific and a legal necessity. DNA evidence quickly gained acceptance in courts (although not without challenge). Initially, some expert witnesses provided a set of probabilities of error for each DNA match. They might say, for example (as in the O. J. Simpson case of 1994–95) that there was a 57-billion-to-1 chance that the blood sample in question came from a person other than the suspect. By 1999, however, the FBI began to question the necessity of producing such figures, which sometimes surpassed not only the present population of the world, but also even the number of people who had ever lived in several centuries of recorded history. Other authorities, however, have been more cautious, and statistical probability is still cited.

This degree of certainty in matching presents difficulties for defence counsel of clients whose DNA has been connected to a crime. Put yourself in the position of the defence counsel in such a case. If the DNA analysis itself seems virtually undeniable, one of the areas you may naturally wish to examine most closely in trying to build a defence for your client is the way that evidence was acquired. Was the crime scene properly protected? Was the evidence collected and handled appropriately? Was continuity of evidence preserved? Might officers have allowed cross-contamination of the crime scene sample with the defendant's DNA? In other words, were the investigators honest and professional in their dealings with evidence and suspect? This increased scrutiny of some aspects of forensic work need not be a cause for undue concern among law enforcement officers. But it does point out the need for professional care and integrity in carefully and properly managing and processing a crime scene in the new age of forensic science.

The DNA molecule so instrumental to the science of detection is essentially the substance of our genes. Every human body contains trillions of **cells**, and every cell **nucleus** 23 pairs of **chromosomes**. Inside the chromosomes is the code that determines the various aspects of our bodily makeup: the colour of our eyes, the natural curl of our hair, and other characteristics such as our vulnerability to certain diseases. This code is arrayed along the strands of **deoxyribonucleic acid** or **DNA** that are packed in tight coils in each chromosome. The tens of thousands of sections of DNA in each chromosome that cause cells to manufacture the proteins or enzymes that construct our physical being are the **genes**. DNA strands are aligned together in an intersecting spiral arrangement, usually called a **double helix**. Along it are chemicals called **nucleotides**, joined in pairs by a hydrogen bond. Each gene is made up of a set of three nucleotides. While there are only four different types of DNA nucleotides, they are arranged in many different sequences of varying lengths, and given the number of these units, the possibilities for genetic variety and genetic manipulation are immense. It is precisely the variations in human DNA that have given rise to its use as a forensic tool.

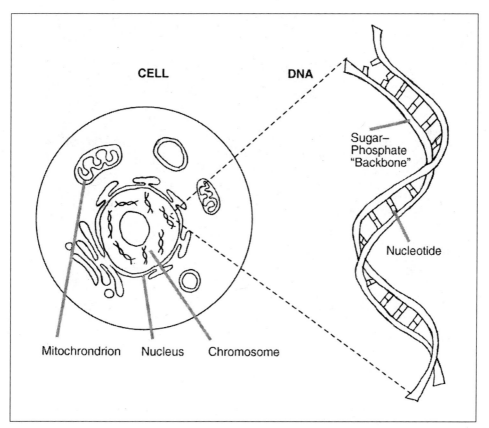

CELL       DNA

Sugar–
Phosphate
"Backbone"

Nucleotide

Mitochrondrion    Nucleus    Chromosome

**Illustration 5-2.** Cell structure and DNA.

As scientists studied DNA, it became apparent that some sections contained distinctive, perhaps even unique, sequences of nucleotides. Dr. Alec Jeffreys of the University of Leicester in England was able in 1983 to use a probe that isolated these DNA sequences and to show the "DNA fingerprint" that could be derived from a sample. Now a known blood sample from a suspect, for example, could be compared to an unknown, crime-scene sample. If the unique DNA "fingerprint" was present in both samples, investigators could be reasonably sure that both samples came from the same person or an identical twin. Jeffreys and others continued to work on the development of better probes and analytical methods.

In one method of **DNA typing**, the DNA in samples to be compared was cut up with the use of special enzymes and subjected to a process called **polyacrylamide gel electrophoresis**. Each sample was placed in its own section of a comparison plate containing gel. Under the influence of an electric charge, the DNA fragments moved through the gel. Because smaller fragments move more quickly in the gel than larger ones, in each sample the fragments were separated from each other into bands

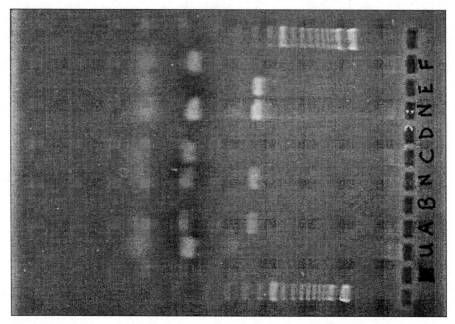

**Illustration 5-3.** A gel electrophoresis for the comparison of DNA in human saliva. **U**: unknown crime-scene sample; **N**: negative control; **A, B, C, D, E,** and **F**: known comparison samples. **C** and **F** match the unknown, **U**.

of different sizes. Transferred to a membrane, these bands were then treated with radioactive **DNA probes**. (Or they could be dyed, viewed with an alternative light source, and then photographed.) When x-ray film was placed over the radioactive bands, the result was a picture of the DNA fingerprint of each sample. Side by side, these pictures allowed the comparison of one DNA sample to another, much the way one could compare two bar codes on merchandise in a store. With these and other methods, scientists were able to compare accurately the DNA from various samples.

One of the problems of analyzing unknown crime scene DNA was that it is often found in minute traces. In order to obtain sufficient quantities for analysis, scientists needed a method of replicating or multiplying the amount of DNA. One of the most successful methods of replication was the **polymerase chain reaction**, sometimes called PCR. Using the enzyme DNA polymerase, scientists were able to mutiply the DNA from a sample millions of times in a relatively short period. The amplified sample was then of sufficient size to undergo analyses such as the one above. Now slight traces of DNA evidence could be amplified, analyzed, and compared as never before. For the investigator at the crime scene, the possibility of DNA typing means that the minutest piece of evidence may be traceable to its source. With the development of extensive databanks of DNA, there is an increasing likelihood that the individual who deposited the DNA can be quickly identified. Extraordinary alertness to trace evidence and great care in its collection, recording, packaging, transportation, and storage are absolutely essential.

While the DNA used for the identification of individuals is **nuclear DNA** (i.e., DNA from the cell nucleus), there is also a type of DNA located outside the nucleus. It is found in a specialized structure called the **mitochondrion** of a cell. This **mitochondrial DNA** is passed exclusively and identically *from mother to child*, and changes only slightly over many generations. It can therefore identify the biological family of its donor body. Biologists find it useful for studying the long-term development of organisms. Projects using mitochondrial DNA are under way in England and elsewhere to map the development of the human race over tens of thousands of years. Participants need only brush a sterile swab across the face and send it to the scientists to find out a great deal about their origins in the distant past. Usable mitochondrial DNA can be obtained from very old skeletons and hair shafts, among other things, and therefore it presents interesting forensic possibilities when nuclear DNA no longer survives. It has been used to identify long-buried victims of political death squads, the burnt corpses from airline crashes, and other unknown human remains. Its analytical possibilities have given bits of hair or bone great evidential value.

## Forensic Pathology

**Forensic pathologists** are medical doctors who have done extensive further study in pathology, the causes of human death, disease, or injury, and their legal implications. Before qualifying, they may also have served a further period of apprenticeship or practice in dealing with cases of unnatural or suspicious deaths. Pathologists are particularly required for the examination of bodies after death, which is done both at the site where a body is found and later in an autopsy room. They may also examine living persons to determine the age of injuries, or to record evidence in cases of crimes such as child or spousal abuse.

Pathologists attempt to determine the time and causes of death. Their determination will sometimes be crucial in deciding whether a criminal offence has occurred. Perhaps foul play has caused a death that appeared accidental. An apparent drowning victim might turn out to have been poisoned, or a suicide to have been a homicide, "staged" to remove suspicion from the murderer. In each case, the pathologist's conclusions about how a victim died can be the crucial factor in the reconstruction of the crime. The examination of wounds, their comparison to possible weapons, the condition of the internal organs and body fluids, and the presence of any foreign substance in the body are all taken into consideration. Sometimes, with the help of specialists in other fields, the pathologist painstakingly and thoroughly attempts to explore all the possible causes of death.

Determination of time of death is probably the most familiar example of the pathologist's activity. The pathologist has several means of measurement in addition to the entomological ones mentioned above. Most readers will have seen or read about some of them. For example, the pathologist might take the victim's body temperature. A body will cool to the temperature of its immediate environment, at a rate depending on how it is clothed, the temperature to which it has been exposed, and its size. Making a calculation accounting for all of these factors, the pathologist can establish the probable rate of cooling and decide on the time elapsed since the victim was alive.

Some of the indications of time of death noted by pathologists can also be observed by homicide investigators. You have probably heard of **rigor mortis**, the rigidity of a body after death. Sometime after about two hours and usually within the space of four hours, chemical changes in the muscles cause them to begin stiffening all over the body. This muscle contraction usually shows first in the neck or jaws, and affects the entire body within something between eight and twelve hours, after which a corpse is extremely stiff for twelve to twenty-four hours. Rigor then begins to disappear and within forty-eight to sixty hours after death the body is completely flaccid.

Immediately after a person dies, the blood, which is no longer circulating, begins to flow to the lowest areas of the body, usually those on the surface where the body lies. The skin covering these places acquires a bruised look called **lividity**. "Livid" literally means "blue" and the livid areas of a body are often a bluish or purplish colour, although loss of blood may prevent lividity. The colour may be affected by other causes, such as carbon monoxide poisoning, which turns the livid areas red. There is also sometimes an absence of lividity in areas of the body that have been in direct contact with a surface such as a floor or hard object. While lividity is not an exact measure of the time of death, it can give the pathologist some notion. It usually starts a short time after the heart stops pumping, beginning to appear in about half an hour, and after about eight hours it is fixed in the livid areas. If **livor mortis** appears on the front of a body found lying on its back, then an investigator can conclude that the body has been moved some time after death.

In addition to these signs, pathologists may examine other features of a body that indicate the time and sometimes the cause of death. The contents of the digestive system can be important to an investigation. The degree to which food has been digested can suggest time of death, reveal poisons, or perhaps even give a clue about where the deceased ate a last meal and thereby help to reconstruct a victim's actions before death. Other indications such as a cloudy film in the normally clear sections of the eyes (eight to ten hours after death), the degree of rotting or **putrefaction**, or of **mummification** (a hardening of the body tissues in dry conditions), may also be of help.

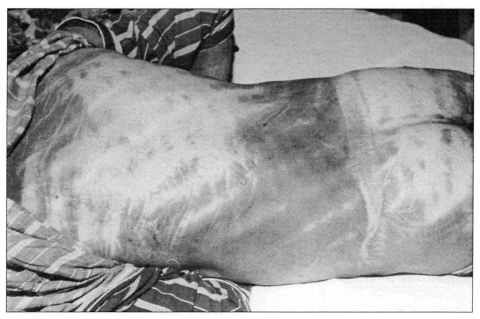

**Illustration 5-4.** Post-mortem lividity constitutes an investigational aid, because it provides an indication of the position or movement of the body after death and can also help in the estimation of time of death.

The pathologist or medical examiner has a highly complex job that is critical to an investigator's success. The major task for medical examiners in a homicide is the **autopsy**, sometimes also called a **necropsy** or a **postmortem**—an examination of the body to determine the cause and manner of death and the identity of the deceased. A medical examiner often inspects the crime scene. A preliminary examination and identification of the body for characteristics such as temperature, lividity, rigor mortis, wounds, and other features may reveal much, but pathologists move onto a more detailed examination under laboratory conditions. The exterior of the body is carefully inspected, and then the pathologist proceeds to an internal examination. At every stage, all of the pathologist's observations are recorded in detail.

## Toxicology

The dissection of the body allows the pathologist to examine the internal organs and to extract organs, tissues, and fluids for the **toxicologist**, who can then report on their contents. At the crime scene, the homicide investigator is most useful in keeping the scene protected so that the medical examiner can work. It is also advised that the investigator be present at the autopsy. The pathologist often requires the officer's information from the crime scene, and the investigator can benefit from the discoveries at the autopsy table. The investigator can provide crime-scene photographs, notes, sketches, and information about the circumstances of the death, the initial state of the body suspected weapons, suspects, and witnesses. The autopsy may give rise to new theories about the crime, reveal inconsistencies in other evidence, or confirm what an investigator already suspects.

The work of the forensic pathologist and the investigator is supplemented in the laboratory by knowledge from many other scientific disciplines. **Toxicology** is the study of poisons or toxins, the effects of poisons, and the methods of detecting such substances. The most common result of this science to most of us is the calculation of alcohol content in the body, which can now be done rapidly by ordinary officers administering breath tests. But today the consumption of other drugs is so widespread that toxicologists are often called upon to identify unknown toxic substances and the levels at which they occupy the body. Fortunately, the variety of types of drugs that are frequently abused is not so great as trade names might indicate; alcohol and cocaine usually top the list. With sophisticated analytical techniques, it is possible to narrow an unknown drug down to one of the narcotics, hallucinogens, depressants, or stimulants in common use.

But, of course, toxicologists must be prepared to encounter a vast number of other substances. Among the most frequently found of these, for example, is carbon monoxide. Toxicologists often work with very little corroborating information about what a substance could be. Moreover, they are required to give opinions on the likely effect on a person of a given toxic substance at a given level. These are sometimes complex matters, with a number of factors to consider; hence, the forensic toxicologist must have considerable education and experience.

The analysis of many other substances, from explosives to traces of chemical pollutants, is another form of **forensic chemistry** (a more general term than "toxicology") and may often employ some of the same principles, techniques, and scientific knowledge as toxicology.

## Dentistry

The crime laboratory or the investigator may call on other sorts of medical experts to examine physical evidence. **Forensic dentistry or odontology** has developed into a highly useful means of identification. In the case of mass deaths by highly destructive accidents,, wartime atrocities, and other mass disasters, dental records have allowed the identification of victims. They have also been used in individual crimes to identify both victims and suspects. In addition to identifying the deceased, dental evidence can help investigators to find and name the living. Probably the best example of such identification is the interpretation of bite marks to link a suspect to a crime. Such evidence was found in the case of the sadistic serial killer Ted Bundy in the United States, and forensic odontologists have since developed considerable expertise in such cases. They may link the crime or skin impressions themselves directly to tooth impressions made by the suspect or use dental records to identify the source of the marks. (See Chapter 7, "Impressions.")

## Psychology and Psychiatry

**Forensic psychiatry or psychology** and related disciplines deal with the human mind and behaviour. Psychiatrists are medical doctors who have done extensive further study and practical work in psychiatry. They may be required to determine the mental competence of persons who are making decisions regarding the disposal of property or the acceptance of medical help. In addition to these civil matters, they, along with other health and counselling professionals, may also be experts in criminal matters, called upon to comment on the mental fitness of a suspect to stand trial. At first glance, however, they may not seem important to the study of physical evidence.

But there is also sometimes a psychological aspect to the physical evidence in an investigation. Not only can research in psychology and psychiatry be important to an understanding of offenders' motives and behaviour, identifying mental disorders such as pyromania (which may characterize arsonists) or the various mental diseases that may issue in violence; it can also help in the interpretation of physical evidence. The **psychological profiling** that has gained increasing credibility among some authorities draws many of its conclusions about the psychological condition and perhaps some other characteristics of the offender from the physical evidence carefully collected by investigators. For example, the arrangement of a homicide scene will often tell the expert whether the crime was committed by an "organized" or a "disorganized" offender. **Disorganized** offenders will often commit spontaneous crimes, leave "messy" crime scenes that indicate the randomness and opportunistic nature of their crimes. Their lives will often reflect their disorganization in various "failures" or inadequacies in interpersonal relations and career progress. **Organized** offenders, on the other hand, who target their victims and plan their offences carefully, often leave physical indications of control at the scene, including the fact that much evidence has been "cleaned up." Despite their acts of violence, they may in fact seem relatively well integrated socially.

In further examining physical evidence, those trained and experienced in the psychology of offenders can speculate intelligently and often accurately about a great many probable characteristics of the unknown criminal: age, sex, race, intelligence, education, occupation, residence in relation to the crime scene, motive, personality, and even family history. A murderer may also provide further clues by the way in which the body of the victim has been treated. Some killers "pose" their victims' bodies grotesquely or obscenely, or in other ways "make a statement" about

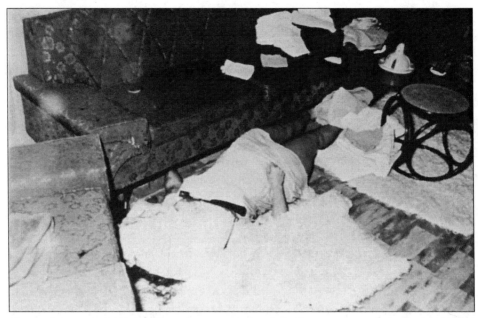

**Illustration 5-5.**  When this homicide victim was found, the face was covered; this fact could provide investigators with some indication of the relationship between victim and murderer.

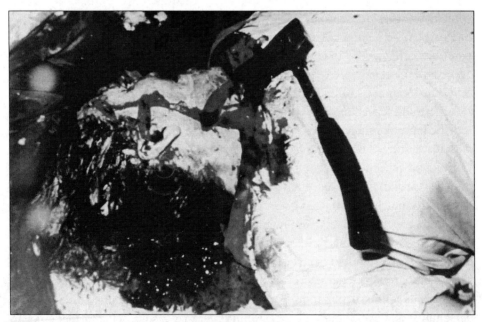

**Illustration 5-6.**  Uncovering the head of the victim revealed the intensity of this attack, a further clue that might indicate the intensity of feeling in the attacker.

their hatreds or obsessions. Others may leave specific objects or marks of their identity. Particular attention of the assault to various parts of the body can sometimes tell the profiler more about the offender. Extraordinary mutilation of the face and head, for instance, is sometimes considered an indication that the victim had a previous relationship with the assailant. Some profilers, such as John E. Douglas, the FBI agent who became a specialist in profiling serial murderers, have become widely renowned for their skill. The greatest help an officer can give to these experts is a careful, detailed recording of the crime scene and all the evidence associated with it.

The health-related sciences are often central to the investigation of crimes, particularly those involving violence. New means of identification and examination are emerging out of a constant, ingenious search for knowledge and justice. There has even been recent interest in **forensic optometry**. Experts in optical problems and the correction of vision can aid in identifying suspects by analyzing their eyeglasses. The size and structure of the face and other characteristics can be inferred from precise measurements of eyewear. But crime and its investigation are highly complex matters that often require expertise beyond the health sciences.

## Anthropology

Anthropology is a natural and social science devoted to the study of human beings in a very wide context: social, cultural, and physical. Understandably such a broad discipline has many specialized areas. The subdivision most directly useful to the examination and analysis of physical evidence is physical anthropology, which examines physical development and its variations in human beings and other primate species. **Forensic anthropologists** draw on this field, which can give an investigator help in estimating the age, sex, and race of, and possible injuries suffered by, a body consisting of skeletal or badly decomposed remains—which might amount to only a few bones. An interesting activity, sometimes assisted by these experts, is facial reconstruction using the skull of the deceased.

Many other forms of study may be applied to the problem of crime investigation. **Forensic engineers**, for example, are sometimes called in to investigate accidents or sabotage. They apply the principles of physics and engineering to evaluate stress and damage in vehicles, aircraft, industrial machinery, and other structures. They are central to solving the problem of finding the causes of structural or mechanical failure. **Forensic geologists** may be required to identify the sources of soil or other materials of geological origin.

While these and other sciences are valuable to police investigation, many areas of expertise were developed exclusively for criminal investigation: fingerprints, tool impressions, tire impressions, questioned documents, firearms, etc. They will be discussed in the following chapters. Although many veteran specialists in these subjects have developed a sophisticated technique of observation and analysis, some have had little formal scientific training. Nowadays, however, formal training in these subjects is common. Forensic technicians, trained to collect and analyze such physical evidence, are practising a highly specialized science. Police officers, whenever they undertake any investigation involving physical evidence, are on the front line of scientific inquiry.

# LABORATORY PROCESSES

Although much of its equipment and many of its processes can be found in other laboratories, a complete forensics laboratory is a unique assemblage of expertise and instruments. The expense of assembling all the equipment and analysts necessary for every possible kind of analysis means that complete laboratories are relatively few. In many cases, specific types of analysis may well be contracted to other labs that possess specialized staff and equipment. The growth of private forensic devices in the United States has meant an increasing reliance on private firms whose staff are specifically trained for the task, rather than officers who have many other tasks to perform.

## Means of Forensic Examination in the Laboratory

The basic instrument of forensic examination, and one of the earliest, common to all forensic laboratories, is the microscope. The ability to magnify objects was crucial to the initial forensic work of Edmond Locard in his groundbreaking examination of the transfer of trace evidence. It is still central to forensic investigation, although in a greater variety of different forms. A simple magnification (such as that through a magnifying glass) is caused by the bending (refraction) of light rays as they go through a lens and into the air again. The **compound microscope** is capable of much greater magnification. It is made up of two lenses, one at either end of a hollow cylinder or tube, and can increase the image of an object over 1000 times.

Beginning with the addition of artificial light, modern microscopy has benefited from a variety of developments. The **comparison microscope** consists of two compound microscopes in a single instrument. It enables the user to magnify and compare two images side by side. With this instrument, comparison of physical evidence, such as the marks on shell casings or the striations on bullets, hairs, fibres, and other sorts of physical identification are made much easier. Another combination of two microscopes is the **stereoscopic microscope**. While its magnification is not particularly great, it gives the viewer a fuller three-dimensional image of objects, and its structure allows the user to examine larger pieces of evidence. The **polarized-light microscope** is useful for identifying minerals, glass, and other materials by their

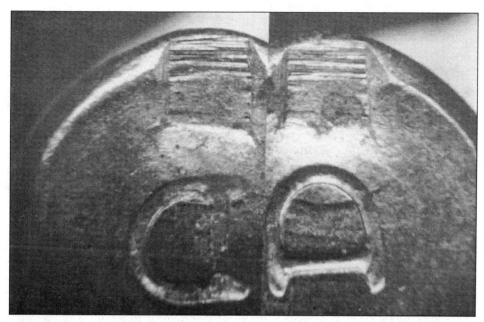

**Illustration 5-7.** .22-calibre rim-fire cartridge cases examined under a comparison microscope.

optical properties and structure. For much greater magnification, the most advanced laboratory is equipped with a **scanning electron microscope**. It is capable of magnifying an image up to in the range of 1,000,000 times, by bombarding objects with electrons. It can also create x-rays. At this degree of magnification the minutest traces of gunpowder can be detected on the skin of a person who has fired a gun, or even of someone who was close to a gunshot.

Various kinds of microscopes can assist in the examination, identification, comparison, and matching of the shape, colour, and structure of objects, fragments, and substances. When more information about unknown evidence is required, forensic analysts can turn to a host of other devices and processes. While we shall not examine all of these, it is useful for investigators to be aware of some of the main methods and instruments in use. Among others, these include **chromatography**, **spectroscopy**, **spectrophotometry**, **laser**, and **alternative light sources**, and various methods of distillation, separation, isolation, x-ray, and photography that we shall encounter as we examine the problems of dealing with physical evidence.

As we have seen, microscopy may be crucial to examining the physical properties of an object such as its structure and refractive index. We must not forget as well that many of the basic physical measurements taken, such as weight, mass, volume, and density, will require the use of principles and equipment that many students became familiar with in high-school science—high-precision balances for weight and mass, the use of liquid displacement to calculate volume, and thermometers for temperature measurement. Beyond these measures, scientists must often identify or compare mixed substances. In comparing the density of soils or glass, they may use the **density gradient tubes**, described in Chapter 11.

To attempt identification of the various constituents of other mixtures, one of the major methods of separating and sometimes identifying the parts of an unknown mixture is **chromatography**. In **pyrolysis gas chromatography**, for instance, the different speeds of each the various gases in a moving, vaporized mixture cause the constituents gradually to separate, until the amount of each separate component can be measured and shown in a **chromatogram**. This process is accomplished by the injection of the heated sample into a tube heated to maintain the vaporization of the mixture. As the various gases in the sample move along the tube they separate. The time it takes for each gas to move through the tube (**retention time**) is recorded by a detection device and automatically graphed. The chromatogram of the unknown mixture can then be compared to those of known substances, and the identity of constituents in the unknown reduced to a narrow range of possibilities. The gas chromatograph can rapidly detect minute traces of a substance in a mixture, but it cannot distinguish between gases with the same retention time. It is a valuable tool for identifying and matching the components of accelerants used to start arson fires, and for the analysis of drugs, alcohol, and other materials. Even paint chips, plastics, and other solids can be analyzed by a special process that uses extremely high temperature to vaporize the samples.

Other forms of chromatography, such as **thin-layer chromatography**, and **liquid chromatography** also separate the constituents of a mixture according to their rate of movement, but instead of gases, these processes use the movement of molecules in the liquid form of the substance to achieve the task. Both of these methods can be employed at room temperature, and **thin-layer chromatography** in particular is relatively inexpensive. The thin-layer process is somewhat like the electrophoresis described above. A spot of the sample in liquid form is placed on the lower edge of a glass plate coated with a gritty material such as silica gel. The plate is placed into a container of liquid that reaches a level just below the sample. The container is closed and capillary action begins to move the liquid up the gel toward the unknown substance. The moving liquid encounters the unknown substance. As the liquid rises, the components of the sample that are most amenable to the liquid move up the plate most quickly. At the end of the separation, the components of the sample are spread out in a line from bottom to top of the plate. Dried, dyed, and exposed to ultraviolet light, the plate contains a chromatogram that appears as a vertical column of spots. The substance in each spot along the column can be identified according to the precise distance it has moved.

Another means of identifying and measuring the presence and concentration of various components in an unknown substance is **spectroscopy**, by which scientists can measure the radiant energy or light absorbed or reflected by a compound. Every kind of radiation has a different **wavelength** and **frequency**. Every compound has a specific degree of absorption of the waves of each kind of radiation. A **spectrophotometer** can measure the absorption of visible light as well as the invisible light rays of **ultraviolet light** and **infrared light**, and thus identify the substance under examination. The basic components of the spectrophotometer are a source of radiation, a container for the sample, and a detector that measures radiation absorption.

In many cases, evidence consists of minute traces of a substance, too small for a conventional spectrophotometer. A solution to this problem is provided by the **microspectrophotometer**, which combines microscopy with spectrophotometry and allows the scientists to both view trace evidence and derive its absorption spectrum. For a highly accurate identification of a substance, laboratories sometimes use **mass spectrometry**. In order to prepare a sample, scientists first separate its components with a gas chromatograph. This then feeds the components into the **mass spectrometer**. The mass spectrometer uses a beam of electrons to fragment the molecules of a sample. These smaller particles of the substance are then gathered into separate groups according to their mass by a magnetic field. This fragmentation pattern is distinctive for every substance. These and other, related techniques such as atomic absorption spectrometry and neutron activation analysis use the emission and absorption of the different sorts of rays on the electromagnetic spectrum to identify the nature of substances down to the type and quantity of the basic elements they contain.

While laboratories rely on increasingly sophisticated techniques, it must be remembered that many processes of examination begin with basic observation and a background of knowledge, experience, and judgement. Many analyses of evidence, such as the comparison of fingerprints or the examination of documents, can be conducted with few complex and expensive scientific instruments, although the computer has advanced even such processes as these. Programs for fingerprint comparison, bloodstain pattern analysis, and other essential tools of investigation have appeared over the past few years to help investigators bring more rapid and accurate conclusions to their cases. As we consider the various kinds of evidence, it is well to remember too that the whole process begins with the professionalism and care of the police officer who answers the first call.

# PHYSICAL EVIDENCE AND MAJOR CRIMES

Before we leave the general discussion of forensic science to examine in more detail the collection of specific types of evidence, it is useful to look at some of the evidential possibilities of the crime scene. How many of the types of evidence and the scientific specialties we have mentioned could be important to the investigation of offences that involve violence to human beings? Let us consider two of the most serious crimes: homicide and sexual assault.

# Homicide

*Remember that before seizure, all evidence is photographed, first as it was found on the scene and then with a scale ruler and markers; notes must also be taken and the scene sketched.*

*The body and clothing of the victim* of a suspected homicide may carry a great deal of evidence transferred by the murderer:

- blood, semen, saliva and other DNA-bearing deposits
- hairs and fibres
- fingerprints
- blood, tissue, fibres, etc. under fingernails ("bag" victim's hands)
- gunshot residues
- possible "staging" of the body, distance from weapon on scene, etc.
- obvious wounds, bruises
- lividity and rigor mortis
- signs of hemorrhaging in the eyelids, trauma to the tongue (indicating strangulation)

Some of this evidence, although observed at the scene, will not be throughly noted and collected until the autopsy.

*At an autopsy* the body undergoes a detailed examination for signs of the time and manner of death and various organs and samples are taken for toxicological and other analysis:

- blood (cardiac and peripheral)
- urine
- liver
- stomach contents
- vitreous humour (from the eyes, for alcohol analysis)
- wounds external and internal
- bullets or other foreign objects
- flesh samples from the areas surrounding wounds

Pathologists may also collect lungs, brain tissue, bile, and cerebrospinal fluid.

*The surrounding scene* must be meticulously searched for a great range of items:

- weapons (firearms or others) and ammunition
- toolmarks, broken glass, and other signs of forced entry
- fingerprints
- blood and bloodstain pattern evidence
- drugs, intoxicants, unknown substances, and drug paraphenalia
- tissue, hairs, and fibres
- possible possessions of the suspect: cigarette butts, clothing, buttons, etc.
- documents, possible suicide notes, diaries, handwriting samples
- foot and tire impressions if appropriate
- arson evidence if appropriate
- cosmetics
- biological, soil, and other samples from outdoor scenes

*The suspect's person and residence* may be examined and the following seized or sampled:

- blood, urine, and breath may be analyzed for drugs and alcohol and for standard samples to compare with crime-scene evidence
- suspects may be searched for evidence of blood, hair, fibres, cosmetics, and other evidence transferred to them from the victim and the scene
- any possessions of the victim
- weapons
- comparison samples of the suspect's hair
- the suspect's clothing

## Sexual Assault

In cases of sexual assault many of the same sorts of physical evidence are collected as in homicide cases. Because certain kinds of evidence collection are routinely required, sexual assault kits are used, usually by medical personnel. In addition to ensuring the thorough processing of relevant physical evidence, officers must also ensure that they employ great tact, politeness, and sensitivity in dealing with victims, who are often likely to have been severely taumatized.

*From the victim and the scene*:

- where necessary, vaginal, anal, and oral swabs
- hair samples

- blood samples
- under the victim's fingernails, tissue or fibres from the suspect
- traces of blood
- seminal stains
- saliva traces
- fingerprints
- lubricant
- hairs, fibres, clothing, and underclothing
- drugs, alcohol, bottles, etc.
- torn fabric, buttons, cigarette butts
- any possessions of the suspect
- signs of forced entry as above
- other evidence, such as broken glass etc.

*The suspect's person and residence* are examined in much the same way as in cases of homicide, except that emphasis is often on the collection of evidence related to the type of crime—pubic hairs, hairs and fibres transferred from the victim, cosmetics, lubricants, saliva—as well as the usual types of evidence described for homicide scenes such as blood, urine, hair, and fibre samples from the suspect.

While there are standard requirements for these investigations, every scene is unique and may present the investigator with unexpected evidence. Can you think of other possible evidence types and scenarios? In the chapters following, we shall examine some of the ways in which a range of types of physical evidence are collected and brought to bear on the problem of crime.

# FINGERPRINTS

A **fingerprint** is an impression of the friction ridges found on the inner surface of a finger or thumb. Prints can also be made by the palms (thenar surfaces) and the feet (plantar surfaces), which bear other friction ridge detail. A **friction ridge** is a corrugated condition of the skin that gives a gripping surface to the hands and feet.

## IDENTIFICATION OF CRIMINALS ACT

The **Identification of Criminals Act** (see Appendix B) permits police to photograph and fingerprint suspects. There are two ways in which fingerprints can be obtained in Canada: voluntarily and involuntarily. If a person agrees to have fingerprints taken, the procedure is straightforward. If, however, a suspect or other individual does not agree to supply prints, the prints can be taken under the Act. The person to be fingerprinted or photographed must be: *in lawful custody*; *charged with a criminal indictable offence*; *or convicted of a criminal offence*. There are also provisions for fingerprinting suspects charged under the Official Secrets Act, the Fugitive Offenders Act, and the Extradition Act. (See Appendix B for a fuller description.)

While these conditions seem clear, officers should be aware of some ambiguities that may arise in the matter of voluntary fingerprinting. For example, a suspect who has received a notice to appear in court (appearance notice, summons, undertaking, recognizance) may not think that suspects can legally be made to give prints; in fact, such persons are compelled to supply them. Refusing to do so can be considered a further criminal offence. The necessity to supply prints may be confusing to the accused. In the case of an appearance notice or field release, suspects can read clearly that they are "not yet charged with an offence." Reading more carefully, however, they will find a statement to the effect that failing to appear for finger-printing may result in a charge under the Criminal Code.

Police powers to take fingerprints depend on the nature of the charges preferred. In Canada, there are three types of offence with which a person can be charged: (1) **indictable**, (2) **dual-procedure** (hybrid), and (3) **summary conviction**. Fingerprints cannot be compelled from a person charged with a summary conviction offence, such as trespass by night. For the most serious offences (i.e., indictable), it is clear that fingerprints can be compelled. Dual-procedure or hybrid offences are more complex. They may or may not be declared indictable in court. Until such time as this election is made by the crown prosecutor, however, *these offences are considered to be proceeding by indictment and therefore fingerprints may be taken from an involuntary suspect.* Moreover, Subsection 2 states clearly that in taking these prints, as much force as necessary may be used.

There are two main reasons for taking involuntary fingerprints. The first is for purposes of identification, to link the person fingerprinted to criminal acts; police may also need to identify an unknown cadaver, both for purposes of burial and to eliminate from the file the fingerprint records of the deceased. The second is for the compilation of data on offenders—in other words, to keep a criminal record. Fingerprints are kept locally, regionally, and nationally, and are accessible internationally. The more complete and accurate such records are, the more rapid and effective criminal investigation can be.

Whenever police officers in Canada take a set of fingerprints from a suspect, they forward a copy to the national repository on Ottawa. The prints are entered into a computer database and given Fingerprint Section (FPS) and Fingerprint Classification (FPC) numbers. With every police inquiry about a person, the numbers enable a rapid retrieval of records, and hence of fingerprints for comparison. If a person who has already been fingerprinted is suspected of committing a further offence, the prints taken and sent to Ottawa because of the subsequent offence are compared with those already on record. When the new prints are verified as belonging to the same person, they are added to that person's existing file under the same FPS and FPC numbers. Fingerprint records can follow a person through a lifetime despite aliases or attempts at disguise. Thus fingerprints can be used to link accused persons to their past criminal records. But of course good record-keeping alone is not enough. The comparison of friction ridge characteristics is the activity essential to the successful use of fingerprints in criminal investigations.

Police services may ask for voluntary fingerprints in several cases. An investigator wishing to eliminate persons from suspicion may take prints that can be distinguished from the "unknown" culprit print, and thereby eliminate extraneous evidence from the investigation. In a break-and-enter, for instance, the prints of persons who have legal access must be eliminated so that investigators can focus on those of suspects. Citizens should not fear giving these elimination prints, for they will be returned or destroyed on request. The major reason for voluntary prints is the increasingly frequent practice by employers of criminal record checks on job applicants, especially those who apply for positions of trust. The most obvious such case is that of applicants for police service, who must undergo extensive background checks and will be asked for fingerprints.

# HISTORY OF FINGERPRINT IDENTIFICATION

To this day, fingerprints are the only infallible means of identification known. Throughout recorded history, observers have noted the existence and uniqueness of the prints left by human hands. Prehistoric art bears witness to an early awareness of ridge patterns and prints were later used in ancient times as a sort of signature to seal business deals. Prints piqued the curiosity of early scientists such as **Marcello Malpighi**, who in 1686 identified some of the distinctive shapes in fingerprints. In his honour, the layer of skin that generates prints is sometimes called the **Malpighi layer** (although most authorities in fingerprinting refer to the **epidermis** and **dermis**). Despite the observations of many, it was not until the 1800s that the notion of using fingerprints for a system of identification was seriously proposed. In 1858, **Sir William Herschel**, a British official in India, started demanding that Indian businessmen leave a hand impression on the back of every contract they signed. While Herschel only intended to intimidate the signers, who believed that touching a contract made it more legitimate, he soon observed that prints were unique to individuals, and he began using them as a means of identifying employees and others.

The first person to use fingerprint identification as a forensic tool was **Dr. Henry Faulds**, a British surgeon working in Japan. Faulds, who knew of Herschel's earlier work, saw the potential importance of fingerprints as source of identification. He is even said to have solved a crime using the fingerprints left on a wall by the criminal, matching the print at the scene with one taken from the accused. Faulds suggested the development of a system of fingerprint identification to the biologist **Charles Darwin**, who passed the suggestion on to his cousin **Sir Francis Galton**. Galton, after many observations in the 1880s, was convinced that fingerprints could be used as an infallible means of identification that does not change over the lifetime of an individual. "Galton's Details" were the characteristics of prints that he described and that are used to this day and his book *Finger Prints* (1892) established the first practical classification system. By the early twentieth century, fingerprinting was widely accepted as *the only sure means of identification.*

In Canada, **Edward Foster** of the Dominion Police began in 1904 to advocate the adoption of fingerprint identification methods. The federal government eventually permitted the use of fingerprints, making the appropriate additions to the Identification of Criminals Act. In 1911, Inspector Foster's persistent advocacy was rewarded with the opening of a Fingerprint Bureau, of which he took charge. Many police services across Canada were already aware of fingerprinting, and they made extensive use of the new Bureau. With the absorption of the Dominion Police into the RCMP, Foster continued to run the Fingerprint Bureau under RCMP aegis until his retirement in 1932.

Until the late 1900s, the **Henry Classification System**, the standard ten-print system of organization of Galton's observations by **Sir Edward Richard Henry**, was used by police in the British Commonwealth and other English-speaking areas.

Although authorities all came to agree on the value of fingerprints, the debate over how many matching characteristics are required for a positive match has never been completely settled. The evolution of computer-assisted comparisons may well be the solution to this debate. When the new computer technology appeared, police soon took advantage of it, and the need for complex systems of classification by humans has been diminishing ever since. The Royal Canadian Mounted Police began to computerize their fingerprint records in the 1970s and the concept of automated fingerprint identification systems gradually developed. At first, classifiers entered fingerprints previously read and classified by human beings, but as the potential of the technology became apparent, identifications became more truly automated.

The detection, enhancement, and lifting of prints, however, is still the job of people processing a crime scene. Every match must be verified by fingerprint technicians. And positive identification for presentation in court still requires expert testimony by a technician.

# HOW FINGERPRINTS ARE MADE

It is helpful for investigators to understand the characteristics of our make up that contribute to the existence of these distinctive marks. Two basic attributes of human beings are important: the structure of the skin and the nature of perspiration or sweat. The prints themselves, as we have seen, are the impressions left on a surface by the friction ridges of the skin. In many cases, the ridges leave these impressions because the skin is moist from the secretions of its glands.

# The Skin and Its Secretions

The layers of cells that make up the skin comprise the **epidermis** or outer layer and the dermis that lies beneath it. Between these two layers is a band of **dermal papillae**, cells that shape the friction ridges of the epidermis. These decisive cells form in the fetus, giving every person a lifetime pattern of ridges and pores. The pores on the friction ridges are connected to the sweat glands in the dermis. Every pore is also a lifetime distinction. When the pores secrete sweat from the glands and the finger comes into contact with a surface, the sweat-covered friction ridges leave their distinctive pattern or "fingerprint." The sweat in a fingerprint may be from other parts of the body as well. The secretions from the hairless surfaces of the hands and feet (mainly the palms and soles) are called **ecrine sweat**. It is about 99.0% to 99.5% water. The solids that make up the other 0.5% to 1% of ecrine sweat are about half inorganic substances such as the salts sodium chloride and potassium chloride and half organic materials, mainly amino acids, along with very small amounts of urea and albumin. In some cases, prints may also contain **sebum sweat** secreted from the **sebaceous glands** in areas of the body containing hair follicles. Sebum sweat, containing oils and fats, is found on the hands usually because of contact with other parts of the body, particularly the face. Chemical analyses of surfaces for latent fingerprints usually therefore include primarily a search for oils, amino acids, and salts.

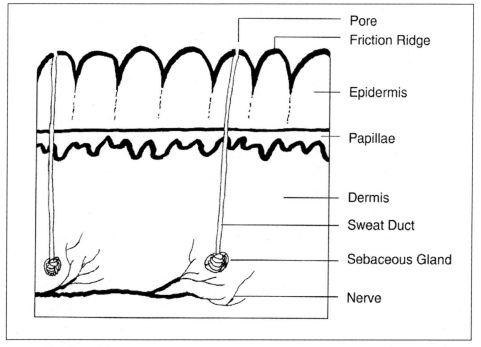

**Illustration 6-1.** Human skin structure.

## Factors Affecting the Condition of Fingerprints

1. *Skin condition.* The presence of disease, dryness of skin, the tendency to perspire, the performance of continued manual labour, and other such factors may affect the state of the skin. They cause its dryness, scarring, or other surface characteristics and hence affect the fingerprint. Skin may also be affected by a person's reaction at the crime scene. Nervousness may enhance the tendency to secrete perspiration, for example. Contamination of the skin by foreign substances will also leave its mark.

2. *Type of surface.* Whether a surface is porous or nonporous, hard or soft, smooth or rough, clean or dirty, will affect its ability to accept a fingerprint.

3. *Atmospheric conditions.* Temperature, humidity, wind, dust, and other environmental factors may affect the ability to deposit fingerprints and their durability. Investigators should not be unduly alarmed by atmospheric conditions. In many cases they will be less damaging to fingerprints than you might expect. Fingerprints can often persist well through rain, wind, and other adverse conditions. One of the authors made a fingerprint under water, left it there for six months, lifted the print with tape (still under water) and found a perfectly readable impression when the fingerprint tape was placed against a black background for contrast.

4. *Pressure of the finger or digit.* The pressure of the finger on the surface must be sufficient to leave a print, but too much pressure can obscure ridges and ridge patterns.

5. *Age of the print.* In combination with atmospheric conditions and other factors, fingerprints may become harder to process with the passage of time. The secretions in an older print, for example, may have dried out, becoming less amenable to powders and other tools of detection. Moreover, without lifting a print, it is difficult if not impossible to tell whether age has made the print unsuitable for lifting. While researchers are currently experimenting, no one has yet discovered how to detect the age of a fingerprint.

# POSITIVE IDENTIFICATION

Positive identification through fingerprints "is established by the agreement of friction ridge formations in sequence, having sufficient uniqueness to establish individuality" (Sgt. Paul Morin, *RCMP Fingerprint Manual*, p. 50). In other words, fingerprints are compared on the basis of friction ridge formations, which must occur in the same order and bear the same characteristics to be considered matching. The two properties of fingerprints that make them invaluable for identification are:

- **Persistency.** Friction ridges are formed before birth (about five weeks after conception) and remain the same, barring accidental changes, until the skin decomposes after death. Prints will grow larger with the growth of fingers but they retain the same ridge formations. The other exception to the rule of persistency occurs in the case of accidental or intentional alteration of the skin's surface.

- **Uniqueness.** No two persons have been discovered to have the same prints, even in the case of identical twins.

Together these two properties of fingerprints make them a permanent and accurate record of every individual. Unfortunately, it is not an indelible record, because friction ridges can be removed chemically or surgically, or even replaced or covered by skin grafts, or scar tissue. In these cases of print alteration, however, some of the original ridge formations may still be readable, or the scars and grafts themselves can make unique impressions which may assist in identification.

There are two general categories of prints we shall examine in this chapter: (1) **known impressions** (traditionally, "inked")—this is the voluntary or involuntary print made by a person for police and other records; (2) **scene-of-crime impressions**—these are **unknown** fingerprints found at the scene of a crime. Finding the latter type can require a more skilled and complex technique and special equipment that we shall describe.

# MAKING KNOWN OR INKED FINGERPRINTS

Whether they are voluntary or compelled under the Identification of Criminals Act, "known" impressions have traditionally been inked impressions made with the assistance of police services and other law enforcement agencies in a controlled environment.

Because one may get only one chance to take these prints, and they will often become the permanent impressions on record, the most important consideration is quality. A sloppy job can have serious consequences that may not be evident at the time of "printing." In one Canadian town, an investigating officer attempting to identify a woman who had been dead about six months was able with great care to make clear impressions from the second layer of skin. But when he tried to identify the cadaver from a set of rolled impressions taken at the time of an offence, he discovered that a previous officer had done a worse job with the live subject than he himself had done with the dead woman's amputated finger. It was only with considerable difficulty and expense that eventually a positive identification became possible.

While technological developments now allow a variety of means of taking impressions, the rolled ink impression has been generally accepted as providing high quality.

# Rolled Ink Impressions

Perhaps it is best to remember the saying "You never get a second chance to make a first impression." Under the Identification of Criminals Act, the subject, having complied with the law in giving you prints, is not obliged to come back to your office to provide better impressions. *Take good prints when you have the chance.* Points to remember:

## A. Equipment

1. *Ink and tools.* You need (1) either tubes of fingerprinting ink, a glass surface, and a roller or commercially made ink strips and (2) an ink pad.

2. *Forms.* In most law enforcement agencies, a variety of forms is required, providing both information on the subject and a surface in which impressions are made. The RCMP provides Form C-216 to be sent to the national repository in Ottawa. One of these forms will usually be kept locally as well, along with another card containing prints that can be used in the Automated Fingerprinting System. Forms are usually completed after prints have been obtained.

3. *Fingerprint form holder.* This is a commercially available device that holds the form as illustrated so that successive clear impressions can be rolled with as much ease as possible.

## B. Method

1. Ink must be spread thinly and evenly with a roller on the glass surface or officers can use pre-inked strips with an adhesive strip holder.

2. Forms will have a section assigned for each impression. The required impressions are spelled out clearly in each box, beginning with the right thumb and proceeding through the left little finger. In each case, you will make impressions of the thumb, index (forefinger), middle, ring, and little fingers. At the bottom of the form are spaces for "plain impressions," that is prints of four fingers of each hand pressed flat on the paper with the fingers straightened, usually at an angle to fit the appropriate box. Here no rolling is required. The Identification of Criminals Act also allows for the taking of flat-palm impressions for which a separate card is usually provided. With the heel of one hand you put pressure on the middle of the back of the other to make a complete impression. The print

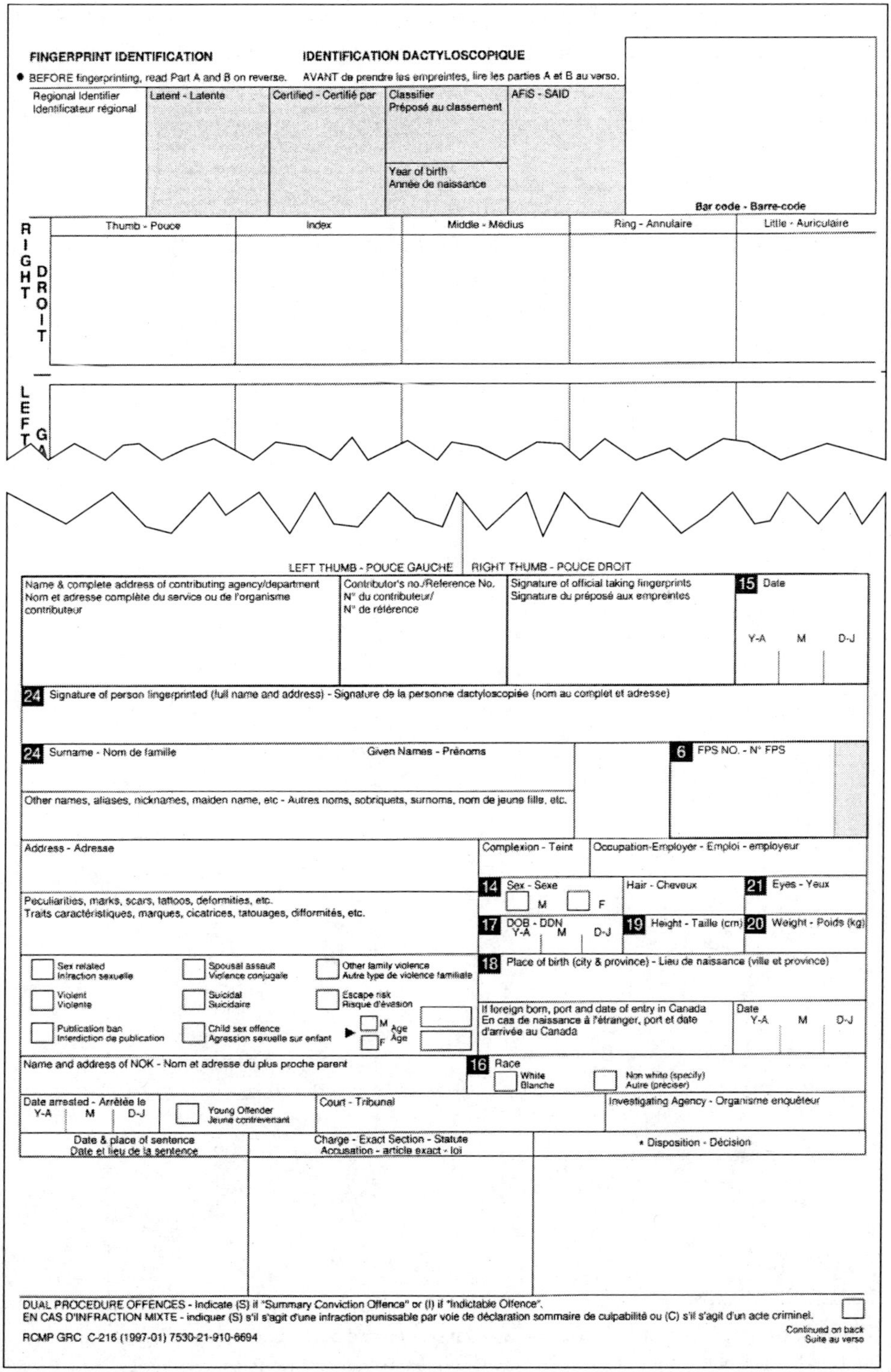

FINGERPRINT IDENTIFICATION IDENTIFICATION DACTYLOSCOPIQUE

• BEFORE fingerprinting, read Part A and B on reverse. AVANT de prendre les empreintes, lire les parties A et B au verso.

Regional Identifier / Identificateur régional | Latent - Latente | Certified - Certifié par | Classifier / Préposé au classement | AFIS - SAID

Year of birth / Année de naissance

Bar code - Barre-code

RIGHT / DROIT: Thumb - Pouce | Index | Middle - Médius | Ring - Annulaire | Little - Auriculaire

LEFT / GA…

LEFT THUMB - POUCE GAUCHE | RIGHT THUMB - POUCE DROIT

Name & complete address of contributing agency/department / Nom et adresse complète du service ou de l'organisme contributeur

Contributor's no./Reference No. / N° du contributeur/ N° de référence

Signature of official taking fingerprints / Signature du préposé aux empreintes

15 Date Y-A M D-J

24 Signature of person fingerprinted (full name and address) - Signature de la personne dactyloscopiée (nom au complet et adresse)

24 Surname - Nom de famille Given Names - Prénoms

6 FPS NO. - N° FPS

Other names, aliases, nicknames, maiden name, etc - Autres noms, sobriquets, surnoms, nom de jeune fille, etc.

Address - Adresse

Complexion - Teint

Occupation-Employer - Emploi - employeur

14 Sex - Sexe M F

Hair - Cheveux

21 Eyes - Yeux

Peculiarities, marks, scars, tattoos, deformities, etc. / Traits caractéristiques, marques, cicatrices, tatouages, difformités, etc.

17 DOB - DDN Y-A M D-J

19 Height - Taille (cm)

20 Weight - Poids (kg)

Sex related / Infraction sexuelle

Spousal assault / Violence conjugale

Other family violence / Autre type de violence familiale

Violent / Violente

Suicidal / Suicidaire

Escape risk / Risque d'évasion

Publication ban / Interdiction de publication

Child sex offence / Agression sexuelle sur enfant ▶ M Age / F Âge

18 Place of birth (city & province) - Lieu de naissance (ville et province)

If foreign born, port and date of entry in Canada / En cas de naissance à l'étranger, port et date d'arrivée au Canada

Date Y-A M D-J

Name and address of NOK - Nom et adresse du plus proche parent

16 Race

White / Blanche

Non white (specify) / Autre (préciser)

Date arrested - Arrêtée le Y-A M D-J

Young Offender / Jeune contrevenant

Court - Tribunal

Investigating Agency - Organisme enquêteur

Date & place of sentence / Date et lieu de la sentence

Charge - Exact Section - Statute / Accusation - article exact - loi

* Disposition - Décision

DUAL PROCEDURE OFFENCES - Indicate (S) if "Summary Conviction Offence" or (I) if "Indictable Offence".
EN CAS D'INFRACTION MIXTE - indiquer (S) s'il s'agit d'une infraction punissable par voie de déclaration sommaire de culpabilité ou (C) s'il s'agit d'un acte criminel.

RCMP GRC C-216 (1997-01) 7530-21-910-6694

Continued on back / Suite au verso

**Illustration 6-2.** RCMP fingerprint form, Form C-216.

should include the whole hand. Amputations must be noted by printing "AMPT" in the appropriate box, or you can attempt to roll the remnant of a partially amputated finger. You should position the form holder so that the section of paper taking the print is at the edge of the counter or surface on which the fingerprinting is done.

3.  The person taking the print must have control of the subject's hand, arm, and body and the subject should be encouraged to look away and allow the officer to do the work. Placing one arm over that of the subject and holding the subject's hand, the officer takes the top or nail of each digit, rolls the digit in the ink, and then in one deliberate and continuous movement places the digit evenly on the paper, rolling it from one side of the nail to the other. The result should be a clear, "nail to nail" fingerprint. You should try to achieve even pressure throughout to make sure that the print is clear from top to bottom as well as from side to

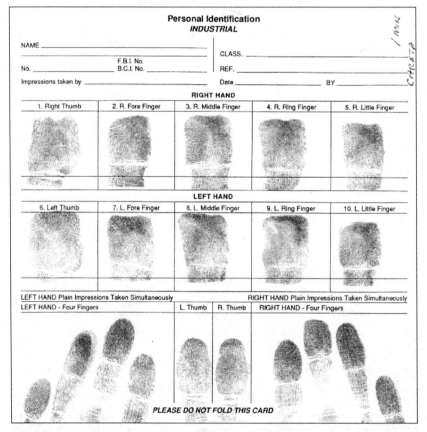

**Illustration 6-3(a) and 6-3(b).** Twins, born one minute apart, show pattern similarity in the sets of ten prints. (See page 83.) Close examination of ridge characteristics, however, reinforces the principle that no two persons have the same fingerprints.

side. The impression should not exceed the sides of the box on the form. Some ridge detail below the line is acceptable, provided it does not interfere with the box needed for another print. Good fingerprinting is a result of experience and care, and it will take practice and concentration to achieve a satisfactory method.

## C. Problems Making Known Impressions

**Skin Conditions** You may discover that any one of a number of conditions will affect the quality of the rolled impressions. The most common is perspiration on the subject's hands. If you notice excessive hand sweat, it is a sound precaution to wash and air-dry the subject's hands. Some excessively dry hands may require soaking to moisturize them. Air-dry the hands to the point where they will absorb ink. You should also be aware of problem skin conditions, but here no general rule applies.

**Safety** *Remember first of all that the subject is standing behind you and could be a threat to you.* You should not wear your sidearm, pepper spray, handcuffs, or any other weapon or constraint when fingerprinting a subject, nor should any of these things be within easy reach. Internal policy and common sense both dictate these measures. *You should also ensure your own health.* The subject may have open cuts or sores; rubber gloves are a wise precaution.

## Taking Fingerprints from Cadavers

At times investigators may need to take fingerprints from deceased victims or other dead persons, either at the crime scene or at the morgue. Usually this practice is performed for two reasons: (1) to eliminate the dead person's fingerprints from criminal record files and (2) to identify the cadaver's prints so that they can be identified or eliminated from among the suspect prints at the crime scene.

For this task a specialized kit is commercially available. It contains an ink pad and a specially formed **cadaver spoon**, which is designed to assist fingerprinting the dead, whose stiff fingers cannot be "rolled." The spoon has slots or guides in it that will take a strip-shaped form containing the boxes present on a fingerprint form. There are two strips, one for each hand, and each strip contains five boxes, one for each digit. The investigator inks the digits of the deceased thoroughly, puts the strip form through the slots in the cadaver spoon, and flattens the form to the curve of the spoon. Holding the spoon up to each digit, the investigator presses each finger of the deceased into the appropriate box of the form, which can be gradually slid through the slots of the spoon as each print is taken. The curved sides of the spoon eliminate the need for rolling.

## CRIME SCENE FINGERPRINTS

The fingerprints you encounter at the crime scene have not been put there for you to discover and they will appear in a great variety of places and substances and in various degrees of completeness. The science of fingerprint analysis has therefore classified fingerprints into three basic types according to the state in which they are found:

1. *Latent (invisible).* These are invisible to the naked eye, usually because of the surface they are on. They must be enhanced by powders, chemicals, or light sources to render them visible and collectible. This enhancement is often performed after suspicious surfaces have been seized and brought to a controlled, equipped environment.

2. *Visible.* These are visible to the naked eye.

3. *Molded (plastic).* This term is applied to prints made in a soft surface such as putty, clay, soap, or even skin.

While these three terms are used widely and you must know them, the crucial scientific distinction is between **latent** and **visible** fingerprints. A molded print is always either simply latent or visible. The distinction between molded prints and others is only useful when an investigator is considering how to collect the prints.

# Development

Technicians and some investigators lift prints from surfaces so that they can be analyzed. In the event that prints are not readily collectible or visible, they must be **developed**. The purposes of development are

1. to render a latent print visible

2. to create a contrast, usually for photographic reproduction

3. to permit the lifting of prints from a surface

   Various methods are used for the development of fingerprints, and they fall into two categories: powders and chemical enhancement.

## *Powders*

There are special **fingerprint powders** that adhere to the substances in fingerprints. The prints can then be "seized" (collected) and taken to the controlled police environment for analysis. While manufacturers produce myriad powder colours, several types of powders for different conditions are in common use: **lightening grey**, **chemist grey, white, black, fluorescent (red wop), magnetic powder**, or the authors' favorite, a combination powder with a mixture of **black and grey** that can be used in a wide variety of situations. Each powder is particularly suited to a specific type of background. Fluorescent powder, for example, is often the most effective powder for a multicoloured surface, showing high contrast when subjected to ultraviolet (UV) light. It can also be photographed under UV light. In addition to having these qualities, fingerprint powders are made in a variety of **textures** from **coarse** to **fine**. The general rule is that fine powders are suited to smooth surfaces while coarser powders work better on rough or greasy surfaces. You can apply powders with various brushes, including a **zephyr brush**, a **camelhair brush**, a **feather duster,** and, for the magnetic powder, a **magnetic wand**.

## *Chemical Enhancement*

**Iodine crystals** are used for **iodine fuming** in a **fuming cabinet**, a process that turns prints brown and does not ruin the document or other surface on which prints have been discovered. Because the iodine enhancement may fade over time, the enhanced prints must be photographed. Iodine fuming is a relatively dangerous process, now less often employed, although it can be useful for fingerprints on skin when the fumed area is sprayed with **napthhoflavone**.

**Ninhydrin** reacts with the amino acids in fingerprints, turning them purple. The speed of the reaction can be increased by the application of steam (some officers simply use a steam iron or kettle). Ninhydrin is particularly effective for prints that are suspected to be very old. This process is best performed in a fuming cabinet because ninhydrin can be toxic if inhaled.

**Silver nitrate** reacts to salts in perspiration to turn prints dark brown. Exposure to sources of UV light such as natural sunlight accelerates the process. Silver nitrate can damage a document irreparably. It will make ink run, and moreover may continue to darken until a document is unreadable. When processing documents for fingerprints, investigators generally use **iodine fuming** first, after which they may try **ninhydrin**, and then **silver nitrate**.

**Cyanoacrylate**, one of the chemicals in super glue, vaporizes and then crystallizes and hardens on the components of sweat in a fingerprint, concentrating on the ridges, making a clear white print. It is commercially readily available to police services and applicable to the widest variety of surfaces. Heat and humidity combined accelerate this process. Users should be aware that the resulting developed print is hard and permanent, and except in serious cases cyanoacrylate should not be used on the surfaces of valuable articles. It is also toxic if inhaled. Cyanoacrylate fuming and powder can be used for fingerprints on the skin of dead persons.

**Amido black** can be sprayed on fingerprints that have been made with blood to enhance their visibility. It is also used extensively as a blood detector.

The above treatments are but a few of the many in use. There is a great range of other chemical techniques used to detect latent fingerprints. Most of them, like those above, are performed in the identification section of a police service or in a forensic laboratory, rather than on the crime scene. Dyes such as Ardrox, Brilliant Yellow 40, and Rhodamine 6G can be used in combination with alternative light sources, such as Luma-Lite®, to enhance cyanoacrylate-treated prints. Other treatments, such as Crystal Violet and Sticky Slide Powder, can be used on adhesive-tape-bearing prints. Molybdenum disulfide is useful for raising prints on large, nonporous surfaces that have been wet. The vacuum deposition technique is well adapted to old, molded prints. They can be suspended inside a vacuum chamber and submitted to evaporating gold and zinc.

# COLLECTION PROCEDURES

The collection of fingerprint evidence at the crime scene is increasingly the exclusive work of forensic specialists, crime-scene technicians familiar with an array of methods, equipment, and problems. You may not, at least not immediately in your career, perform the techniques of processing that we are about to describe. But on the other hand, you may well assist in such matters, or be the first officer on a scene

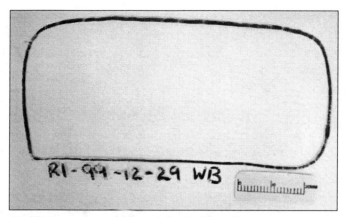

**Illustration 6-4.** Exhibit treated with chemical dye.

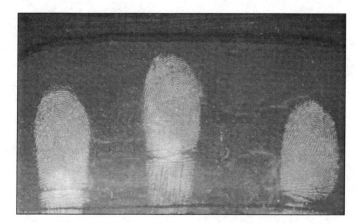

**Illustration 6-5.** Exhibit examined with alternative light source to reveal latent prints.

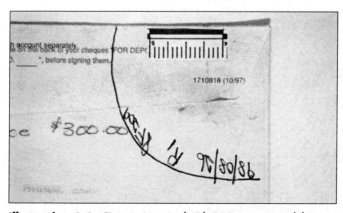

**Illustration 6-6.** Fingerprint raised with DFO on paper exhibit.

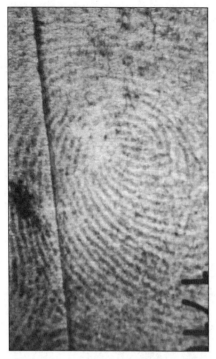

**Illustration 6-7.** Close-up photograph of fingerprint.

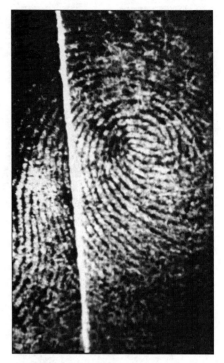

**Illustration 6-8.** Fingerprint photographed using Polaroid HC51 high-contrast film and a red barrier filter.

**Illustration 6-9.** Suspect police file fingerprint enlarged to five times for comparison.

that requires processing. You must have in mind the forensic possibilities of, and the consequent necessity of protecting, the scene. *Remember also your duties of photographing, sketching, and taking proper notes.*

## Exterior to Interior and Visible to Invisible (Latent)

As you process a scene for fingerprints, normally you will *deal first with the exterior and the visible, and last with the interior and the invisible.* The prints at a point of entry outside a building may be in danger of erasure or degradation by weather or other forces. The obvious potential sources of incriminating prints will be in places such as the broken glass of a forced entry, window- and doorframes, surfaces such as weapons, dressers, or drawers, and any items out of place on the path of contamination.

The obviously visible prints in substances such as dust, grease, blood, and paint, or on receptive surfaces such as glass, can also be dealt with right away. *You should photograph and process these immediately, including a scale ruler in pictures to allow 1:1 photographs.* In processing visible prints, your decision about whether to attempt lifting them will depend on their nature and the type and condition of the surface. Technicians will seldom attempt to lift a print in dried blood on a wall. It will be dealt with by photographing the print **overall**—to show its location in the scene, and **close-up**—to reveal clearly the ridge detail. In some cases, investigators will cut out a piece of a wall in order to seize and analyze its impressions. More commonly, technicians will have a surface from which they can seize a print made by human secretions. The surface will dictate the type of processing and lifting required. Think first of the size of the surface on which the visible print is found. In many cases if the object is relatively small and easily moved (e.g., a sheet of paper, a small piece of glass or a metal cash box) it is sometimes better to seize the entire object, after photographing the scene.

Both visible and latent prints will otherwise be lifted in the same manner. If the print is latent, to find its location it must be made visible. Once you have considered the scene for the most likely surfaces, you must choose the optimum process to raise the prints. In the case of suspected latent prints that you cannot raise at the scene, seize the suspect object for laboratory enhancement procedures.

## Using Powders

The most commonly used method of raising a fingerprint is **fingerprint powder**. On dark surfaces, a light or grey powder is usually most effective, while on lighter surfaces a dark powder works best. Again, for general use the authors recommend **grey-black powder**, the best all-purpose powder that is commercially available. On dark surfaces it appears grey or light and on light surfaces the black powder in the combination shows up as dark ridges on a light background. But you should always try to employ the most appropriate powder for each surface. (Different powders also have different degrees of coarseness. With practice you may find, for example, that a fine powder works well on a mirror, while a coarser one is more effective on a greasy kitchen counter.) Powders are available in almost every conceivable colour although many colours are seldom used. A multicoloured, busy background is best processed with a **fluorescent powder** which shows good contrast when subjected to ultraviolet (UV) light. It is best used on a glossy surface such as plastic or glass. It can be photographed under UV light, and can also be lifted like other powders.

To raise prints, dip a brush gently into the powder, being careful not to overload it (too much powder will clog the print). Apply the powder to the surface in question, barely touching the surface. Too light a touch will apply no powder; too heavy will clog or even erase the fingerprint. One experienced technician suggests that the most successful motion for application is one in which the brush handle is rotated back and forth between the thumb and forefinger causing the brush to swirl.

If you have occasion to use a **magna brush** or **magnetic wand**, which is most commonly used on paper and works wonderfully on styrofoam, dip the wand into the iron filings and keep the wand above the surface, allowing the filings that hang from it to come into contact with the surface until you begin to see evidence of a print. Then move the wand, following the pattern of friction ridges (dragging it across will often cause the filings to clog the print).

## Deciding What to Lift

Once prints have been dusted or are otherwise ready to be lifted, you must decide whether they are worth lifting or need to be lifted. This requires a visual inspection of the quantity, quality, and size of the impressions. If, for example, there is the impression of several digits and a palm, you may decide to lift them all together. Experience is necessary for several decisions regarding quality; you may eventually decide that some prints are simply too smudged or dirty to provide any ridge detail. When deciding on the size of your "lift," you will be limited by the size of the commercially available fingerprint tape. You must be careful therefore to avoid breaking up a single set of impressions. Four fingers on one side of a beer bottle and the accompanying thumb may sometimes be impossible to lift all at once; but you must remember that the two or three lifts together form one set of prints. Remember: *Before applying fingerprint tape always photograph the raised impressions, and include a scale ruler in your photographs.*

In some cases, the surface bearing the prints can be transported; if so, you should seize it for presentation in court. In a sense, this practice is an extension of the **best**

**evidence rule**, which is often applied to documents, but can also be pertinent to fingerprints and other physical evidence: Whenever possible the original of a document or of other physical evidence must be produced. While photographs and other representations may be highly accurate, the best evidence is always the document, object, or impression itself. Again, before seizing a surface or cutting out the portion of the surface that contains fingerprints, you should always photograph it as it was found. If a lift should prove unsuccessful, you will at least have clear photographs of the print at every stage of development.

## Marking Developed Prints

Using a grease pencil or other marker to which fingerprint powder will adhere, you must now identify this lift. Draw a circle around the impressions to be lifted. Write the time, date, and place of discovery along with your initials. Identify each lift with the letter "R" and a number indicating the order in which lifts are being made. "R" is the universally recognized way of ensuring that the print is displayed with the same orientation it had at discovery (is laterally correct) or that the display has been explainably reversed (with a rubber lifter). A typical exhibit is thereby marked as shown in Illustration 6-10.

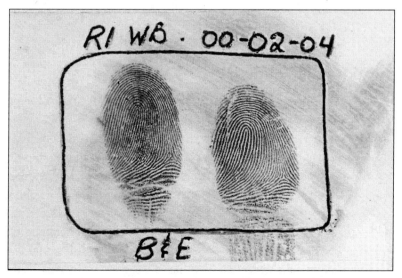

**Illustration 6-10.** Fingerprint raised and properly marked for investigational purposes.

The next step is to powder lightly the entire impression and markings again as you did prior to marking the print.. The print is now ready to lift. *Make sure that at this point the print and markings are clearly photographed in case of accidents in lifting.*

## Fingerprint Tape

Remove an appropriately sized piece of tape (slightly larger than the area marked). Place the tape securely on one side of the marked circle and hold the other end above the print. Lower the tape over the print, gradually flattening it to the print(s) and markings with your finger, beginning with the end already on the surface bearing the print. Work through the centre of the tape straight across to the other side of the marked circle. To ensure that there are no air bubbles that will damage the detail of the print, flatten the tape with your finger, rubbing outward from the original zone of pressure in the centre of the tape. The tape end that you have held while applying tape to the print should be left loose, because you will want to lift the tape. Once you have removed all bubbles, very carefully and slowly pull the tape back from the impression towards the point where the tape was originally secured. Make sure that you keep the tape taut so that it does not roll up after being removed from the print. You now place the tape on an appropriate fingerprint card. Use the same motions that you used to apply the tape before, again making sure there are no air bubbles. The print exhibit is now marked, lifted, seized, and in your possession. *Remember that you are accountable for the continuity of the evidence that you have seized.* Record carefully all of your actions involving the evidence from the time you have seized until it is presented in court.

## Rubber Lifters

On some occasions you may wish to use commercially made **rubber print lifters**. The print is prepared for lifting in the same way. The lifter is a strip of rubber bearing an adhesive side covered with a removable piece of clear plastic. Remove the plastic and apply the adhesive rubber surface to the print in a fashion similar to taping. Peel it back carefully and replace the plastic sheet over the fingerprint on the adhesive surface. You now have a seized print. But remember *the print will now appear as the mirror image of the way it was discovered* and therefore *your marked "R" is particularly important.* If you have had no room for markings, anyone reading the print might think that the flow pattern indicates a left hand when it is actually a right-hand print. Some technicians will often therefore photographically correct the exhibit in the dark room to show a properly oriented chart for ease of court presentation.

# COMPARING PRINTS

The lifted "unknown" print is now ready for comparison and possible positive identification with "known" prints. While automated fingerprint identification systems are now well established, investigators will also often make manual comparisons for a possible match with a known suspect. This traditional method requires two magnifying glasses and fingerprint picks with which the investigator searches for commonalities and differences in two sets of prints. Remember that the minutiae of a print are compared for "**continuous agreement of ridge characteristics in sequence, with no unexplainable differences**" or a **positive identification**. If a positive identification is made, the prints are powerful evidence to be used in court by an expert witness. For courtroom presentation, the prints are usually photographically enlarged and each characteristic is labelled. Labelled charts of the "known" and "unknown" prints are then effective in illustrating a positive identification.

To compare prints, you will usually place the known and unknown prints side by side under magnification. If there is a clear indication of a pattern type on both prints, some technicians will immediately see this as a good first reference. The essential subjects of comparison, however, are **friction ridge characteristics or minutiae**. These may be outside a normal pattern or, if you are examining the friction ridge prints from other skin surfaces such as the palm or foot, there may be no classifiable pattern at all.

First, you must find a starting-point from which to begin examining and comparing ridge characteristics. For example, on one print you may find one of the four characteristic ridge formations with another clear formation beside it. If you can find the same combination on the other print, you can begin to count ridge characteristics on both prints from this starting-point. If you find that the same number of the same ridge characteristics in the same sequence appears on both prints, you have begun to establish a positive match. While the condition of the unknown print may limit the number of similarities you find (it may be only a partial impression, for example), expert opinion will finally decide whether the matching ridge formations are sufficient to provide a positive identification. Remember, you must also be sure that there are no unexplainable differences between the ridge formations of the two prints.

Some clear prints can be magnified so that experts can compare them for the position and shape of pores (poroscopy) and the shapes of the edges of friction ridges (edgeoscopy); matching these features can further strengthen identification evidence.

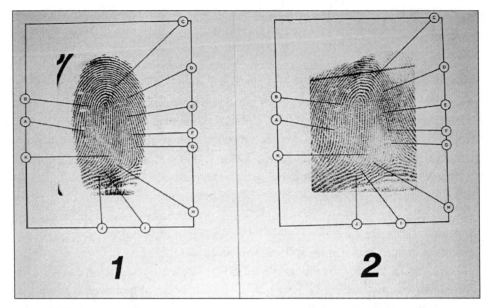

**Illustration 6-11.** Two fingerprints, positively identified, can be enlarged photographically, charted to show similarities used to make the identification, and used as a visual presentation to the courts. The charted numbers or letters serve as a reference point between the "known" (**k**) sample and the "unknown" (**u**) or "questioned" (**Q**) sample.

## Friction Ridge Characteristics

*The* **minutiae** (friction ridge formations) *are the basic elements of fingerprint identification.* In Canada fingerprint technicians recognize four basic types of friction ridge formations:

1. *Ridge ending.* A ridge that stops abruptly.

2. *Bifurcation.* A ridge that splits to form two ridges.

3. *Island.* A short ridge whose length is at least twice its width.

4. *Lake.* A ridge that bifurcates then closes again forming an enclosure.

As we take a more detailed look at the analysis and comparison of "unknown" to "known" fingerprints, there are several questions that need to be asked about fingerprint evidence. The answers to these questions help to determine the nature and the evidential value of fingerprints:

1. *Completeness of pattern.* What is the extent of the friction ridge area discovered at the crime scene?

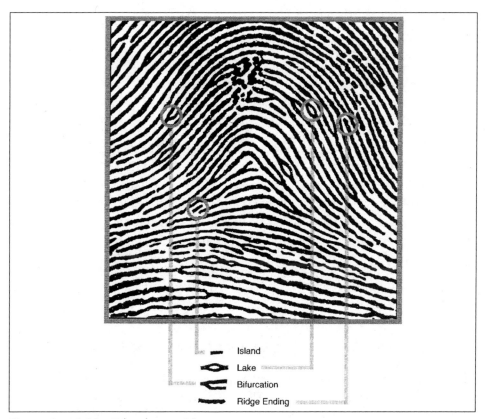

Island

Lake

Bifurcation

Ridge Ending

**Illustration 6-12.** Ridge characteristics.

2. *Rarity of pattern.* How frequently does this pattern type occur in the population? Some types are common and some are rare.

3. *Clarity of pattern.* How clearly defined and readable are the overall fingerprint patterns?

4. *Clarity of ridge characteristics.* Can the distinctive minutiae of the print be identified? Can a ridge ending be distinguished from a bifurcating ridge?

5. *Presence and clarity of sweat pores.* Are the sweat pores visible enough that you can see the detail around the pore microscopically? A fingerprint without sweat pores can be made through a fine rubber glove, for example. The absence of sweat pores is also a characteristic of planted fingerprints taken from an inked or other impression which is relatively easy to move.

6. *Rarity of characteristic type and combination.* Even if the pattern is common, does an unusual combination of minutiae occur? For example, a series of five lakes in close sequence would be extremely rare.

7. *Ridge edge shape (edgeoscopy).* Using a microscope, can you see a distinctive cell pattern on the edges of friction ridges (somewhat like the distinctive pattern of a shoreline)? Is it identical in the "known" print?

8. *Position and shape of pores (poroscopy).* Does a microscopic observation of pores produce distinctive positioning and shapes of the pore on the friction ridge that are seen in the "known" sample?

9. *Presence and clarity of incipient (false) ridges.* Are there incipient or false ridges in the fingerprint? These are not true friction ridges but rather raised areas of skin between two friction ridges. They contain one sweat pore and are usually thinner than the true ridges. Quite rare, they most commonly arise with age. While they are not used in fingerprint classifications they could contribute a positive link from the known to the unknown print because of their rarity.

10. *Technician's experience.* What degree of experience in fingerprint analysis, education, training, and overall record qualify the technician analyzing the prints?

# FINGERPRINT CLASSIFICATION SYSTEMS

Systems of classification have been developed in order to organize the classification, storage, and retrieval of fingerprints. The ability to retrieve prints of a configuration similar to a print that police have submitted allows investigators to identify rapidly a range of suspect prints so that the more detailed work of comparing ridge formations closely can begin. Ultimately, computer-based automation can allow comparison without classification; but it is still useful for investigators to familiarize themselves with the general character of the traditional classification systems.

While many systems have been tried since the acceptance of fingerprint evidence, police services in the English-speaking world have come to rely on various versions of the **Henry System**, adopted by Scotland Yard in 1901. It is the most useful of the traditional approaches; even the relatively recent automated systems began with the input of Henry-based characteristics. The general principles of this system form the basis of the various pattern classifications adopted by several countries. In the United States version of the system, police have used nine basic fingerprint patterns. Canada's Henry System was similar, but broke the pattern into further categories. Whatever manual classification system was employed, the various pattern types identified were usually elaborations of the three basic patterns: **arches**, **loops**, and **whorls**.

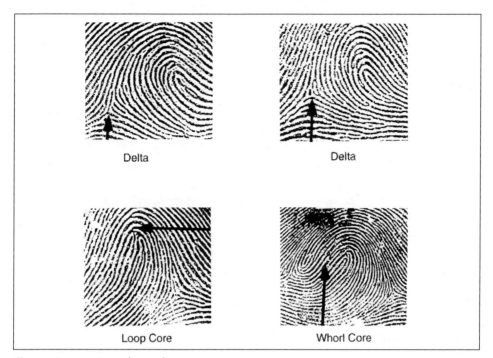

Delta

Delta

Loop Core

Whorl Core

**Illustration 6-13.** Deltas and cores.

## Deltas and Cores in Fingerprints

Two important features of fingerprint patterns identified under the Henry System are deltas and cores. The nail-to-nail roll in making inked impressions is important, because if done properly such a print will include any points of delta on either side of the pattern. The **delta** is a focal point found outside the central pattern, to the sides and below it. From its triangular shape, ridges tend to surround the centre of the pattern area. The **core** of a fingerprint is the area in the centre of the pattern, an inner focal point. Deltas and cores are still used as beginning reference points in many classification systems, both manual and automated.

## Automated Fingerprint Identification Systems (AFIS)

The automation of fingerprint analysis has revolutionized the entire process of identification. It has replaced long and painstaking searches for matching prints with a rapid and accurate comparison of "unknown" prints with a large database of "known" impressions. The **Auto-Class System** used by the RCMP is a case in point: the number of pattern types is simplified to five basic classifications: **arches, tented arches, radial loops, ulnar loops,** and **whorls.**

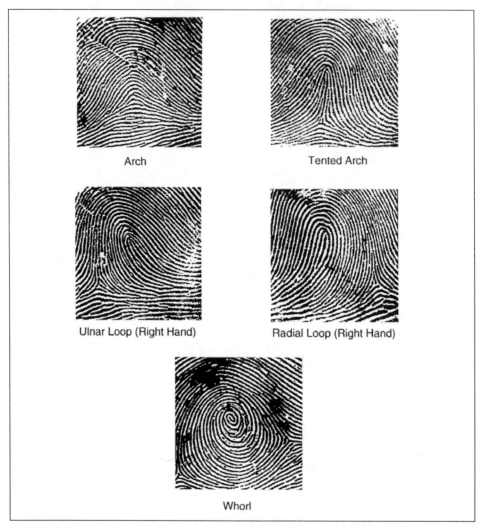

**Illustration 6-14.** Examples of pattern types.

    While the number of pattern types has been reduced, the computer, creating a spatial geometry of fingerprint minutiae, can rapidly identify and compare thousands of characteristics. Technicians must still, however, take account of exceptional prints, particularly those made by amputated, tip-amputated, and abnormal or temporarily injured fingers. Those intending to use the system should also be aware of other exceptions to the basic classifications of Auto-Class identified in user manuals.

    Auto-Class is only one of several systems in use. Another example is the **NEC®** **Technology System**, which uses several more distinct pattern types, each symbolized by a letter: "**A**" arch; "**T**" tented arch; "**W**" whorl; "**R**" right-slant loop; "**L**" left-slant loop; "**S**" scar (includes unknown); and "**N**" none (amputation etc.).

The above systems are only two of several AFIS developments that have emerged, and the fingerprint revolution continues. Various police services have adopted or are considering the adoption of new systems as you read this. While the technological sophistication of newer methods such as DNA typing may make fingerprinting seem relatively old-fashioned, it must be remembered that fingerprint comparison has stood the test of time. After a century of use in many millions of cases, *no two persons have ever been found to have the same fingerprints.* It is still a highly reliable means of identification, and it can be conducted manually at very little expense. Moreover, with the development of computer-assisted comparisons, it is likely that many of the complexities of various fingerprint identification systems will disappear. In their place, a computer program will perform the continuous comparison of characteristics or identification of differences.

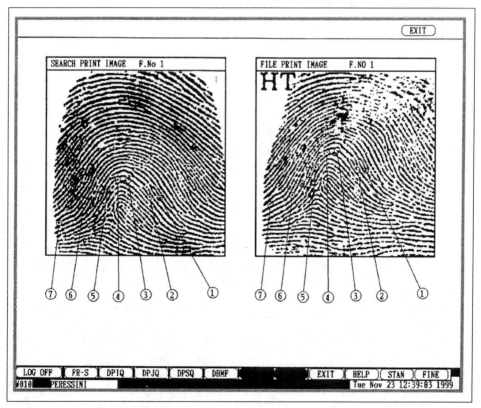

**Illustration 6-15.** An AFIS fingerprint chart.

*C h a p t e r*

# IMPRESSIONS

It is the hope of every investigator that the criminal will "make an impression" at the crime scene, so that this "unknown" mark or print can be connected with a "known" suspect's impression. Television shows, crime novels, and news reports have made the public aware of fingerprint evidence. As a result of this general knowledge, criminals will often take elaborate precautions, wearing gloves and cleaning up the crime scene to avoid leaving fingerprints. But criminals often leave a variety of other impressions at or near the scene of a crime. They must walk to the scene or drive a vehicle, often leaving footwear or tire impressions. Attempting to gain access to the objects of their desire, they may leave tool marks and other impressions. After a struggle with a victim, or in partially eaten food, suspects sometimes leave teeth impressions. All of these traces can constitute important circumstantial evidence. In order to achieve a thorough investigation of the scene, officers must take account of this kind of evidence and learn to gather, record, and compare unknown to known impressions.

There are basically two general types of impressions you may find:

1. **Two-dimensional impressions**, which are flat—without depth or texture.

2. **Three-dimensional impressions**, found on surfaces that are soft at the time impressions are made—most commonly mud, soft dirt, and snow.

# PRECAUTIONS

Remember you will be looking at the approach to a crime, the point of entry, the path of contamination, the focal point(s), and the point of exit. All of these, properly protected and processed, may yield valuable physical evidence, pieces in the puzzle of a crime. You may be under pressure to process a scene quickly, but haste may cause you to destroy or overlook evidence. No two crime scenes are alike and one mistake by a criminal can leave the evidence you need. It is important to keep in mind the lessons you have learned about avoiding crime-scene contamination. Avoid indiscriminate walking about until the scene has been processed, and try to control others attempting to enter the scene. Otherwise you may find that the impressions gathered from a scene are all too often those of investigators, you included. Of course, the initial priority of ensuring safety on the scene may unavoidably contaminate it, but there should be no further contamination.

# FOOTWEAR IMPRESSIONS

Footwear impressions can tell quite a story when fully analyzed. An investigator may be able to discover the number of suspects, their range of movements, their size, abnormalities of stride, whether they ran from the crime scene, signs of a struggle, the degree of planning in a crime, and even in some cases whether the suspect is male or female. You should always be conscious that footprints are trace evidence. They are usually transient in nature, and must be well protected, well photographed, and quickly processed.

## Characteristics of a Footprint

In footwear impressions you will be looking for two distinctive characteristics:

- **Class characteristics.** These are characteristics created by the manufacturer in the mass-production of footwear. Every manufacturer makes shoe soles with a unique pattern for particular purposes such as an individual sport or activity. A smooth-soled dress shoe may give you very little indication of class characteristics, and you must often be content with determining size. A running shoe, however, usually possesses distinctive class characteristics that can be matched to a particular manufacturer and model. The size of a shoe narrows the class to which the shoe belongs. The class characteristics of a shoe would therefore include a pattern type, size, and manufacturer.

- **Individual (accidental) characteristics.** These are characteristics that a piece of footwear acquires through wear. As soon as a person wears a shoe, it is made unique. It acquires cuts, pits, stones, scars, abrasions, and **anthropo-**

**logical wear** (the wear inside and outside the shoe made by the foot and walking style of the wearer). These marks, detected in an impression, are unique to every shoe. Once the class characteristics of an impression have been identified it is these individual characteristics that will enable the investigator to make a positive match with a known shoe.

Even if it is not possible to find individual characteristics, you should be aware that a match of class characteristics can still add to the weight of circumstantial evidence. Class characteristics recently helped to convict an arsonist in a small Canadian city. Someone threw a Molotov cocktail through the window of an apartment in which a woman and her children were living. While the assailant left an indistinct footprint partly on gravel and partly on snow, investigators were able to enhance the print in snow with black fingerprint powder and to take a photograph revealing the pattern and size of the impression. The print matched the shoe of the prime suspect, the woman's estranged ex-husband. In this case investigators made a transparency of the known footwear seized from the accused and superimposed it on the crime scene photograph to show very effectively the match of size and pattern in court. Along with other pieces of physical evidence the footwear impression completed the investigator's puzzle of evidence.

## Developing Footwear Impressions

Like fingerprints, footwear impressions must be photographed first. If they are not visible, they must first be rendered visible by various means of enhancement. If three-dimensional, they must be photographed first and then cast.

### *Two-Dimensional Prints—Visible Impressions*

As with every footwear impression, the investigator should first photograph the print. Include a scale ruler to indicate size. Photographs should include one that shows the position of the impression in the overall crime. Another should be taken from directly above the print at 90 degrees to the surface so that there is no distortion. The impression should be photographed so that it fills the negative as much as possible.

*Enhancement* With many impressions, it may also be possible to lift a print, but some form of enhancement is necessary. Even in the case of visible impressions, enhancement can greatly improve the quality of a photograph. Be aware that if the impression is a dust print (made by the dust from the sole of a shoe or boot), it is extremely transient in nature and must *never* be lifted without photographing first. If the impression has been made with a sticky substance such as cooking grease from a restaurant kitchen or motor oil, which has been tracked onto a relatively clean surface, you can use powders to enhance the impression. For an impression made with grease, for example, you can use magnetic powder and the magnetic wand as you did with fingerprints in Chapter 6. Experimenting with various powders on a variety of substances can yield impressive results and heighten the contrast of the impression against its background. There are also commercially available chemicals used to enhance bloody footprints. (Blood enhancement is discussed in Chapter 9.)

*Lifting* Once an impression has been enhanced with powder you must lift it, preferably on a lifter large enough to hold the entire impression. A device in common use is the **hinged lifter**, which is a clear sheet of plastic hinged in the middle. On one side of the hinge, the plastic has an adhesive surface that is applied to the enhanced impression and pressed or rolled to get rid of air bubbles. The adhesive surface is then folded back to the non-adhesive plastic, resulting in an enhanced, preserved footwear impression. Dust prints can also be lifted with electrostatic devices that use static electricity and Mylar film to gather dust impressions from floors, walls, furniture, and other surfaces. Some investigators have also demonstrated the practicality of carbon paper (increasingly rare) in lifting dust impressions.

### *Two-Dimensional Prints—Invisible Impressions*

In many cases you may think the scene is free of footwear impressions. But in order to be sure you must use various means of enhancement to reveal any invisible impressions. Light sources and contrasting surfaces can be extremely useful in

**Illustration 7-1.** Footwear seized from a suspect.

**Illustration 7-2.** Footwear impression in soil. Footwear impressions at a crime scene often reveal class and individual characteristics. Photographs, including a scale ruler, should be taken of the impressions before any attempts are made to enhance, raise, or, in this case, cast the impression. The photographic evidence itself is valuable.

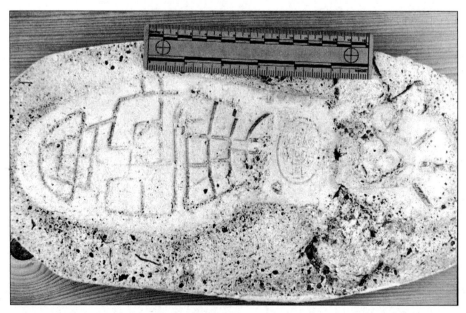

**Illustration 7-3.** Footwear casts too can be used for an identification. A good-quality cast may reveal distinct individual characteristics. (See pages 107–110 for casting methods.)

**Illustration 7-4.** Inked test impressions made from the suspect's footwear can be used to compare characteristics found in the crime-scene impression. (See pages 110–113 for methods for making test impressions.)

**Illustration 7-5.** Once the hardener has been allowed to dry, a light powder release agent can be applied. Do not hold the atomizer too close or the forced air may damage the print.

**Illustration 7-6.** Pour the mixture into the mold using a deflector. This too minimizes the risk of damage.

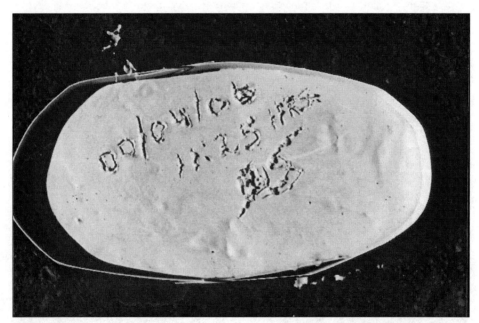

**Illustration 7-7.** This is the cast in Illustration 7-3 made of the suspect shoe and footprint in Illustrations 7-1 and 7-2. Allow the mixture to set up or begin to dry. You should notice a colour change and the mixture will feel warm to the touch. When you can scratch the surface with your fingernail, you will know the drying action is taking place. Do not forget to put the time, the date, and your initials in the cast. This can be done with any sharp object as the mixture dries. You may add any other identifiers you want at the time as well.

enhancing footwear impressions. You can enhance the visibility of an impression yourself simply by using a flashlight as an oblique light source. Try it:

1. Turn off all overhead lights.

2. Turn on a flashlight and lay it on the floor.

3. Observe the enhanced prints.

Most police services or their support units have high-intensity light sources that are used to render impressions visible. These often reveal impressions on surfaces that have been washed or even painted.

Whether or not you intend to lift footwear impressions, you should always photograph them again after they have been enhanced, using the methods mentioned above. Footwear impressions can also be further enhanced by the use of filters in the darkroom to create greater contrast. You can also use ordinary light sources to reveal footwear impressions on glass by simply back-lighting the glass. Alternatively, technicians will sometimes place a contrasting colour, usually white or black, behind a piece of glass to reveal impressions in sharp contrast.

## Casting Three-Dimensional Impressions

If you find three-dimensional prints at a crime scene, photograph them for both position and detail, including a ruler in the close-up photographs after you have photographed them as you first found them. For better contrast in your photograph and to create more depth and show the three-dimensional nature of the impression, use oblique (side) lighting or use a white piece of paper to reveal detail in shadowed areas. Make sure that they are protected, and then you may attempt to make casts of the impressions. Caution: if you have managed to apprehend a suspect and wish to match the suspect's footwear with the print, *do not, under any circumstances, put the shoe back into the impression.* Even if the shoe fits, you have compromised your evidence and could even be accused of falsifying evidence.

Let us suppose you are casting an impression using a quick-setting dental stone. If you wish to make a cast you will need:

(a) cardboard strips, a tin rectangle, or other materials suitable for making a form around the impression and the cast

(b) a mixing container that holds about 4 litres or 1 gallon

(c) dental stone and water

(d) potassium sulfate to accelerate hardening of dental stone

(e) a hardening spray (hair spray works well)

(f)  a fine powder, talcum or baby powder, for use as a release agent

(g)  a wide paint scraper or putty knife

To make your cast, follow the steps below. (See Illustrations 7-5 to 7-7.)

1.  Place a retaining wall around the impression. Be careful not to disturb the impression or contaminate with dirt.

2.  If there is debris in the impression such as windblown leaves, you may remove it with tweezers, but you must avoid touching the print. Do not try to remove anything that may disturb the print.

3.  From a height of about 30 centimetres or one foot, gently spray the print with your hardening agent. Take account of conditions to make sure that the force of the spray does not disturb the impression.

4.  Use an atomizer of baby powder to dust the impression lightly when the hardener has dried. Do not spray the powder directly into the impression at close range. Spray it against a deflector (a card or your hand) so that a light dusting lies evenly on the print. Remember: you must not fill any detail of the impression with powder. Properly applied, the powder will act as a release, enabling you to produce a clean cast.

5.  Mix the water, potassium sulfate, and dental stone. In a four-litre ice cream bucket, you should have about 3–4 centimetres of water. Put about a teaspoon of potassium sulfate into the water first. You can put the dental stone powder into a measuring cup. Pour the powder slowly into the water until it begins to form a pyramid above the surface. Then mix the dental stone into the solution. You must be ready to use the mixture immediately, because dental stone will harden very quickly. If it hardens, you will have to start all over again. The mixture should be about the consistency of a milkshake or pancake batter.

6.  Pour the mixture quickly into the impression, starting at one end and pouring evenly along the impression. As you pour, deflect the stream with a putty knife or piece of cardboard so that the pouring mixture does not alter the impression.

7.  As soon as the cast has begun to harden, mark it with the time, date, place, and investigator's initials.

8.  As the dental stone hardens it will be warm to the touch and gradually become lighter in colour. Wait until it has cooled down and ceased changing (usually about 15 minutes to 1/2 hour). Scratch the surface with your fingernail to see if the cast is hard.

9. When the cast has hardened, remove the barrier gently and then very carefully lift the cast. Do not worry if the cast is covered with dirt and *do not* attempt to clean it. Let the cast finish setting up for 24 hours and then wash the dirt away. Wash the impression gently with water and scrub it lightly with a brush.

You may also wish to try making a cast with **plaster of Paris**; mixture is not so crucial, but setup time is much slower. The steps for making a plaster of Paris cast are the same as for one of dental stone, except that you need not worry so much about working quickly. When you have carefully poured the layer that takes the impression, you may wish to reinforce the cast with mesh, screen, or reinforcing sticks that are commercially available. Set the reinforcing material on the poured surface very gently and then continue to pour the remainder of your casting material. The completed cast is fragile and must be handled with much greater care than a dental stone cast.

*Impressions Under Water*  Don't be afraid to try casting impressions in puddles of water. While it is not always successful, you should never leave valuable evidence behind. It is important to note that such impressions are often made outdoors and can be extremely transient, so they must be processed immediately. Use a larger barrier whose edges will be farther away from the impression. Otherwise you may disturb soft mud. Remove debris carefully. Sprinkle potassium sulfate sparsely into the form and let the crystals dissolve. Carefully sprinkle the dental stone powder evenly over the entire impression and keep sprinkling until you've filled as much of the form as possible or until the powder is above the water. If successful, the cast will set the same way as others. You can mark it and collect it.

*Footprints in Snow*  Snow can be an excellent medium for impressions, but such prints are often difficult to cast. Be sure to photograph fully before attempting a cast. To ensure contrast, dust the print very lightly from above with a black fingerprint powder or black spray paint. Remember to light the impression from the side, at a 45 degree angle. Your goal at this point is to capture clearly the class characteristics of the impression. The camera should always be held straight above the impression to avoid distortion. Include a scale ruler in all photographs.

*Snowprint Sprays and Dental Stone*  The hardeners that can be sprayed into snowprints are useful additions to the investigator's kit. Snowprint® wax, for example, can be sprayed into snow impressions for photography and casting with either dental stone or sulfur. Spray carefully, making three layers on the impressions. Snowprint wax also acts as an enhancer for photographs. Photograph the print in the same way as others. A clear, obliquely lighted photograph of a "waxed" snowprint may yield individual as well as class characteristics. After photographing, place a form around the print and pour in dental stone mixed with potassium sulfate and lukewarm water. The cast will need a longer time to set in freezing weather, perhaps as long as 90 minutes. Some technicians also place a box over the treated impression to prevent freezing.

*Sulfur Casts*  Despite the usefulness of the above method, for more fine detail authorities recommend the more traditional use of sulfur in casting snow impressions. Above all, remember that the use of sulfur can be dangerous and it is wise to have masks or respirators on hand. To make a sulfur cast, you need a camp stove, a three-litre cooking pot with a handle and enough sulfur to fill two-thirds of the pot. Either place a form around the impression, or if the snow is suitable ("sticky"), build a snow barrier around the impression. In both cases, build a snow ramp leading to the impression. The ramp should be concave and formed so that the molten sulfur can run down the ramp and flow into the impression. Heat the sulfur to a liquid state, stirring constantly. Be careful not to overheat it, or it will begin to thicken. Allow the liquid sulfur to cool slightly by setting the pot in the snow, continuing to stir. Pour the liquid sulfur onto the ramp in one continuous stream. It will quickly fill the impression, setting up on contact. You must remove the cast carefully, because it is brittle. Some technicians place the sulfur cast into a dental stone protector once they are indoors.

Casting in snow can be an excellent method of collecting footwear evidence and other impressions, but it is uncertain. The varying conditions of snow may make it difficult if not impossible. Winter wind, rain, and other factors can be troublesome and working conditions are often hard. But snowprints can be crucial physical evidence. The most important step therefore, in all cases is: *Photograph all impressions (with the appropriate ruler) before casting.*

## Test Impressions

Having collected the "unknown" impressions at the crime scene, it is time to make "known" impressions for comparison. If you are fortunate enough to have a suspect, you will need to seize that person's footwear and also to eliminate extraneous impressions from the crime scene. Remember that not all crime-scene impressions are those of suspects. Check the footwear of complainants, police, and other authorized persons quickly before you begin the elaborate work of casting.

You must take great care in casting test impressions. These are the prints to which crime-scene impressions will be compared. You can make them in a controlled environment and you must optimize this opportunity. Think carefully when making them. Try to replicate as closely as possible the weight and movement of the suspect and make several impressions until you are satisfied with the quality of the detail for comparison. Students of this science will often attempt to make a hasty impression by putting a hand on a shoe and pushing down. The best method is to put yourself, as it were, in the suspect's shoes.

There are several ways to make successful test impressions. Among the recommended methods with readily available materials, you may wish to try some of the following.

## Inked Test Impressions

For inked test impressions you will need: (a) a fingerprint ink roller, (b) fingerprint ink or black printer's ink, (c) a piece of glass for rolling the ink evenly, and (d) white bond paper of sufficient size to accept an entire impression (see Illustration 7-4).

1. Spread the ink evenly on the glass so that the roller can be coated evenly.

2. Run the ink-covered roller over the sole of the footwear thinly but completely. (Too much ink will fill in detail; too little will make a poor impression.)

3. Place sheets of paper in piles on a firm flat surface where walking is possible. You need to make the impression on a small pile of paper (10 to 20 sheets) because one sheet alone may not be soft enough to produce a detailed impression, and may also allow characteristics of the floor or other firm surface (grit, cracks, etc.) into your test impression. To achieve best results experiment with various thicknesses of paper piles.

4. Put the shoe on your foot. (You may wish to wear a plastic covering on your foot before donning a suspect's shoe.) Walk across the paper piles, using a normal heel-to-toe step. Do not smudge by stepping side to side or by sliding your foot. You may wish to try several different steps. It is best to try making several impressions before re-inking the shoe, because the first impression will often remove excess ink, so that the second or third has just the right amount.

5. Mark your test impressions with time, date, and investigator's signature or initials. Number your exhibits to keep them in order.

## Cooking Oils and Magnetic Powder

1. Apply a thin layer of cooking oil (spray oil is most convenient), margarine or butter to the sole of test footwear.

2. Walk heel to toe across piled white bond paper.

3. Apply magnetic filings to the impression with the magnetic wand in the usual manner, avoiding contact between the metal wand and the oil surface. Use a

careful back-and-forth motion across the print to reveal the print pattern detail. Shake the excess filings from the paper or pick them up with the wand.

4.  To avoid smudging it is best to protect them by covering them with a large adhesive lifter.

## Helpful Hint: Using Toner

You can also use the **black toner powder** made for photocopy machines or printers to enhance an oil test impression. Place a line of toner along the side of the paper outside the impression. Shake the paper laterally so that the powder dusts the print lightly. Shake the excess toner off the paper. With this method, you can heat the toner-covered oil impression under a photo-lamp or other heat lamp. This process bakes the toner into a permanent exhibit that will not smudge. Try it! Be careful to avoid turning the paper brown from the heat of the lamp.

## Black Fingerprint Powder and Adhesive Lifter

You will need a large **hinged adhesive lifter** for this method.

1.  Peel open the lifter. Mark the adhesive surface lifter with a dark felt marker, including time, date, initials, and the letter "R," the universal symbol of laterality. An easy method of keeping order is to label your test impressions in the sequence "R1," "R2," "R3," etc.

2.  Lightly dust the sole of the footwear with black fingerprint powder.

3.  Lay the lifter, adhesive surface upward, supported with a pile of paper on the walking surface.

4.  Step on the adhesive surface heel to toe with the dusted footwear. You may need assistance in holding the lifter down so it does not stick to the footwear.

5.  To enhance contrast of the impression, place a piece of white paper over the entire adhesive surface. Be careful not to crease the paper or create air bubbles.

6.  When you fold the lifter you should have a high-quality, clearly contrasted print that is well protected. But note that the impression is a laterally reversed or mirror image. Your left shoe will look like a right shoe and all your markings will be backwards. That is why the letter "R" is, in this case, a necessary mark. It will appear in reverse on this exhibit. When comparing the test impression to a cast, this is an important point.

### *Dust Impressions*

This is a "quick and dirty" impression that you can test easily. Using the suspect footwear, you simply walk through dust and step on a piece of clean, white bond paper (preferably stacked). This method will yield a dust print and it is sometimes used at the crime scene for a quick comparison. It is highly transient and not recommended unless no other means is available. To render the impression permanent, it should be photographed. You can also make a dust impression less transient by using a plastic cover or adhesive lifter.

## Footwear Impression Comparisons

Investigators usually make comparison charts on photographs of scene of crime and test impressions. Remember to include the all-important ruler in all photographs. In many cases, you are best to enlarge photographs of impressions to clarify individual characteristics. Generally, class characteristics are not charted, although the investigator and the presenter of such evidence must be ready to give a detailed account of the size, manufacturer, model, and pattern of each piece of footwear as far as possible. Individual characteristics will be identified and marked numerically on charts of both the "known" and "unknown" impressions, clearly and systematically, so as to eliminate any doubt as to a positive match. The uniqueness of the footwear should be established and the match demonstrated in vivid, graphic fashion.

## Non-matching Individual Characteristics

In many cases, the suspect may wear the footwear in question after the crime has been committed. The sole of a shoe or boot will thus acquire new marks that are not on the impression collected at the scene of the crime. These must be considered and shown to be "explainable differences" due to subsequent wear.

## Anthropological Wear

In some instances, investigators can also compare the wear on the inside of a shoe with the barefoot impression of a suspect. This could be the comparison of a suspect's interior shoe wear pattern with a bare footprint at the crime scene. This sort of comparison requires considerable expertise and will often be assigned to forensic anthropologists. In Ottawa, the RCMP has done considerable work with computer imaging in developing anthropological wear evidence.

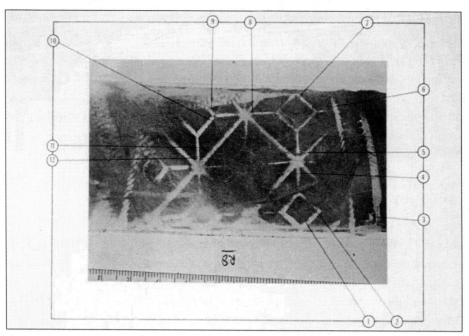

**Illustration 7-8.** Suspect footwear impression raised on a telephone receiver at a crime scene.

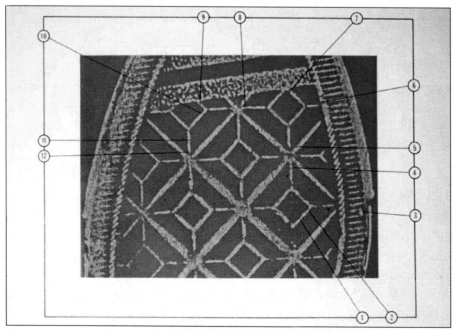

**Illustration 7-9.** Test impression of suspect footwear. These impressions were compared, identified, photographed, and charted for court presentation.

# TIRE IMPRESSIONS

Mobility is important to the criminal; in a high proportion of offences, a vehicle is used. In discussing the approach to the crime scene, one warning worth repeating in this book is: Be careful not to destroy tire impressions. Tire impressions can be invaluable physical evidence, narrowing down the search for suspects and providing important supportive circumstantial evidence. Tires, like footwear, have a story to tell from their birth in the factory to their presence at a crime scene.

## Class Characteristics

To improve tire performance, manufacturers add distinctive characteristics to their products. These characteristics, which include the composition of the tire, the tread characteristics, and the sidewall markings, are valuable identifiers with which investigators can narrow the search for evidence.

Not every tire impression will reveal sufficient accidental characteristics to enable a positive identification. Class characteristics can therefore be vital investigative leads, narrowing considerably the population of suspect vehicles. A combination of different tires can even enable you to establish the uniqueness of a vehicle from class characteristics alone. Imagine that a suspect's vehicle has two, three, or even four mismatched tires. The class characteristics of the impressions left by the vehicle could form a unique combination of patterns that would enable you to say with certainty, or at least would add considerably to the weight of the evidence for saying, that those impressions were made by the vehicle bearing that unusual combination of tires.

## Composition of Tires

Tires are manufactured in a range of types. Three of the most common for commercial and personal use are bias-ply, belted-bias, and radials. Radial tires, developed for long wear and safety, have become the most widespread on ordinary passenger vehicles, although new designs are constantly evolving.

The **carcass** of a tire is the structure of the tire not including the tread and sidewall. A **liner** is like an attached inner tube, a thin rubber layer at the innermost part of the tire. The liner is bonded to the **plies**, which are made of chord fabric and run in layers from one bead of the tire to the other. The **beads** are simply the edges on the inside radius of the tire, which form a seal with the wheel or wheel-rim of a vehicle. **Belts** are layers beneath the tire's **tread** made of steel cords or fabric. Between the bead and the tread are the **sidewalls**. The area at the edge of the tread, leading on to the sidewall, is known as the **shoulder**.

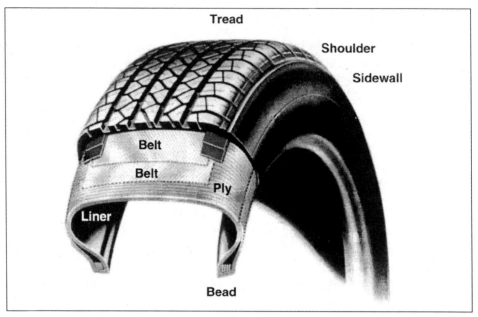

**Illustration 7-10.** Radial tire structure.

While all these parts may be of interest in general identification, accident analysis, or descriptions of extreme wear, the area of principal interest for tire impression evidence is the tread—the part of the tire that comes into contact with the travelling surface. It is usually made up of rubber and other materials molded into a tread design with five distinctive class characteristics, as follows:

- **Ribs** are the most noticeable part of the tread pattern. They run around the surface of the circumference of the tire. You can identify a pattern firstly by counting the number of ribs. (*Note:* Be careful not to count the shoulders as ribs.)
- **Grooves** are the channels that separate the ribs of a tread.
- **Sipes** are the smaller grooves in the ribs of the tread.
- **Elements** are the sections of the rib separated by grooves and sipes.
- **Blades** are the edges of the ribs and therefore also of the elements.

In addition to these basic tread components, manufacturers add the following class characteristics:

- **Arc width** is the width of the tread.
- **Stud holes** are holes in the tires designed to accept studs for winter driving.
- **Tread wear indicators** (sometimes called **wearbars**) are strips that run in a straight line across the tread pattern. Because they are set below the surface of the ribs, indicators are usually only visible in the grooves.

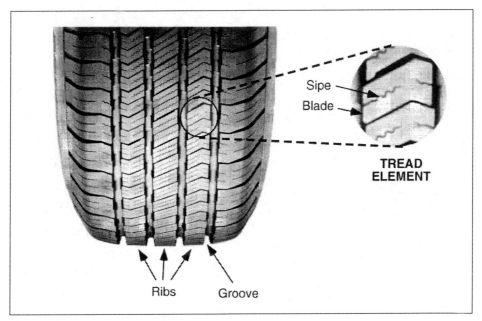

**Illustration 7-11.** Tire tread design.

- **Noise treatment** (variable pitch tread design) refers to the variation in the size and position of tread elements—a feature of most tires introduced to reduce noise of constant pitch.

## Tire Sidewall Markings

The sidewall of a tire is virtually a catalogue of class characteristics. It can enable you to pinpoint the origin of the tire, sometimes down to the specific weeks or months of its manufacture. The company name, tire name, size, place of manufacture, serial number, identifying product codes, basic construction, ply type, recommended inflation, and load range are all usually marked here.

## Accidental (Individual) Characteristics

Accidental characteristics are all those properties a tire acquires after manufacture, through use and exposure to the elements. Every tire wears uniquely with the nature of the vehicle, style of driving, surfaces travelled, and general environment characteristics. The individuality a tire gradually acquires is often your most valuable aid in identification. An understanding of the terms, nature, and causes of tire wear is essential to the investigator's collection and interpretation of evidence. One matching accidental characteristic may be all that is necessary for a positive identification.

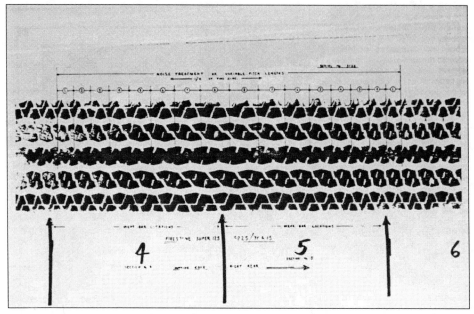

**Illustration 7-12.** Noise treatment of a tire is a pattern of sizing and positioning of tread elements. Generally, the pattern will repeat several times around the circumference.

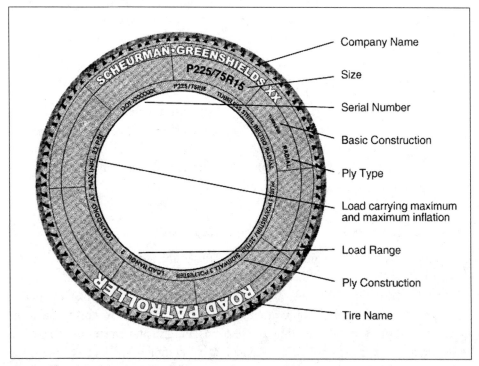

**Illustration 7-13.** Sidewall markings.

### General Characteristics of Tire Wear

Some accidental characteristics are found in varying degrees on most tires. They include:

- **Tread measure and circular wear.** All tires wear as they rotate in contact with a surface. This circular wear can be assessed accurately in some "unknown" impressions and in all "known" tires, by a measurement of tread depth.
- **Skid depth.** Tires subject to skidding will show flat spots at which tread wear will be greater than on the rest of the tire.
- **Toe-in, toe-out.** Think of looking at a vehicle from above, with a line drawn through the centre from bumper to bumper. The degree to which tires are toed towards or away from the centre of the vehicle is toe-in, toe-out. If tires are incorrectly toed the tread will wear improperly, feathering (losing their distinctness of pattern) because the tires are sliding slightly as they roll.
- **Camber wear.** If tires are tilted incorrectly they will wear on one edge only.
- **Incorrect inflation.** Overinflation causes a tire to wear at the centre, while underinflation causes wear at the shoulders or edges on the treas.
- **Cupping.** Various mechanical problems can cause a tire to wear unevenly at the outer edges of the tread.

### Specific Accidental Characteristics

Specific injuries to tires may produce valuable unique impressions:

- **Cuts.** Will produce small interruptions of the general pattern on a tire impression. In a three-dimensional impression they will fill with road surface material, giving the investigator a unique raised surface.
- **Abrasions.** Can also produce unique tread patterns.
- **Tears** on the rubber surface of a tire will also produce unique marks.
- **"Chunk-outs."** "Chunking" is the loosening or loss of a tire tread portion through centrifugal force. It can produce a dramatic interruption in the tire tread pattern.
- **Stoneholding.** Stones stuck in tire treads can also leave their unique mark.

# Crime-Scene Impressions

The principles, methods, and materials employed in gathering tire impression evidence are basically the same as those you have studied for footwear. The major differences are those of scale. Unlike the collector of footwear impressions, you cannot expect to incorporate some tire impressions in a single cast or photograph. You must adjust your methods to the situation. Experience will teach you how much of an impression can be collected, but as with other evidence you are processing, the ideal is collect as much as possible.

Remember the crucial steps in recording and seizing impression evidence.

1. **Photograph and mark the impression** including a scale ruler. In the case of tire impressions, include if possible the likely direction of travel (perhaps with an arrow) and the position of the tire on the vehicle ("LF" = left front, "RR" = right rear, etc.).

2. **Cast or lift the impression.** If you are lucky, the suspect has driven over a board, cardboard, or other surface that you can seize. Otherwise you cast substantial three-dimensional impressions or attempt to lift two-dimensional ones. Again, you must be guided by the nature of the impression. It may be possible to dust and lift impressions made by oily tires, or to use adhesive lifters to seize dust impressions on a smooth surface. Most impressions, however, will probably be seized as casts and/or photographs.

## Test Impressions

As is the case with test impressions of footwear, the known impressions you may make include mainly inked and vegetable oil impressions. In practice, however, the nature of tires and vehicles demands some adjustments of your methods. Test impressions of tires are best made with the tire on the vehicle so that the tread pattern is pressed on a surface with the same vehicle weight as the "unknown" crime-scene impression.

1. Raise the vehicle with a jack or on a hoist.

2. Coat the tire evenly. If using **ink**, apply with roller and glass; make sure the tread and the shoulder are completely and evenly covered. If using **cooking oil**, coat the tread and shoulder evenly with a spray can. If using **fingerprint powder**, dust lightly, evenly, and completely with a brush.

3. Mark the tire sidewall. Put a chalk or felt pen line on the tire to indicate the point at which the impression starts.

4. Set out a clean, white surface long and wide enough to accommodate the impression of a complete rotation of the tire. You may wish to calculate the outer circumference of the tire to find how long your impression will be. If so, use the formula $2\pi r$, where $r$ is the radius of the tire. You will find that the complete impression will be between six and seven times the radius of the tire. Allow a

small extra space at each end of the impression (before and after your mark) to ensure a complete pattern.

5. Lower the vehicle and move it continuously along the length of your test surface.

6. Enhance oiled impressions with magnetic powder and wand, with fingerprint powder, or with copier toner as in the case of footwear. In the latter case again, you can place the toner to the side of the print and shake it gently across the surface, shaking off excess powder. Remember that heat from a photo-lamp on oil and toner impressions will create a fused, permanent print.

## Comparing Tire Impressions

For rapid and easy comparison, make a positive transparency of your photograph of the crime-scene impression. If your test impression is not in toner and oil, it can be smudged easily. You may wish to cover it with a sheet of clear plastic to protect it. You can slide the transparency along your test impression until you have found the crime-scene impression location on your test impression. *You can look for noise treatment features first as quick reference*, if such features are present on the tire in question. If you are able to find identical class characteristics on both impressions,

**Illustration 7-14.** Crime-scene photograph reveals suspect vehicle was equipped with three different tread pattern types. This unusual combination of pattern types provided strong physical evidence in court that the impressions were unique to the vehicle equipped with those tires.

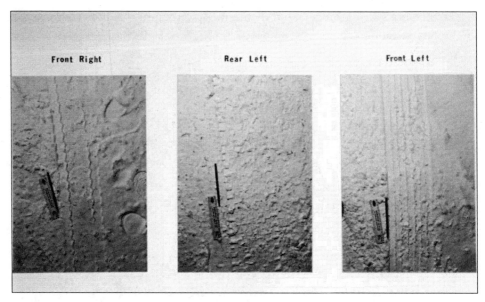

**Illustration 7-15.** Crime-scene impressions of the suspect vehicle.

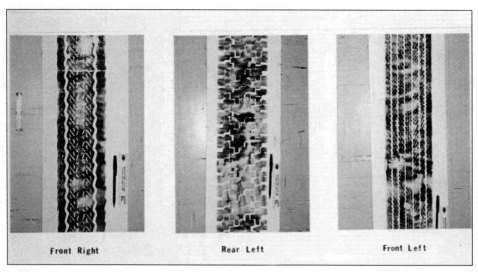

**Illustration 7-16.** Test impressions showing class characterization of the three pattern types.

the accidental characteristics you have already identified on the unknown impression should match your test impression exactly. Keep in mind that your test impression may also show accidental characteristics acquired after the crime that involved the suspect vehicle.

### Comparison Charts

Assume that you have acquired expertise in tire identification. Whether you are comparing a crime-scene cast to a seized tire or photograph, or a crime-scene photograph to a test impression, you will need to prepare comparison charts, which consist of photographs of both "known" and "unknown" evidence. If you are using accidental characteristics to make a positive identification, you must chart them for court presentation.

# Determining Direction of Travel

In order to fit more pieces into the puzzle of a crime, it is often useful if you can interpret a tire impression to determine the direction in which a suspect vehicle has travelled. First of all the direction of travel can help you to find out which tires of the vehicle made the impressions. You can also sometimes discover the trail of exit from a crime scene and any further evidence left along the trail. In addition, you may be able to reconstruct the chronology of a series of offences, such as break-and-enters. If a vehicle has been used as a weapon, you can add a great deal to crime reconstruction by determining direction of travel. Look for the following indications of direction:

1. **Acceleration residue.** When a vehicle starts off from a point, particularly if it is on a soft surface, it will leave a deposit on the surface behind the drive wheels. In soft earth, the investigator should look for small mounds of dirt and for debris thrown behind the vehicle. This is particularly true if the tires have spun on damp soil. On pavement, a spinning tire will leave deposits of rubber which are darkest at the starting point, and fade in the direction of travel.

2. **Stopping and changing direction.** Impressions can tell you when a vehicle stopped by a deeper mark on a soft surface and turning marks. If the vehicle has skidded to a stop on pavement the residue will be heavier and darker towards the point of stopping (the reverse of "spinning out").

3. **Steering of front tires.** Even if a car is driving "straight" ahead, the driver will make constant adjustments of the front wheels to correct the course. These result in a steering pattern that, with other indicators, can help to determine the vehicle's direction.

4. **Overlapping tire tracks.** Manufacturers often make vehicles with wider track width on the front. This variation in track width is also useful in showing vehicle direction. In order to use this characteristic, you need to track the vehicle over a distance.

5. **Examination of vegetation.** If you can see the way in which grass or plants have been bent by a vehicle, these can act as an indictor, bending in the direction of travel.

6. **Directional tires.** The treads of tires on working vehicles such as tractors, high-performance cars, and off-road vehicles are often called "directional" and the treads will therefore indicate direction of travel.

7. **Soil displacement.** A vehicle rolling over damp soil will often lift the soil as it progresses. The soil settles back down, leaving the back edge of the lifted portion above the surface level of the rest of the impression.

8. **Vehicle deposits.** As a vehicle progresses, it may drip fluids, or drop excess snow, mud, or other materials whose trail may indicate direction. This indicator is often important in investigations of hit-and-run accidents.

## Vehicle Searches and Impression Measurement

Tire impressions can help you to narrow down the population of suspect vehicles even if you have no particular suspect in mind. Computer-assisted searches of vehicle types are possible, if you are able to take accurate measurements from tire impressions. A search can tell you the possible type, model, and year of vehicles that match your measurements. The crucial factor in the success and utility of such a search is the number and accuracy of measurements you are able to take from crime-scene impressions. The following are the measurements needed for such a search:

1. **Wheelbase.** This is the perpendicular distance between the axles of a vehicle. To find the wheelbase from tire impressions, you measure from the leading of the rear tire to the leading edge of the front tire. In order for you to take this measurement, the impressions must indicate where a vehicle stopped, paused, or turned, so that you can see the leading edge of the tire in the impression. In the case of front tires that are turned, you can find the wheelbase by measuring from the inside leading edge of the rear track to the inside leading edge of the front track.

2. **Front track width.** The vehicle's track width is the distance from the centre of one tire to the centre of the other (e.g., from the centre of the left front to the centre of the right front). You can also find this distance by measuring from the

inner side of one tire impression to the outside of the other (or vice versa), or by measuring between the inner sides of the impressions and adding the tread width, or the outer sides and subtracting the tread width.

3. **Rear track width.** Remember you should measure the rear track width in the same fashion. While wheelbase and front and rear track width are the most important measurements, you should gather as much information from impressions as possible. Be aware too that camber and toe-in, toe-out can affect track width.

4. **Turning diameter.** Although this is sometimes called "turning radius," it is actually the diameter of the smallest circle a vehicle can make when turning. This calculation can be one of the specifications

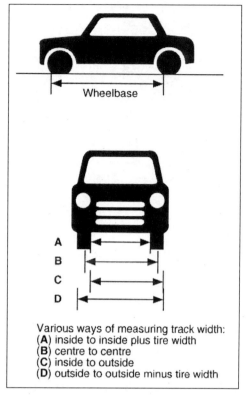

Various ways of measuring track width:
(**A**) inside to inside plus tire width
(**B**) centre to centre
(**C**) inside to outside
(**D**) outside to outside minus tire width

**Illustration 7-17.** Wheelbase and track width.

listed by automobile manufacturers, and is part of the computer database identifying makes, years, and types of vehicles. To find the turning diameter, you must measure the outer edge of the arc made by the outermost front tire in an impression, and then calculate the diameter of the arc:

• Draw a line (B) across the arc.

• Find the centre of the line.

• Draw a perpendicular line (A) from the centre of your horizontal line to the arc.

• Calculate with this formula:

$$\text{Turning diameter} = (B^2 \div A) + A$$

To pin down further the identity of the suspect vehicle, you can add two features we have discussed already:

5. **Tread design width.**

6. **Tread depth.**

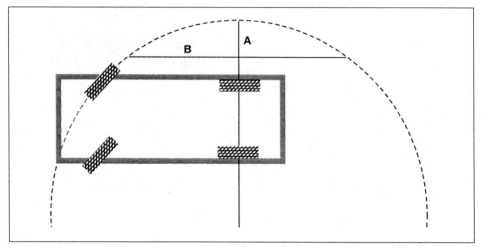

**Illustration 7-18.** Measuring turning diameter.

In summary, remember six possible measurements you can take to provide further precision and weight of evidence when interpreting tire impressions. Remember as well that the first four of these are frequently used in computer searches to identify vehicles:

1. wheelbase

2. front track width

3. rear track width

4. turning diameter

5. tread design width

6. tread depth

## Research Data on Tires

For purposes of comparison and identification, a tire design database called Tracs Searches is available from RCMP headquarters. Investigators can also rely on these important resources available from tire manufacturers: *The Tread Design Guide, Tire Guide, Who Makes It and Where, The Oldtimer's Tire Guide.* Contact: *Tire Guide,* The Tire Information Center, 1101—6 South Rogers Circle, Boca Raton, FL 33431.

# Snowmobile Impressions

It is also possible to gain considerable information from the impressions left by snowmobiles. From their various characteristics investigators can narrow down the range of suspect vehicles and sometimes make a positive identification.

## Characteristics

Identification is possible from both the skis that steer a snowmobile and the tracks that propel it. RCMP research in cooperation with snowmobile manufacturers has identified several important features and measurements of both class and accidental characteristics.

*Ski Stance*  The distance between the centres of the ski tracks. Skis usually have one or more wearbars on them. The wear on these (or even its absence) can be taken as an accidental characteristic. Ski stance, as well as in camber placement and number, can often be detected even in scratches on pavement or ice and enable identification. Accidental characteristics such as bar wear are more easily visible in snow. Ski width can also be important, especially if the suspect has used distinctive replacement skis.

*Track Width*  The measurement of the complete width of the track can also be used for identification, although there are relatively few width variations.

*Track Pattern*  Because of the great variety of track designs, this can be an important identifier. Some have an alternating zigzag track pattern, others have snow holes in the tracks, and older models will sometimes have metal traction bars across the tracks. Tracks can be replaced and exchanged between machines, but generally it requires considerable expense to do so and tracks are usually quite durable.

*Track Pitch*  This is the distance between traction bars, or the size of each link in the track. If possible, it is best to measure eleven traction bars and divide by ten for more accuracy. Be aware that tracks also skip and you should try to measure the impressions made by a stationary machine or measure in several locations.

*Track Length*  If you can find one recurring track detail in an impression or a piece of wood or ice stuck to a track, you measure the total length of the track. Simply find two points at which the identical detail occurs and measure the length between them. You can also measure length by counting the number of pitch lengths or links between these two points and multiply by the number of links.

***Detailed Measurements and Impressions***   In particular track impressions, you should also measure various distances such as the distance between vent holes or from such features to the edge of the track. Some tracks will also have cleats or spikes on them which may be distinctive and give the impression individual characteristics. It may also be possible to discover serial numbers and other distinctive features from a clear impression.

***Evidence Seizure***   Black-and-white photographs made with oblique lighting as in the case of other impressions are the usual method of seizure. Include a visible scale ruler in every photograph. In some cases you may wish to cast a impression. Follow the same procedure as in other snow casts.

***Research***   Serial numbers and other data are available for most currently running snow machines of North American manufacturers and can be obtained from the RCMP.

# TOOL IMPRESSIONS

The tools of the criminal's trade are often just that—tools. Consequently, the investigator must learn to recognize, seize, analyze, and appreciate the evidential value of tool marks as physical evidence. Recall again the principles of alternation. Tool marks can be the most subtle visible changes of a crime scene, but they are often important evidence, occurring frequently at points of entry or the focal points of crime scenes. Investigators must be vigilant in the detection and presentation of such evidence. Moreover, in remembering your other crucial investigative principle, that of physical matching, you must be aware of the kinds of marks made by a wide variety of tools.

*A tool mark is any impression made by a tool on another object.* The impression may be a cut, an abrasion, a gouge, or a depression made by the presence of the tool. Specialists classify tool marks into at least three types: (1) **compression marks,** caused by a blow; (2) **scraping marks,** caused by lateral movement; (3) **shearing**, caused by a cutting action. You should note that many marks will contain some combination of two or all of these types.

Your objective as an investigator is, ideally, to match tool marks found at the crime scene with a tool or tools found in the possession of a suspect. Several problems may arise: (1) the criminal may have left the tool at the crime scene; (2) it may be difficult to find the tool in question; (3) even if found, the tool may not allow a positive identification.

# Seizing Tool Mark Evidence

After the important first step of taking overall and close-up photographs of the evidence, the best way to seize a tool mark is to transport the object marked by the tool or to remove and transport the marked portion of the object. For example, you can cut out part of a wooden doorframe, or seize an entire damaged door. If these options are not reasonable, you should, after photography at various angles, make casts of tool impressions. Caution: inspect tool marks for any transferred material. In other words, look carefully to see whether a piece of the tool has been broken off and left in the tool mark, or any other substance has been either deposited or carried off by the tool.

## *Casting*

The simplest casting technique is to fill the impression with silicone rubber that you have mixed with a hardening agent. Press the mixture into the impression with a tongue depressor or spatula. Allow it to set for 15 to 30 minutes until it is firm but

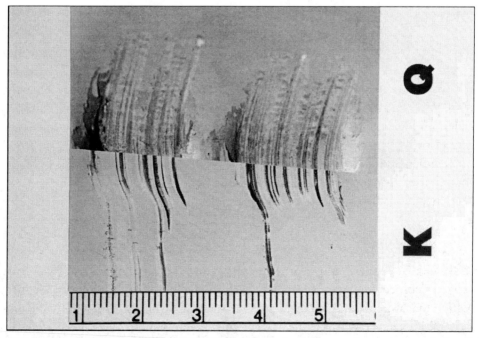

**Illustration 7-19.** Questioned tool impression compared to known impression. Tool marks found at a crime scene can be compared with tools found in the possession of a suspect. Test impressions are often hard to reproduce accurately because of additional wear and tear on the tool, the angle at which the tool was used, and the pressure used to make the different impressions.

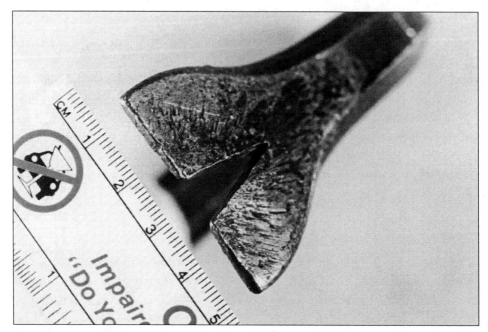

**Illustration 7-20.** Tools can have individual markings right from the point of manufacture, especially if they are machined metal objects.

pliable and dry to the touch. Peel off the silicone and you have a cast. Package it to avoid damage.

Casts are sometimes made with other materials, such as dental stone. Recently, forensic scientists have tested various forms of the dental casting material **vinylpolysiloxane**, which is made in a number of commercial applications, including Panasil® Light Body, Reprosil® Medium Viscosity, 3MExpress® Light Body or Regular Body, and 3M Imprint® 1:4. A product called Mikrosil® is also commonly used. An applicator or gun is used to apply the material, which produces tool mark casts that are accurate in size and detail.

### Testing the Tool

Assume that you wish to perform the task of an expert in tool marks. If you have seized a suspect tool, you are ready to perform the three steps essential to identification that were mentioned in Chapter 4: Analysis, Comparison, and Evaluation (ACE). Remember to protect the tool carefully before testing. *Never place a suspect tool back into a tool mark. You may be fabricating evidence.*

The steps in testing a tool are:

1. Photograph the tool first as you have found it, and then again including a scale ruler. Photographs should be of extremely high clarity and, ideally, taken under a microscope (usually forensic laboratories will perform the most demanding close-up work).

2. Make a test impression, preferably on a surface similar to the one bearing the crime-scene impression. In the case where the latter was made in steel, however, you might wish to use a softer surface such as lead or plasticine to avoid damaging the tool. Again, this will usually be the work of crime-scene technician. In any event, it is important to make only the impressions necessary to avoid further wear on the tool.

***Problems of ACE***  In examining test and crime scene impressions, consider the following questions:

1. Was the impression made at an angle similar to that of the crime-scene impression?

2. Was the degree of pressure on the tool equal to that which made the crime-scene impression?

3. Was the area of the tool which made the two impressions the same?

4. Has the tool been subject to wear after the crime scene impression was made? Comparison methods may include:

   - The microscopic comparison of a tool with the seized tool mark. (The best means for this is a comparison microscope, which allows side-by-side viewing.)
   - The imposition of a transparent overlay of the tool over the tool mark or of the tool mark over the tool. In some cases you may have to compare an overlay with a photograph of the impression.
   - The comparison of a crime-scene cast with a test-impression cast.

There are many possible means of comparison. Whatever method you use, your task will be to chart the comparable class and accidental characteristics. For the most part, cheap, modern, mass-produced tools bear few individual or accidental characteristics when new. Most of the distinctive characteristics of the tool will be acquired through use. Many will be microscopic chips or striations, although well-worn tools may exhibit various stresses such as rounding at the tips of screwdrivers, significant voids in the sharp end of a chisel, or indentations in the striking surface of a hammer. These marks will usually cause their reverse impression on the object contacted. The pits in a hammer will become raised bumps in a wood or paper surface, just as chipped-out sections of a chisel blade may leave raised marks on a chiselled surface.

You can also use the principles of tool mark comparison in examining human bodies. Stab wounds in human cartilage and saw marks on human bones can both be compared profitably with the tools that caused them. Evaluation of tool and tool mark comparisons requires the careful use of the matching principle, which involves a search for similarities and an explanation of differences. Experience and training in this science are essential if you wish to acquire competence.

# SERIAL NUMBER RESTORATION

Serial numbers or identifying numbers of various kinds are sequences of numbers or of number-letter combinations on some manufactured goods. Usually, they are stamped, cast, etched, or routed on surfaces such as steel (metal plates), aluminum, or cast iron. They can show where in a series an item was made and can also be used to protect the owner of the product. Such an identifying mark can be invaluable in an investigation. If an article is stolen, these quick identifiers can help the police connect it to its original owner. It makes sense that for criminals trying to destroy evidence of their crime, these marks are obvious targets. Fortunately for investigators, many attempts to destroy serial numbers are unsophisticated indeed.

**Illustration 7-21.** Serial number restoration performed using an acid method.

These numbers mean nothing if a careful tracking system is not in place. The serial numbers of handguns in Canada, for example, are kept in a central repository, and any sale or transfer of a handgun should be recorded accordingly. A criminal wishing to hide the evidence of a gun theft and subsequent crimes with that gun will no doubt try to obliterate the entire serial number. In an automobile theft, on the other hand, the thief may attempt to alter the serial number of the vehicle and make some quick cash on the legitimate used-car market. In fact, cash is usually the motive in most attempts to destroy or change numbers. Most items bearing serial numbers are relatively expensive: vehicles, boats, trailers, firearms, electric appliances, cameras, agricultural implements, and jewelry are some of the many targets of theft and resale that are numbered.

## Obliteration, Alteration, and Restoration

When numbers are stamped on an object the pressure of the process alters the structure of the metal below the surface of the stamp. The depth of this disturbed area varies; but such stamping may create an area of distinct structure beneath the stamp that is equal in depth to the stamp above it. In other words, a stamp that is 10 millimetres deep may actually disturb the structure to a depth of up to 20 millimetres below the original surface of the metal. Some authorities argue that this disturbed area is shallower usually by about half the depth of the stamped numbers.

Most thieves make fairly crude attempts to destroy serial numbers by **scratching**, **filing**, or **grinding** them down. In other cases, they go further and use a **hammer** over their obliterations, or they may work the numbers with a **punch**. Once a number has been effaced, some may use nickel or chrome plating to cover the signs of removal. More professional thieves will often try to replace serial numbers as well as to obliterate them. After grinding the number off, some will **overstamp** a new number in place of the original to give the appearance of legitimacy. The most sophisticated thieves will sometimes **drill** out the original numbers and **weld** a new surface on which they stamp new numbers.

The chances of successful restoration depend heavily on the means used to destroy or alter the numbers in the first place. Although there are several methods for restoring markings on various kinds of surfaces, the most common is **chemical etching with a solution of hydrochloric acid (HCl), distilled water($H_2O$), and copper chloride (CuCl)**. The proportions are usually close to equal parts of each substance, although various other mixtures and various other proportions of this mixture are used. It is best to consult an experienced technician if you wish to experiment with this method. In summary, this method consists in the following steps:

1. The acid used in the solution is dangerous and must not be allowed to contact the skin or eyes. You must also be sure that the restoration is performed in a well-ventilated room.

2. Photograph the surface and make thorough notes about it. Any numbers or other marks should be noted and all possible attempts to enhance and lift fingerprints made before proceeding.

3. The surface must then be cleaned and polished. Filing and sanding are often used to remove projecting pieces of metal. But care must be taken not to deepen any already existing marks. After polishing, the surface is cleaned completely.

4. The area that bore the serial numbers should be removed from the larger item if possible. If not, a dam of wax or clay can be built around the area to be etched.

5. The etching solution is applied, and after a time the numbers begin to appear. To speed up the process, some technicians run a current of electricity through the surface and the swab. In either case, the investigator should record numbers as they appear. Clean off the surface and repeat the process if not successful in the first attempt.

Remember that this process is futile if the investigator has no information on the meaning of the marks being raised. It is also unlikely to work if the surface bearing the numbers has been ground too deeply, or if intense heat or pressure have damaged the distinctive structural deformities beneath the serial number area.

# TEETH AND BITE MARKS

An increasingly useful means of criminal identification is the comparison of bite marks with the teeth of suspects. Bite marks have sometimes been called "dental fingerprints," and every individual has a unique set of teeth. Of course, unlike fingerprints, teeth change, fall out with age, and can be altered by dental work; nevertheless, bite mark analysis and forensic odontology have repeatedly proven their usefulness. While these are sophisticated comparisons, completed by forensic odontologists, the essential groundwork must be done by investigators who detect, preserve, and seize the evidence analyzed by scientists.

A bite mark investigation involves several steps:

1. the recognition of bite marks

2. the careful recording and collection of evidence

3. the preservation of bite mark evidence

4. the comparison by a scientist of the bite mark with the teeth of a suspect

The first three of these steps may be the work of investigators and forensic technicians.

## Bite Mark Locations

Forensically useful bite marks or tooth patterns are usually found in a number of locations:

1. on food or other objects (such as pencils) at a crime scene

2. on the body of a victim

3. on the body of a suspect

4. on dentures or teeth at a crime scene

5. on dental x-rays

## Recognition

The most typical pattern of a visible full bite mark is a circular or ovoid injury or impression. There will be two separate arcs of impressions, lacerations, or bruises that are comparable to the upper and lower teeth. In some cases there will also be a contusion at the centre of the mark.

The variations in bite marks are many and may be due to the degree of pressure of the teeth, the nature of the surface bitten (food, live or dead skin, etc.), the shagging of the teeth, the presence or absence of clothing, and the age of the mark.

## Collection and Preservation of Bite Mark Evidence

As with other impression evidence, seizure can be literal in the case of bite marks in foods, pencils, and other objects. In the case of a human body, the most important step in evidence collection is photography. *Do not spare the film.* Colour shots tend to show bruising and other discolourations, and investigators should take numerous close-up shots, position shots on the body, and crime-scene location shots. Be sure to include a scale ruler in all close up shots to enable 1:1 reproduction.

The work of comparison will be done by **forensic odontologists**, who will chart both class and individual characteristics. In some cases, tooth marks can also yield valuable DNA evidence, so they should be swabbed for possible deposits.

By its very nature, bite mark evidence is often a valuable clue in serious and sometimes vicious offences. Take the case of a murderer captured first in Lethbridge, Alberta in 1982. On December 24, 1982 at 9:30 a.m. police were called to secluded rear entrance to an empty building. There they found the naked corpse of a woman.

Detective Gordon Scheurman and Detective Sergeant Bill Plomp carefully processed the scene for physical evidence of every kind. Officers could discover only two types of physical evidence after hours of sifting through the rubble of the alley: a footwear impression on the abdomen of the victim and lacerating bite marks on her right cheek and on each breast. Scheurman took an extensive series of close-up, position, and crime-scene colour photographs, later ensuring complete coverage with further photographs in the morgue. Canvassing of the area yielded a suspect who had been seen leaving a nearby tavern with the victim and returning shortly there-after without her.

A pair of running shoes seized from the suspect's house appeared to have blood on them. The detectives' analysis and comparison of the shoe print with the seized shoe resulted in a match for class characteristics, and the blood drops were of the same type as the victim's blood. The conclusive evidence, however, was that of the bite marks. The suspect volunteered to give test dental impressions from which a cast was made by a denturist. Casts, impressions, and 1:1 (actual-size) photographs were hand-delivered to a forensic odontologist by Detective Scheurman so that continuity was assured. The scientist, Dr. William Blair of Calgary, charted extensive comparisons and established a positive match between suspect and crime-scene

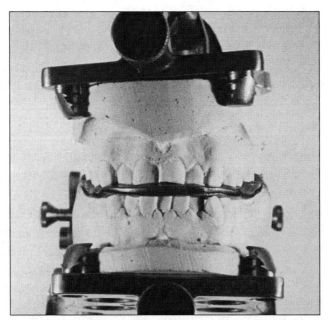

**Illustration 7-22 to 7-26.** These photos (on pages 136 to 138) represent some of the extensive and specialized measurement, casting, charting, and comparison required to make an identification on the basis of bite mark evidence in a homicide.

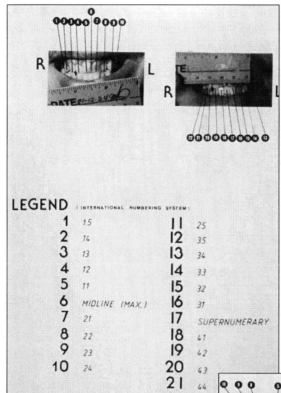

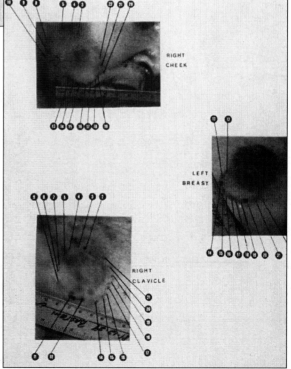

LEGEND (INTERNATIONAL NUMBERING SYSTEM)

| | | | |
|---|---|---|---|
| 1 | 15 | 11 | 25 |
| 2 | 14 | 12 | 35 |
| 3 | 13 | 13 | 34 |
| 4 | 12 | 14 | 33 |
| 5 | 11 | 15 | 32 |
| 6 | MIDLINE (MAX.) | 16 | 31 |
| 7 | 21 | 17 | SUPERNUMERARY |
| 8 | 22 | 18 | 41 |
| 9 | 23 | 19 | 42 |
| 10 | 24 | 20 | 43 |
| | | 21 | 44 |
| | | 22 | 45 |

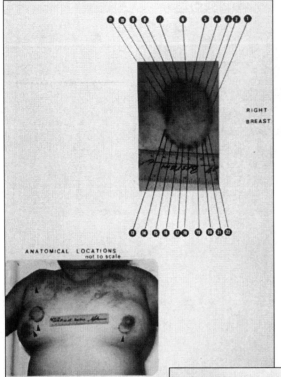

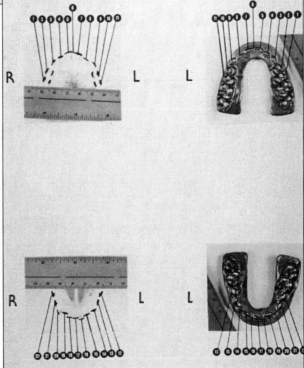

impressions. The resulting weight of evidence was so overwhelming that the suspect pled guilty.

## OTHER IMPRESSION EVIDENCE

While our discussion of impression evidence here may seem long and complex, it barely scratches the surface. In fact, there are so many surfaces and so many means of imprinting them that the possibilities are immense. Just as any heavy object can be a weapon, any textured object may leave an impression on a surface; if it has distinctive characteristics it may also be compared with the original object that made the impression. Textiles, jewelry, ropes: the range of things that could leave an impression is limited only by the imagination, professional skill, and intelligence of the investigator.

Imagination, research, and solid investigative practices led a Calgary investigator to an unusual means of identification in a homicide case. Sergeant R. J. Edwards was a constable in the Identification Section of the Calgary Police Service in the fall of 1992. In the early morning of September 16, a Calgary householder interrupted a burglar. In the ensuing struggle, the burglar stabbed his victim to death, leaving a shattered family and a bloody crime scene. The burglar, now a murderer, fled the scene and Calgary police quickly began to search for suspects. Their efforts were rewarded at 11:00 p.m. the following day when Detective Acheson arrested a young

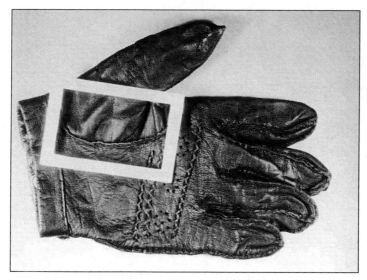

**Illustration 7-27.** Suspected area of the glove where a positive identification was made.

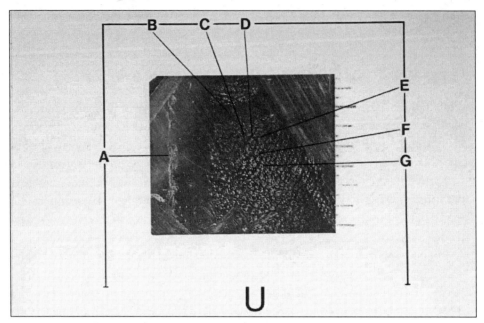

**Illustration 7-28.** Impression raised at the scene of a homicide. "**U**" identifies the unknown impressions for court purposes.

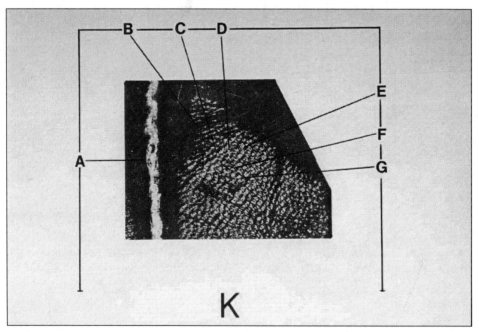

**Illustration 7-29.** Test impression made by Constable (now Sergeant) Edwards of the Calgary Police Service. "**K**" identifies the known impression for court purposes. It was positively identified to the suspect print and charted for court presentation.

man. The suspect fit the description given to police by a taxi driver who had picked up the young man near the scene on the night of the murder.

In a separate case, police had been looking for a stolen 1989 Ford. It was found in the alley behind the murder victim's house. The car's owner had reported that his leather driving gloves should be in the glove compartment of the car. They were missing from the recovered vehicle. A pair of leather gloves was seized from the accused on his arrest and turned over to Detective Johnston, who took them to the Identification Section for examination. There Constable Edwards photographed the gloves and began an interesting journey into new forensic methods. On September 23, he examined a basement window, an attempted point of entry at the homicide scene. On one of the inner window panes, he discovered a small impression that looked as if it could have been made by leather.

Constable Edwards recovered the gloves from the evidence at the Homicide Office, and began to experiment and to do research. He discovered that the gloves had been a gift to the stolen car's owner three years before. The purchaser had bought them from a leather boutique in a Calgary mall to which Edwards went to interview the retailer. The gloves were made in Hungary and the retailer had bought them from a distributor in Montreal. The distributor informed him that such gloves were usually lambskin, and about 12,000 pairs of them were distributed annually throughout Canada. But his quest for information on leather and leather impressions had only begun. He contacted and consulted with a range of experts in a wide variety of places. He contacted the Ontario Police College Identification Training unit, and learned of the extensive glove impression work done by Gerald Lambourne (now retired) of New Scotland Yard in England and of two other glove impression experts in England. He learned about the processing of leather and the fabrication of leather goods from Wolfgang Schluessel, the President of an Edmonton fur and leather company. As we might expect from our general discussion of forensic science in Chapter 5, Constable Edwards' research also led him to the scientific and academic experts. Scientists in the Western College of Veterinary Medicine at the University of Saskatchewan in Saskatoon and at the Veterinary Pathology Laboratory in Edmonton were also on his list of contacts.

The final science, however, was police work. Although they had not previously been involved in leather impression work, officers from the RCMP in Ottawa were nonetheless helpful. RCMP Sergeant Dave Ashbaugh suggested that Constable Edwards examine the principles and procedures used to differentiate human-hand and sole prints. Leathers are treated animal skins that have distinctive follicle and hair growth, and distinctive grains. Even before he had made extensive expert contacts, Constable Edwards had immediately begun to make test impressions and take photographs. He made 20 test impressions of the left palm of the seized glove, and photographed and tested 10 of them for comparison with the crime-scene print.

The ultimate result was a match of the "known" to the "unknown." This comparison lent considerable weight to the evidence against the accused. An enterprising officer had carefully taken an obscure piece of evidence, relentlessly tracked the possibilities of comparison and employed the **matching principle** to a successful conclusion. The murderer was convicted and is now serving his time.

# FIREARMS AND AMMUNITION

Many crimes demand that the investigator discover a "smoking gun." In Canada, about a third of homicides involve the use of firearms. While this rate has not changed appreciably for the past several decades, the use of handguns or pistols has risen as a percentage of total firearms crime. Conservation enforcement officers routinely deal with firearms offences. Proving that firearms have been used in commission of a crime can lead to the discovery of valuable evidence. Every firearm leaves its own distinctive signature that can link a suspect to a crime scene. It is important therefore that investigators be aware of the evidential possibilities of firearms, ammunition, and their effects.

While you may not perform the final ballistics and other weapons analyses, it is often the first officer on the scene who will be responsible for the recognition, collection, and preservation of firearms evidence, especially in a remote police detachment or conservation office. While some students or officers may have extensive firearms knowledge and experience, others must depend entirely upon a systematic study of unfamiliar, dangerous weapons. In any case, you should first of all be familiar with the great variety of firearms in use.

## TYPES OF FIREARMS

Firearms consist of: a **chamber** into which the **ammunition** (**cartridge**) is placed; a **barrel** or tube through which a **projectile** or **bullet** travels; a **hammer**, **pin**, or other source of impact situated behind the chamber so that it can strike and ignite the

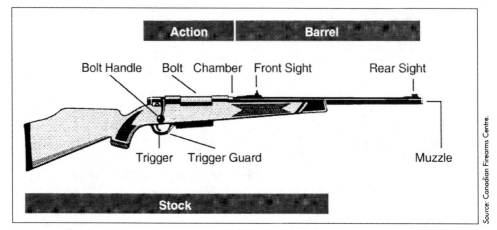

**Illustration 8-1.** Firearm parts.

ammunition—when the hammer is in position to be released, the weapon is said to be **cocked**; the **trigger**, usually located conveniently close to the **grip** or **stock** by which the weapon is held, and by squeezing which the user of the weapon causes the release of the hammer and the firing of the gun.

## Rifles

**Rifles** are usually *long guns, fired from the shoulder, that are characterized by rifling in the barrel*. **Rifling** is a spiral pattern on the inside of a firearm barrel that consists of **grooves** and **lands** (the portions between grooves) that cause a bullet to spin and improve its accuracy. Grooves and lands also leave distinctive markings on bullets, because every weapons manufacturer has its own unique rifling pattern.

## Shotguns

Shotguns are long guns, fired from the shoulder. They are usually smooth-bore weapons, containing no rifling. Today, shotguns conform to a simple measurement of diameter. A 12-gauge has a barrel diameter of 0.730 inches. The higher the gauge of a shotgun, the smaller the barrel diameter. A 16-gauge shotgun has a barrel diameter of 0.670 inches. The .410 gauge is exceptional in that its gauge represents the 0.410 inches of its barrel diameter.

## Revolvers

Generally speaking, revolvers are **handguns**. The cartridges are loaded into a **rotating cylinder**.

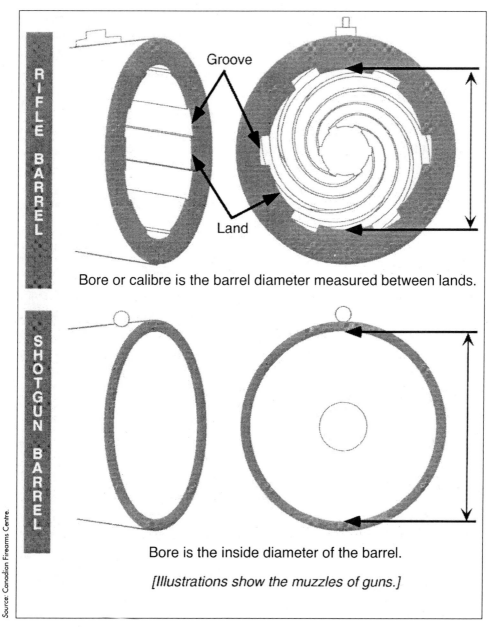

Bore or calibre is the barrel diameter measured between lands.

Bore is the inside diameter of the barrel.

*[Illustrations show the muzzles of guns.]*

Source: Canadian Firearms Centre.

**Illustration 8-2.** Rifling.

# Pistols

The term **pistol** has historically been used to refer to any handgun; in today's descriptions of weaponry, it usually refers to *handguns in which the cartridges are loaded into magazines* rather than a revolving cylinder. The **magazine** often enables the loading of many more cartridges than a revolver can carry, and also makes reloading easier. In addition, pistols are usually **semi-automatic**, that is, they can be fired rapidly by squeezing the trigger for each shot without manual cocking each time. The mechanism uses the gas emitted by the cartridge to eject spent cartridges and load the next round.

Both revolvers and pistols come in single-action and double-action types.

**Single-action** handguns require manual cocking either for each shot, or in the case of semi-automatic pistols an initial cocking for the first round. **Double-action** weapons can be fired either with manual cocking, or simply by squeezing the trigger. Many experts consider double-action firearms to be safer. Police services generally use semi-automatic pistols, which allow officers to have many more rounds of ammunition both in the weapon and in easily carried and loaded extra magazines.

## Bolt-Action

A **bolt-action** weapon is loaded and cocked through the use of a hand-operated **bolt**. The bolt is pulled back to open the action and eject a round, and a new cartridge is fed into the chamber, either manually in the case of a **single-shot** weapon, or automatically in the case of a **repeating** weapon whose cartridge rises into the chamber from a magazine. When the bolt is pushed forward and locked downward, the weapon is loaded. In most cases it is also cocked, although some weapons also require manual cocking before firing.

## Pump-Action

In a **pump-action** weapon, the pump performs tasks similar to those of the bolt, and also enables the user to load a cartridge and fire it without removing the hand from the trigger area. The grip of the pump-action is aligned under the barrel, and when pulled back it ejects a spent cartridge and causes another to rise from the magazine. The pushing-forward of the pump loads the cartridge into the chamber and cocks the weapon. Pump actions are used in the design of both rifles and shotguns.

## Lever-Action

In a **lever-action** weapon, a lever hinged in front of the trigger is pushed down and forward, ejecting spent cartridges and moving new rounds toward the chamber. When the lever is pulled back into place over the trigger, the cartridge is loaded and the weapon is cocked.

# Hinged-Action

In a weapon of this sort the front or barrel is hinged, so that the weapon must be "broken" open. The barrel is pressed downward and the chamber is exposed. Cartridges are inserted manually and the barrel is closed by pulling it upward. In some models, the weapon is then ready to fire, while in others an external hammer behind the barrel must be cocked.

# Semi-automatic

This term refers to weapons which are cocked and reloaded after each firing, usually by the pressure of gases from the exploding cartridge. *In a semi-automatic weapon the trigger must be squeezed for each shot.*

# Automatic Weapons

**Automatic weapons** use mechanisms similar to those of semi-automatic weapons, except that *they fire many rounds continuously as long as the trigger is depressed.*

# Calibre

The **calibre** of a weapon refers to *the diameter of rifled barrels, measured from land to land, as labelled by the manufacturer.* It is calibrated in either inches or metric measurements, and there exists a great range of calibres. In fact the actual land-to-land measurement may differ considerably from the stated calibre. A .22 rifle for example could have a barrel diameter of 0.22 inches, 0.217 inches, 0.221 inches, or some other measurement more or less than 0.22 inches.. Some .303 calibre rifles measure 0.308 inches, while others are 0.312 inches. A .38 calibre pistol might be 0.357 inches.

# Gauge

**Gauge** refers to *the internal diameter of shotgun barrels*. It was originally measured by calculating the number of spherical balls of the barrel's diameter that could be made from a pound of lead. A 12-gauge shotgun had a barrel diameter that could be used in making 12 balls from one pound of lead.

***

The above characteristics of firearms, combined with the nature of the cartridges they shoot, can provide investigators with crucial physical evidence. Keeping in mind

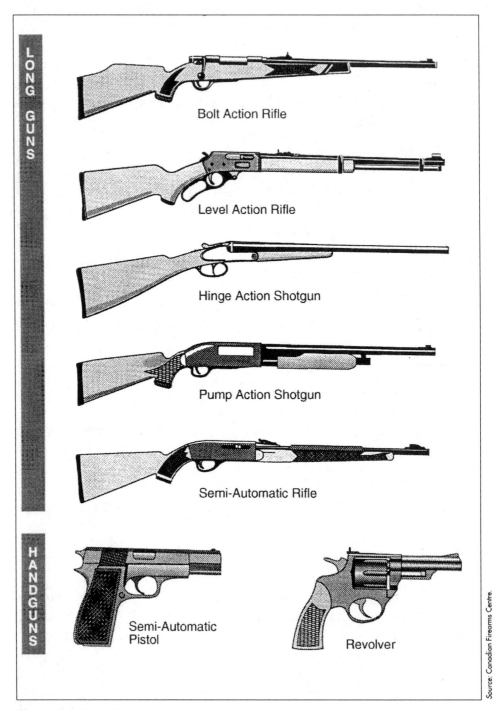

**LONG GUNS**

Bolt Action Rifle

Level Action Rifle

Hinge Action Shotgun

Pump Action Shotgun

Semi-Automatic Rifle

**HANDGUNS**

Semi-Automatic Pistol

Revolver

Source: Canadian Firearms Centre.

**Illustration 8-3.** Firearm types.

the matching principle, you can often determine from which gun a bullet has been fired or a spent cartridge ejected. Manufacturers have unintentionally created some of the surest means of matching projectiles to weapons. Every weapon barrel and action is machined, and this metal-on-metal process creates not only class differences in the pattern of rifling, but also microscopic differences (individual characteristics), even from one weapon to the next of the same model. The manufacturing machinery is altered with every fabrication of a weapon, and hence produces a slightly different weapon each time. In other words, no two weapons are exactly alike. Every barrel, for example, contains unique microscopic **striae**—scratches created by the changing condition of the boring tool. These in turn make **striations** on the bullet. The loading and firing of a weapon produces marks on cartridge and shot shell casings, as well on the bullets that travel through rifled barrels and are marked by the pattern of lands and grooves. Forensic examination of weapons and ammunition can find these marks and use them to make a comparative analysis.

In addition to the marks made by rifling and by the striae of a barrel, there are **breech marks** on the base of the cartridge case caused by the **breech block**. The breech block prevents the backward motion of the cartridge when firing. The pressure of the shell on the breech block leaves readable impressions.

**Magazine marks** result from the movement of the cartridge into and out of the magazine.

**Extractor marks** are caused by the device that grips the cartridge casing for ejection.

**Ejector marks** are caused by the ejector in the breech of the weapon. The **firing pin** which strikes the primer in the end of the cartridge makes a unique

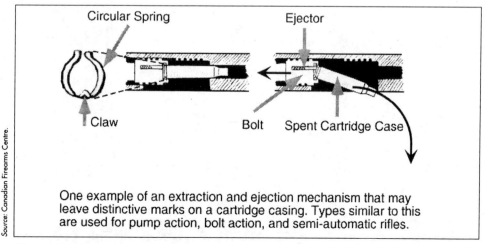

Source: Canadian Firearms Centre.

One example of an extraction and ejection mechanism that may leave distinctive marks on a cartridge casing. Types similar to this are used for pump action, bolt action, and semi-automatic rifles.

**Illustration 8-4.** Extractor and ejector.

impression. In the case of rim-fire cartridges, the impression is made by the striking surface of the hammer.

# AMMUNITION

There are hundreds of kinds of ammunition that can be classified by calibre, gauge, and structure. The three basic kinds are: (1) the **rim-fire** cartridge; (2) the **centre-fire** cartridge; (3) the **shotgun shell** or **shot shell**. Each cartridge or shell consists of a **casing**, **primer** or priming mechanism, **gunpowder**, and a **projectile** or projectiles. The projectile in a rifle cartridge is often called a **bullet**. Shotgun shells may contain many projectiles or **pellets**. When a trigger is squeezed, the firing pin strikes and ignites the primer, causing the gunpowder to ignite. This explosion propels the projectile from the cartridge case.

Shotgun shells also contain a **wad** between the projectiles and the gunpowder. The wad is usually a piece of plastic that maintains the grouping of pellets as they are propelled from the gun. The wad usually accompanies the shot for a distance and then falls away, allowing the pattern of pellets gradually to open up, creating the spread of the pattern. If the barrel is a **full-choke** barrel, constricted for a longer distance, the spread pattern will be tighter. Variations in the choke or length for which the barrel is constricted (modified, improved, or improved cylinder) will produce variations in the spread of the pattern.

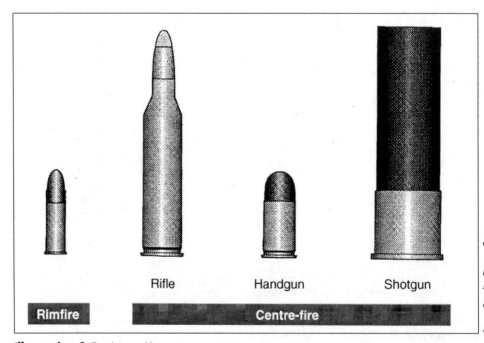

Rifle          Handgun          Shotgun

Rimfire                    Centre-fire

*Source: Canadian Firearms Centre.*

**Illustration 8-5.** Ammunition types.

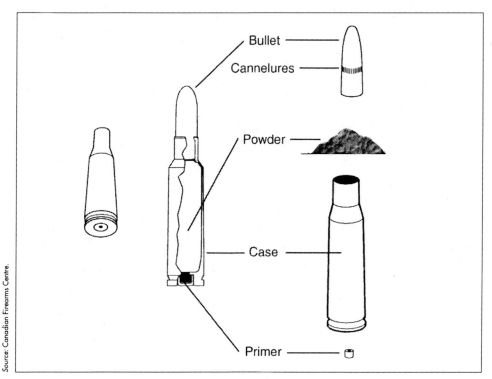

Bullet
Cannelures
Powder
Case
Primer

**Illustration 8-6.** Ammunition structure—rifle cartridge.

## Bullet Types

Because every manufacturer, in competition with others, attempts to improve ammunition, there is a great variety of types on the market. In addition to classification by calibre of the weapon, bullets can be identified by a host of other features. These include structure and materials of manufacture, length, weight of the projectile (usually measured in grams, or in **grains**: 1 grain = 1/7,000 of a pound), and the presence and nature of **cannelures**—the indentations on a bullet where the end of the cartridge casing is crimped to it and that hold lubricating grease.

*Accelerator Cartridges* These are cartridges in which a smaller-calibre bullet can be fired through a larger-calibre weapon. The projectile is encased in a plastic **sabot** that is equal to the calibre of the larger weapon. Thus a .25 calibre projectile could be fired from a .30/06 rifle. The projectile itself does not acquire striations from barrel rifling. In order to find such marks, it is necessary to recover the sabot, a short distance (15 to 30 metres) from the point of firing.

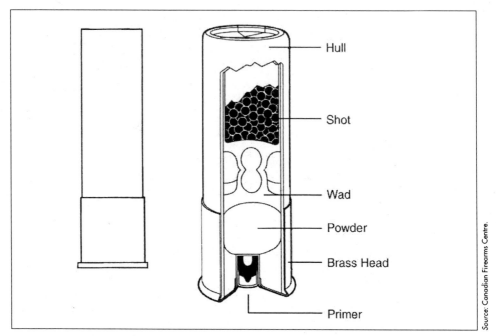

Source: Canadian Firearms Centre.

**Illustration 8-7.** Ammunition structure—shotgun shell.

***Expansion Marks***  When a weapon is fired, the explosion in the cartridge case expands it against the chamber walls. With this great force, the outer surface of the cartridge case is impressed with marks characteristic of that individual chamber. Hence the cartridge case can sometimes be matched to the weapon in which it was fired.

***Chamber Marks***  The injection of a cartridge into the chamber of a weapon may also cause striations.

To sum up, any contact of metal on metal or of cartridge with metal firearm parts can leave useful evidence for the investigator.

## Recovered Ammunition

The ideal situation for the investigator of a firearms crime is the recovery of the weapon, the cartridge casing, and the bullet. In many cases, only a partial recovery is possible. The most crucial item is *the weapon or evidence of possession of a weapon (registration, licensing or other documentation)*. At the crime scene, investigators must search for bullets and cartridge casings. If the suspect fired one shot from a bolt-action rifle and took the weapon away from the scene with the spent casing in it, you may be out of luck. Often in firing a semi-automatic weapon, the suspect will leave ejected casings on the scene. Distances of ejection vary greatly, and the scene must be thoroughly searched. Always take notes, measure, and photograph before you collect firearms evidence. When picking up cartridges, avoid using your bare fingers. If fingers are unavoidable, seize the cartridge casing, touching it as little as possible. Remember that cartridge casings may bear fingerprints. Do not use metal tweezers or forceps unless they are covered with rubber, and avoid any other metal-on-metal contact that could contaminate the evidence with new marks. Casings should be stored and transported separately so that one piece of evidence never comes in contact with another. Wrap each casing in soft facial or toilet tissue and place it in a transparent glass vial. Mark the container rather than the casing itself. Projectiles should be collected and stored in the same way as cartridge casings.

# Bullets

The most likely location for the recovery of projectiles is the **target of fire**—that is, what the bullet hit. This may be anything from the body of a victim to a door or window—in the case of a more random discharge of firearms, there may be bullets everywhere. If a bullet is lodged in a door, wall, or other surface, you may be able to seize and label the surface or the portion of the surface affected. In homicides and woundings, bullet recovery may occur during an autopsy or medical treatment. It is important that as many fragments as possible be recovered to enable the weighing of the bullet. Conservation officers or game wardens may find themselves performing an autopsy on an animal. In this case, proceed methodically, measuring and photographing wounds. When recovering a bullet, be sure again not to damage the bullet with a metal tool. In many cases, conservation officers will package and deliver not only a bullet to the lab but also the portion of an animal containing a wound or an entire small animal. If it is not possible to submit wounded flesh to a lab immediately, officers should freeze it for preservation.

# Recovering Firearms

It is important to remember two things when removing firearms:

- These are dangerous weapons.
- You must be careful to avoid damaging fingerprint evidence.

The classic TV detective often inserts a pencil in the muzzle or in the trigger guard of a weapon to retrieve it without contamination. This is a highly unsafe practice, and what's more, any hard object inserted in the barrel of a weapon may damage the striae which are its mark of distinction. When recovering weapons, handle them as little as possible. They should usually be unloaded at the crime scene, the officer taking care to keep all cartridges. If possible, handle the weapon using the edge of the trigger guard or any knurled or bumpy surface. Mark weapons on the surface least likely to have been handled and mark them as little as possible—a label tag containing full information tied to the trigger guard is an excellent means of marking, and for the necessary marks on the weapon itself, the butt of the stock is a good location. If possible the container appropriate for the type of weapon in question should be obtained from a gun dealer in order to pack firmly and transport weapons. Before submitting firearms, you must make sure that they are dry, especially if there is a possibility of delay and hence rust or corrosion. Air-dry wet weapons, and flush dirty barrels with boiling water so that they dry quickly. If you must clean the inside of a barrel otherwise, avoid brushes and other methods that could damage the striae. A soft cloth on a string is a good cleaner. But remember: any cleaning of evidence may be contamination. If you suspect a contact wound (i.e., a wound caused by a weapon pressed to the body of the victim, which may suck the victim's skin and blood back into the muzzle), do not clean the weapon. If the weapon has been used as a club or if there is any possibility of blood traces on it, air-dry but do not clean the weapon.

*Do not* under any circumstances:

1. "test" the weapon by firing shots; this may alter the evidence.

2. take the weapon apart; send it "as is."

3. check the trigger mechanism. The lab must have the weapon *as it was recovered* to perform the mechanical checks.

4. test the weapon by working ammunition through its action.

## ANALYSIS AND COMPARISON: READING THE STORY OF FIREARMS EVIDENCE

Your carefully seized and packaged evidence can now be analyzed, compared and evaluated. Under a comparison microscope, your recovered cartridge casings will be compared with casings test-fired from the suspect weapon.

- The marks of unique barrels, firing pins, breach blocks, extractors, and ejectors reproduced on a test cartridge can allow a positive identification with a seized weapon.

- Even if no suspect firearm has been recovered, cartridge casings and bullets can still be analyzed to discover the calibre, type, and sometimes the make of the firearm used.

- Recovered shot shells are analyzed in a similar fashion, although it is not possible to match shot or pellets to a particular weapon.

As an investigator, you can get a great deal of information back from the firearm and ammunition evidence you have submitted to the laboratory.

1. If you have submitted a bullet or cartridge casing and a suspect firearm, the lab can tell you if the bullet or casing was fired in the suspect weapon.

2. A bullet or cartridge case, or a fired shot shell alone, can be analyzed to tell you the probable calibre or gauge, type, and make of arm from which it was fired.

3. A cartridge or shotgun shell and a suspect weapon can be analyzed to tell you if the ammunition in question has been loaded into the suspect weapon.

4. More than one bullet cartridge case or shot shell as evidence can be compared and you will discover if they were fired from the same weapon.

5. The size of recovered shotgun ammunition can be compared with the shot size of the pellets originally in an expended shot shell. Wadding can sometimes give you information about the actual firing and the gauge of a gun. There are sometimes indications that a wad was fired from a particular gun.

**Illustration 8-8.** Cartridge cases seized at a crime scene and those test-fired in a controlled environment can be successfully compared as having been fired by the same weapon. Firing pin marks can be readily identified using a comparison microscope.

**Illustration 8-9.** Lands and grooves in the rifling of a barrel leave striation marks on a bullet and enable a positive match.

# EXAMINING THE EFFECTS OF SHOOTING

In the investigation of firearms crimes, the physical evidence includes not only weapons and ammunition, but also the wounds and damage caused by the discharge of weapons, and the residue of guns and gunshot. These can tell a considerable story. An officer receives a call to an alleged suicide. A woman is found dead in bed with a small-calibre gunshot wound to the head. Powder burns on the skin around the wound indicate that the probably fatal shot has been fired at contact with or very close to the woman's skin. A .22 calibre rifle lies far enough from the woman to have been out of her reach. The rifle contains one spent cartridge case. Such a rifle has very little recoil from firing and is not likely to have moved this distance on its own. What are the possibilities? There are no readable fingerprints on the weapon or cartridge cases presented by the physical evidence.

1. Did the person who discovered the body or someone else move the rifle in reaction to this discovery?

2. Did the victim react to the shot with sufficient force to move the rifle?

3. Was the suicide in fact a murder, staged to look like suicide?

This is the sort of puzzle you may encounter on your beat. The above story contains the basic evidence of an old mystery that remains unsolved. The reason that it remains a mystery (which, however, may someday be cleared) is primarily the existence of conflicting firearms evidence. But the wounds and other evidence resulting from shooting can usually give investigators various substantial clues toward the solution of such mysteries.

# Point of Impact and Entrance Wounds

These can yield important evidence to the investigator and must be examined carefully. This may be very unpleasant work that requires complete professionalism if you are required to examine the results of a brutal attack on a human being. If there was an attempt to disguise the crime, the evidence may be extremely gruesome. While the topic can be confusing, the point of impact can usually give some notion about the distance from which the weapon was fired.

## *Contact Wounds*

There are several possible indications that the barrel of the weapon was touching the skin of a victim. You may actually find the imprint of a gun muzzle on the skin, marked by the gas and smoke escaping from the barrel. The appearance and nature of a contact wound will depend on whether it was made in an area where bone is close to the covering of the skin. If yes, the trauma of the entrance wound may cause a star-like ripping of the skin. The ends of the wound may be **everted** (i.e., skin flaps may extend outward) and very little powder residue will appear on the skin's surface.

If the shot has been fired into skin covering soft tissue and organs, the bullet will make a round hole with most of the damage made inside the body. With contact wounds in general, remember that there is a strong likelihood of tissue, blood, and other possible DNA evidence on the weapon. You will also find blood and skin inside the barrel when the phenomenon known as **blow-back** occurs, in which rapidly escaping gases from the barrel create a vacuum that draws skin, blood, and tissue back in.

## *Near-Contact Wounds*

Near-contact wounds (made from up to 5 centimetres away) will usually display (a) a **scorching** of the skin and hair, (b) a **smudge ring**, (c) a ragged wound around which the skin is smudged and **tattooed** or **stippled,** and (d) blood, skin, hair, and tissue deposits on the weapon. As the distance of the weapon from the point of impact becomes greater, there is less likelihood of tissue and other deposits on the weapon and the smudge ring and skin blackening grow fainter.

## Short-Distance Wounds and the Flame Zone

Each combination of weapon and ammunition has a characteristic **flame zone** (usually less than 25 centimetres) within which a shot can cause scorching or burning of skin or other surface (including the clothing of the victim). The size of powder burns may vary with the calibre or gauge of the weapon, the load of the shell or cartridge, and the distance from which the shot was fired. A greater distance, for example, may cause larger a burn area, up to the point where the flame is no longer in contact with the surface and beyond the flame zone. Wounds at close range will also sometimes be characterized by a **halo** or smudge ring of smoke or soot that disappears with an increase in range.

Occasionally you may find a wound that includes no burning on the skin of a victim, but has in fact been made at very close range. In this case the weapon may have been fired through cloth or other obstacles. Sometimes this is done intentionally, to disguise the nature of the shooting. Do not, therefore, automatically conclude that victims without burns have been shot from a distance. First look for trace evidence of a "muffling" device.

## Powder Pattern

Up to about three metres (depending on the type of firearm used), shooting may leave a **powder pattern** around a bullet wound. Burned and unburned gunpowder will **stipple** the skin for some distance around the hole. Taking into account the weapon used, **powder residues** are strong indicators of a shot fired at close range, but not of a contact shot. The farther away the shot has been fired, the wider the powder pattern, until the range of the shot prevents powder deposits. This can be important evidence in considering the possibility of suicide. Powder is usually seized as evidence if possible; other surfaces such as clothing should be seized very carefully. Avoid folding any materials that may contain powder residues and keep them away from other powder-bearing evidence. Remember that powder residues are not necessarily visible and chemical analysis in the laboratory can reveal invisible traces and establish a pattern; so avoid mixture and contamination of possible powder-bearing articles. The pattern made by powder and other ejecta are specific to every firearm and laboratory matching of patterns as well as of the composition of ejecta is possible.

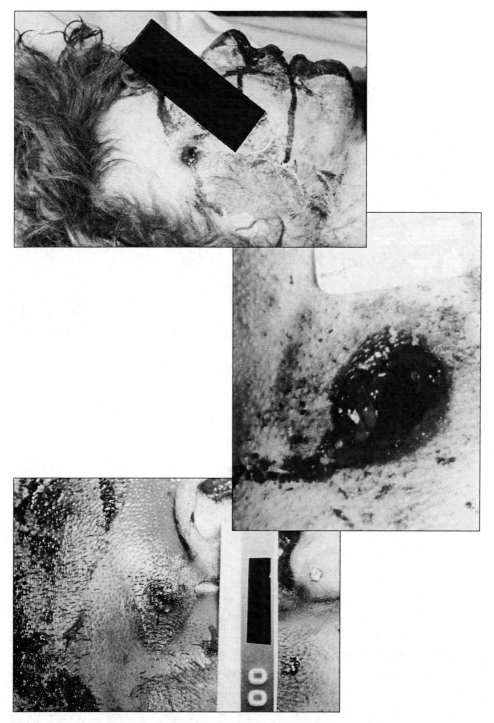

**Illustrations 8-10, 8-11, and 8-12.** Contact and near-contact wounds. Note the presence or absence of scorching, smudge ring, and other evidence of proximity.

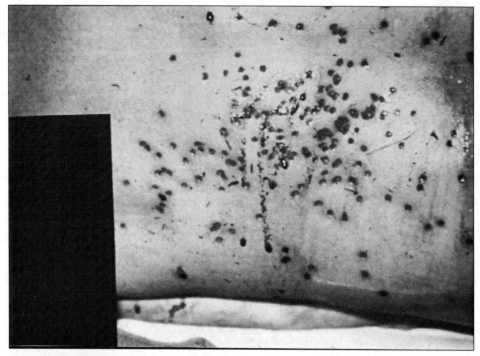

**Illustration 8-13.** The effects of a shotgun fired at a distance. The pattern of the shot is greatly enlarged.

## Bullet Wipe

**Bullet wipe** will be a feature of almost all entrance wounds regardless of distance of fire. Around the edge of a bullet hole in skin or other surfaces, the entering projectile makes a dark ring composed of lead, lubricants, gas residues, and any other substances on the bullet at entry.

## Bullet Track

As it passes through the human body, a projectile creates a path that can be used in your reconstruction of the shooting. This **bullet track** is particularly useful for establishing the direction of fire. An entrance wound and exit wound of a bullet travelling straight through the body can give sound evidence of the direction from which the assailant fired. But various factors may complicate the forensic pathologist's interpretation. The speed of the bullet, the type of bullet (materials of composition), and the deflection or **ricochet** of a bullet can all change the track considerably. These are matters left to the expertise of scientists.

The bullet track will in some cases end inside the victim's body, because of low velocity, bullet composition (e.g., it may have been a "mushrooming," hollow-point bullet), or deflection off obstacles. In some cases a bullet striking bone changes direction radically. Bullets or shots that penetrate the skull may run along the smooth inner contour of the skull and do considerable damage to brain tissue.

## Exit Wounds

The main characteristic of most exit wounds is that they are larger than the entrance wounds of the same projectiles. This is due to the change in shape, the expansion of the projectile, and the **tumbling** or twisting of the projectile as it travels through a body. Several other clues can guide you in deciding whether a wound has been made by the exit of the projectile. The skin around the exit hole is usually everted, and no halo, burning, or ejecta are present. When the projectile has passed through bone, **cratering** or breaking away of bone material usually occurs. Bone fragments may also accompany the projectile farther in the direction of the track.

## Gunshot Residues and Metal Tracing

In addition to deposits on victims and targets, investigators must also consider the possibility of trace evidence on suspected shooters. The most obvious evidence is **back spatter**, which will be discussed later. (See Chapter 9.) But examination can also reveal whether a suspect has fired or even handled a weapon.

## Powder Residues

Depending on the models of firearms and ammunition, the discharge of a weapon may deposit various types of **blow-by** or **blow-back** residues on a shooter, most commonly on the hands, face, and clothing. Gunshot residue kits are available and should be on hand. Traditionally, residues on skin have been collected with cotton swabs moistened with nitric acid and sealed in separate containers. These can later be laboratory-tested for the presence of barium and antimony from the ammunition primers as well as for other components of ammunition and explosions. Gas chromatography and mass spectrometry have long been in use for gunshot residue analysis.

## Trace Metal Detection

Not only ammunition but also the gun itself may leave a "signature." It is possible to determine whether a suspect has held a weapon, and sometimes to identify the type of weapon held. The metal of a firearm, knife, or other weapon sometimes leaves traces on the hand, and these can be found if a suspect has been taken into custody fairly quickly.

One of the early means of detection involved a **Trace Metal Detection Technique** that came into use in the 1970s. A suspect's hands were sprayed with a solution (0.1–0.2%) of 8 hydroxyquinaline. When exposed to ultraviolet light, the sprayed skin bore the imprint of the metal with which it had come into contact. The colour of the imprint could also indicate the type of metal held. Trace metal detection has evolved in the decades since, to the point where a relatively simple field test can be used to detect traces of iron on the suspect's hands. Solutions of pyridyl-diphenyl-triazine (PDT) under the trade names Ferroprint® and Ferrotrace® are sprayed on the suspect's hands. Traces of iron react with the spray to cause a magenta-coloured stain. This "print" often contains enough detail to allow identification of some class characteristics of the weapon. Even in cases where weapons of plastic or handgrips of wood have been the major areas of contact, PDT sprays can reveal the location of screws, triggers, and other parts made from ferrous metals (i.e., metals containing iron). On unwashed hands detection is possible up to seven hours after contact with metal (*Journal of Forensic Identification*, 48(3)(1998): 257–272). Theoretically, if the surface of the handgrip or trigger of a weapon has been significantly altered, it may also be possible to detect some individual characteristics, and make a much stronger match.

*C h a p t e r*

# BLOOD AND BODY EVIDENCE

Important for the investigator is the fact that about 8% of the human body is blood, that is, 5–6 litres for males and 4–5 litres for females. Since the beginning of violent crime, blood evidence has been considered important. Even when crime is not violent, blood at the scene may be of help to the investigator. With the ever-growing ability of scientists to analyze blood samples and interpret bloodstains more accurately, blood evidence tells a greater and greater story. The reconstruction of crimes and the matching of blood evidence are now more than ever possible. Bloodstain pattern interpretation has become a recognized, systematic form of analysis. With the introduction of DNA testing, the possibility of error in matching correctly seized and processed samples is negligible. The acquittal in the celebrated O. J. Simpson case had more to do with the inability of jury members to comprehend the accuracy of DNA testing and the skill of defence attorneys in raising doubts than with any possibility of error in testing.

Blood evidence entered into the English language long ago with reference to a guilty man having "blood on his hands," and long before this, the Biblical murderer Cain was told that his dead brother's blood cried out Cain's guilt from the ground. But the modern analysis of blood evidence was given its greater beginnings in the late 1800s and early 1900s in Europe. A series of murders during the previous century had identified various properties of blood and characteristics of its behaviour as a result of injuries. These discoveries were the background to two major steps crucial to the forensic analysis of blood evidence. First, in 1895 Dr. Edward Piotrowski, a Polish scientist, published his landmark article "Concerning the Origin,

Shape, Direction, and Distribution of Bloodstains Following Head Wounds Caused by Blows" (Vienna, March 1895). For the first time an original, systematic, and comprehensive study depicted extensive data that showed that bloodstain pattern interpretation could be a highly useful forensic discipline. The second great blood discovery in 1901 eventually won the Nobel Prize for Karl Landsteiner. Landsteiner successfully identified and classified the various types of blood; his work led to the A-B-O blood typing system still in use today. By 1937, further blood work had uncovered the Rh factor and the complexity of blood factors slowly began to emerge under the scrutiny of scientists. It was becoming clear that the combination of blood factors in each individual was probably unique. The identification of this uniqueness was difficult until the 1980s, when the work of Dr. Alec Jeffreys and others was the basis for the use of the **deoxyribonucleic acid (DNA)**, of which genes are constructed, as a tool for the identification of individuals. "DNA fingerprinting" has since become the most revolutionary of forensic identification techniques (see Chapter 5). It has been responsible for numerous convictions and for the release of innocent persons, in cases that would previously have been impossible to conclude.

# THE CRIME SCENE: RECOGNITION, COLLECTION, AND PRESERVATION

With current techniques of analysis, the smallest amount of blood or other fluids at a crime can be of tremendous evidential value. Moreover, blood crimes are often of a serious, violent nature. It is important therefore to remember what you have already studied about the careful approach to and treatment of evidence, and the nature of DNA typing. Even if you are dealing with the all-too-frequent break-and-enter, blood and fluid evidence may add yet another important piece to the puzzle of reconstruction. Remember, there are two analytical processes to which you are contributing by collecting blood and fluid evidence. The first process is the interpretation of the distribution and nature of bloodstains; the second is the typing of blood through DNA analysis. Your treatment of evidence must therefore take account of these two separate aims.

## Protection

Remember first of all that if you are likely to be handling or to be frequently in the area of blood and bodily fluids, you must protect yourself from infection and the crime scene from contamination. Rubber gloves are an absolute necessity when collecting bodily fluid evidence and protective clothing is required if you plan, after the initial response, to enter a bloody crime scene. You know well enough by now that all efforts must be made to avoid altering the suspect's path of contamination. This is also sometimes the area most likely to contain blood and other fluids leading to the focal points of crimes.

## Recording

Usually after the scene has been secured to avoid any alteration, you should begin recording immediately, with notes, sketches, and photographs. Your rough sketches will not require extensive measurement but ought to indicate roughly the location of blood and other fluid deposits. As with other scenes, you should take overall, medium-range, and close-up photographs. Photographs should be taken at a 90-degree angle from the surfaces on which fluids are deposited. After shots of the untouched crime scene, include a scale ruler in every shot. After you have inserted rulers, you may wish to take another series of overall shots, which will show the scale of the shot and also indicate the stages of your investigation. Later you can refer to the overall shots with rulers as a general reference to the various close shots. Many investigators now use colour film for a more realistic and vivid presentation of the crime scene. A complete set of photographs can allow a bloodstain pattern interpretation specialist to analyze the scene even if such a specialist is not able to be present.

# IDENTIFICATION AND ENHANCEMENT OF BLOOD AND BODY FLUID STAINS

## Identification of Blood

In some cases you may suspect that deposits are bloodstains, but you need to be sure that they are and are therefore worth a laboratory submission. To verify the likely presence of blood, there are a number of presumptive tests, such as Hemastix®, leucomalachite green, and **phenopthalein**. **Benzidine** and benzidine derivatives such as **o-tolidine** can also be used, but they are now believed to be carcinogens. **Hemastix®** comes in the form of a short stick. When touched to blood and then moistened with distilled water, the reagent at the tip of the stick turns green. (A **reagent** is a substance used to detect by reaction the presence of another substance.) **Leucomalachite green** not only identifies the presence of blood, but also enhances stains for further interpretation and analysis. When applied to a blood sample and then moistened with drops of hydrogen peroxide, the mixture should instantly turn blue-green. Researchers are constantly vigilant for health risks in these reagents and you should always keep up with the latest health bulletins.

# FLUID STAIN ENHANCEMENT

## Visible Stains

For interpreters of bloodstains, investigators examining bloody tool marks or fingerprints, or simply to clarify further photography of a crime scene, visible bloodstains can be chemically enhanced. In addition to leuco malachite, a most commonly used stain enhancer is **amido black**, which turns the protein in blood a blue-black colour. It is particularly useful for raising the contrast in bloody fingerprints.

## Hidden Stains

While an initial survey of the crime scene may seem to reveal no blood traces, it is important that you examine areas where blood may have collected: cracks between floorboards, joints in linoleum, subfloors beneath carpets, tub and sink drains, and traps. Such areas may contain the residues of a criminal's attempt to clean up or remove evidence.

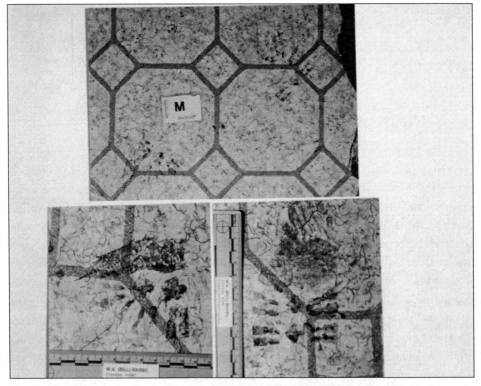

**Illustration 9-1.**  Crime-scene footwear impressions in blood enhanced with amido black.

## Invisible Stains

In some cases, a suspect or someone else may have attempted to "clean up" the crime scene, or conditions may have obscured the evidence of bodily fluids. If this is the situation, there are various techniques of discovery and enhancement of stains. The enhancement of invisible deposits is a steadily evolving science and a few examples will suffice here. High-intensity light sources, ultraviolet lights, and lasers can be used in darkened rooms to detect a variety of latent stains made by semen and other bodily fluids.

## Bloodstain Enhancement

Bloodstains do not usually react to light sources, but they can be chemically treated to emit light or **luminesce**. In a completely darkened room, invisible bloodstains can be made luminescent with **Luminol®**, a mixture of sodium perborate, sodium carbonate, 3-aminothalhydrazide, and distilled water. Luminol is sprayed or otherwise applied to the surface, causing the enzymes and iron in bloodstains to luminesce. It will often reveal extensive staining of surfaces thought to be "clean." Luminol presents some problems because it will also react with cleaning agents, vegetable matter, and some metals, although investigators usually find that enhanced bloodstains will luminesce longer than these other materials. Experience will enable you to discriminate. Another chemical, **Fluorescein®**, has recently been claimed by some

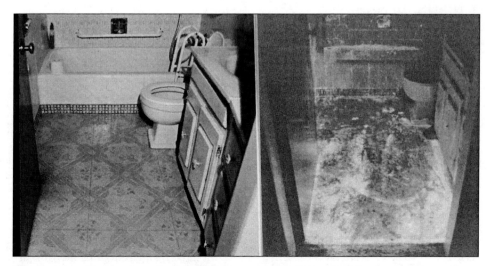

**Illustration 9-2.** A seemingly clean crime scene can reveal a totally different story when enhanced with Luminol. This photograph was taken in total darkness with a long time exposure for the film.

authorities to have a more highly sensitive reaction than luminol, although others regard the two chemicals as having comparable results (R. Cheeseman, *Journal of Forensic Identification*, 49(3)(May-June 1999): 261–268).

## Blood Reagents and DNA

A question that may have occurred to you is "Do the substances used to identify or enhance bloodstains damage the blood's potential for DNA typing?" The RCMP has tested a number of reagents for their effects on the DNA analysis of bloodstains to which they were added. In addition, there was an assessment of the effectiveness and convenience of five of the reagents. The reagents included some we have mentioned before and others in common use. **Ninhydrin**, described in Chapter 6 for the enhancement of fingerprints, was among them. Also tested were **amido black**, **Hungarian red**, **Crowles Double Staining®**, **Leucomalachite Green**, and two substances that cause stains to luminesce: **Luminol** and **DFO (Diazafluoren-9-one)**. Fortunately for investigators, the tests showed that *none of the seven reagents above reduced the usability of bloodstains for DNA analysis*. As for the effectiveness of the chemicals tested, amido black, Hungarian Red, Crowles Double Staining, Luminol, and leucomalachite green showed the presence of blood that had been diluted up to a level of 1:10,000. Leucomalachite green seemed the least sensitive when blood was more diluted, and moreover required preparation immediately before use because of its short shelf life.

## Light Sources

1. **High-intensity light sources** with red, orange, or light yellow filters work best for relatively practical detection.

2. The least expensive method is the use of readily available **ultraviolet light** ("black light"), which will cause some fluids to fluoresce, although not as effectively as high-intensity filtered light.

3. The most effective, but also the most expensive and awkward, source to use is **laser light**, which has great powers of enhancement.

## Outdoor Crime Scenes

As you have read earlier, trace evidence outdoors can be extremely transient. This is certainly true of blood and fluid evidence. You must be an assiduous investigator to locate fluids outdoors, a task that requires hands-and-knees dedication. While the same principles of investigation apply, you must be aware of the effects of rain,

**Illustration 9-3.** An alternative light source can show evidence otherwise not seen by the human eye.

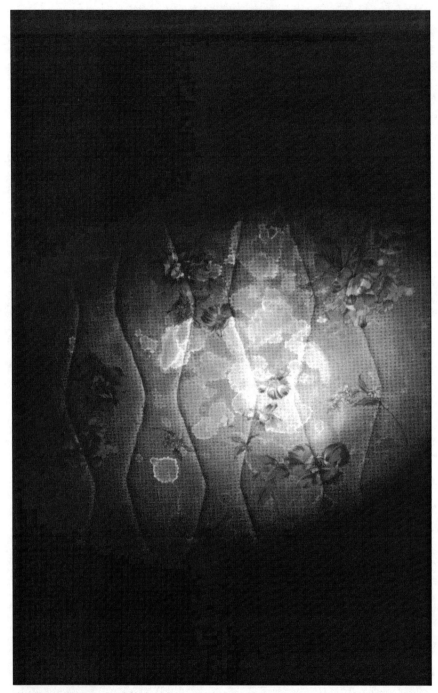

**Illustration 9-3.** Red filter added to the light source reveals more clearly the body fluid stains shown in Illustration 9-3.

snow, and sun. At the same time, while blood and fluid evidence may be altered by these factors, criminals are less likely to attempt to clean up outdoor scenes. Investigators may find it necessary to seize samples of soil, debris, leaves, or snow in order to preserve blood evidence. A search of the area along the patterns we have earlier recommended and the thorough recording of the scene are important in evidence seizure and incident reconstruction.

# DNA TRACE EVIDENCE COLLECTION

In many cases on a major crime scene, you may find smeared fingerprints or handprints that cannot be lifted and interpreted. They may, however, contain the potential to identify a suspect, victim, or other person relevant to the investigation. The key is DNA analysis. In order for this analysis to retain its evidential value, careful crime-scene procedures are essential. Let us consider the problems of collecting minute traces of body fluid evidence. In this case, you are employing one of the most powerful examples of the matching principle. This is also a case where you must be more aware than ever before of the **Principle of Alteration**.

# CONTAMINATION POSSIBILITIES

In Chapter 5, we discussed some basic aspects of DNA analysis. As you may remember, the nuclear DNA of a person's cells is unique to that individual. It can be extracted from blood, semen, saliva, vaginal fluid, and various tissues. The extracted DNA, although it may be a very small sample, can be amplified by the **polymerase chain reaction**. It is then separated through **polyacrylamide gel electrophoresis**. The resulting profile or "DNA fingerprint" of an unknown sample is finally compared with that of a known sample. If the profiles match, there is very little possibility (excluding identical twins) that the DNA samples are not from the same source.

The important aspect of this process for the crime-scene investigator is the fact that the analysis often involves very slight traces of evidence of human origin. The danger is that such minute traces can be ruined by or confused with equally microscopic contaminants from other human beings or samples. It is therefore necessary that all investigators be aware of the potential for DNA contamination when handling evidence. Some recent RCMP experiments have demonstrated that the following possibilities of DNA transfer exist:

1. Some persons slough off **epithelial cells** (cells on the epidermis of the skin) to other objects from the palms of the hands, fingers, and other areas. In some cases, the DNA from these deposits can be collected and analyzed.

2. It is possible for a person handling an object to pick up readable foreign DNA from that object.

3. It is further possible, although extremely unlikely, for a person to pick up foreign DNA from one object and transfer that foreign DNA to another object. This is called **secondary transfer**.

Think for a moment of the importance to you, as an investigator, of the three facts above. First of all, at a crime scene, there can be recoverable DNA on anything that has been extensively handled or used. Most surfaces, however, are likely to bear several unknown profiles, a mixture that cannot be interpreted. The possibility of depositing DNA by touching a surface also means that you must be aware of the dangers of contamination. Handling evidence with the bare hands or sneezing on it could destroy its evidential value with deposits of your DNA. Thirdly, even if you are wearing gloves and a mask, there is a slight possibility of the secondary transfer of DNA. Theoretically, for instance, the DNA on your gloves from a hairbrush at the crime scene could be transferred to the murder weapon if you hold the weapon wearing the same gloves.

# COLLECTION AND PACKAGING OF SMALL TRACES OF DNA EVIDENCE

*Note:* Be sure to photograph everything thoroughly before seizure.

1. In processing DNA evidence, it is not necessary, useful, or practical to attempt collection from all surfaces at a crime scene. Most of them will probably not yield useful results. At major crime scenes, however, you should swab surfaces that contain finger- or handprints too smudged for lifting or other areas that contain, or that may bear, biological evidence. Look for smeared windows, deposits on doorknobs and light switches, saliva on telephone receivers, and so forth. Two of the most important things to remember generally when processing DNA evidence are:

   (a) Avoid contamination.

   (b) Air-dry samples as soon as possible.

2. **Measures you must take to avoid contamination** include the following:

   (a) Wear a face mask to prevent contaminating the evidence with your own DNA by coughing or sneezing. (Naturally you must always wear sterile gloves.)

   (b) To avoid cross-contamination between pieces of evidence, always change your gloves after handling evidence bearing DNA, even if you think they are clean. Some authorities also recommend wearing protective clothing and changing it as you move to different areas of the scene. (See Appendix A for details.)

(c) Always change gloves immediately before touching a possible murder weapon.

(d) Process samples separately, and package them separately.

(e) Do not lick envelopes to seal them. Use water or a glue stick.

3. **Collection methods will vary** according to the state of the sample and the surface on which you find it. The following recommendations should be applied:

(a) For stains on portable objects, seize the entire object and air-dry it. In some cases, you may be able to cut out and seize the relevant portions of such surfaces.

(b) On nonporous surfaces that cannot be seized (wooden floors and walls, tile, linoleum, glass, concrete, etc.), you should use a sterile cotton swab to collect fluids and smudged fingerprints. Moisten the swab with distilled water and rub it on the deposit thoroughly to pick up as much of the material as possible.

(c) On porous surfaces that cannot be seized, use a cotton swab as described above. While you may not be able to remove some porous surfaces (paper or cork wall coverings etc.), you can cut and seize the stained pieces from cloth, carpet, paper, and other such materials. Be sure to allow a generous border around the stained area when cutting.

4. Air-dry completely your samples, including the stained surfaces or objects that you have seized. All DNA samples, even if they appear dry, were originally wet. To prevent damage by bacteria, they must be air-dried thoroughly. You must do this as quickly as possible, but avoid contamination. If a clean drying cabinet is within convenient distance, use it. If not, you may have to package the material appropriately and submit it quickly, as described below.

5. If you must package samples moist, ensure that air is able to flow around the sample. *Do not use waterproof packaging.* Use clean brown paper to wrap the sample and put the wrapped sample in a clean container, but do not seal it. It is essential to air-dry the sample as soon as possible thereafter. Otherwise samples should be sealed in exhibit bags. Remember to avoid contamination and to package all samples so that they can be opened with safety by other personnel.

## Blood Collection

Again, *your personal safety is of primary importance when collecting blood and other body fluid evidence.* Take precautions, using suitable gloves, and protective clothing if required. Remember that these precautions can also prevent the contamination of evidence. After the scene has been recorded, take samples for analysis. You should be able to take sufficient evidence from wet or dry deposits. *The method is as described above for DNA evidence collection.* In the case of large pools of blood, investigators have traditionally collected blood with a sterile hypodermic syringe or eyedropper that was then placed in a stoppered tube provided by the crime lab, and, if not sent immediately, refrigerated. For DNA samples, however, sterile material wiped in the blood and thoroughly air-dried is usually sufficient. **Known comparison standards** of liquid blood are usually taken by medically qualified persons.

## Vaginal and Seminal Fluids

Other than blood, these are among the most common fluids found at violent crime scenes, especially those of a sexual nature. Ideally, if there seems a possibility of semen stains, you should seize all portable surfaces of deposit at the crime scene: the clothing of the victim and if possible the suspect bedding and anything else that can be carried. Other deposits can be removed with a sterile cotton swab, air-dried, and stored in sterile containers. As with blood deposits, for dry stains moisten the swab with distilled water. Vaginal, oral, and anal swabs will usually be performed by medical examiners at an autopsy or a hospital and samples dried and stored similarly.

## Saliva

Saliva can be collected and stored with the same techniques as those used for blood. Saliva deposits may be found on anything that has contact or extensive near-contact with the mouth. Observe the same precautions and procedures that you would with the DNA trace evidence discussed above.

## Urine

This should be collected with the same procedures as blood.

## Feces

*Large deposits* of feces should be collected with a small, clean shovel and allowed to air-dry. Air-dried feces should be stored in sterile containers.

As with wet blood, *small deposits* of feces can be removed with cotton swabs, which are then air-dried and stored in a sterile container.

## Vomit

Deposits can be collected with small shovel, eyedropper, or cotton swab, air-dried, and stored in sterile containers.

There may be other useful bodily excretions at a crime scene and *all* should be considered evidence: perspiration, ear wax, mucous, tissue, or any other deposit from the body. Bloodstains and other such evidence, once identified and collected, can begin to tell its story through the services of skilled interpreters.

# ANALYSIS AND COMPARISON

## Bloodstain Pattern Analysis

Specialists can often draw a great deal of information about the nature of a crime from the appearance of bloodstains. The location of stains, as well as their pattern, size, and shape can be invaluable clues in the reconstruction of a crime. When the closed system of blood circulation is broken open traumatically, the resulting wound often hemorrhages, sometimes with great force. Consequently, bloodstains can help the investigator to estimate:

(a) where persons or objects were situated

(b) where persons or objects moved during bloodshed

(c) the point or points at which bloodshed originated

(d) the type of impact and the direction in which it was made

(e) the type of weapon that made the impact and the number of times it struck or fired

These facts can further assist the investigator to reconstruct the overall sequence of events.

### *Bloodstain Types*

Forensic specialists have developed an increasingly elaborate catalogue of terms to identify various types of bloodstains according to the way in which they were made. These classifications can be extremely useful to any officer looking at crime-scene bloodstains.

***Passive Stains*** These are caused by dripping or flowing onto a surface of blood acted on by nothing other than the force of gravity. Types of passive stains usually identified are:

(a) **Clots**—gelatinous lumps formed of clotting blood which appear as a combination of fibrous material and gelled red blood cells.

(b) **Drip Patterns**—caused by blood dripping into blood, creating a "satellite spatter" around a central stain.

(c) **Drop**—a small quantity of blood falling as a single mass. The size of drops is related, among other things, to the size of the object from which blood is dripping. Larger objects have a tendency to allow greater surface tension and mass created by flowing blood hence a greater weight of blood accumulates before falling. *Drops that fall at a 90-degree angle to a smooth surface will make a circular stain. As the angle of fall becomes more acute (less than 90 degrees), the stain becomes more elliptical.* Textured surfaces such as concrete cause distortions in stain shape.

***Projected Bloodstains*** These are caused by a force other than gravity exerted on an exposed source of blood.
  They include:

(a) **Arterial spurting**—a stain made by blood emitted from a breached artery. The pattern often exhibits large volumes of blood and may also show a series of large stains that reflects the beating of the heart and arcs according to the rise and fall in blood pressure.

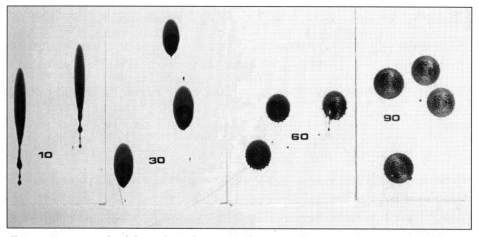

**Illustration 9-5.** Blood drops shown hitting a surface at 10 degrees, 30 degrees, 60 degrees, and 90 degrees.

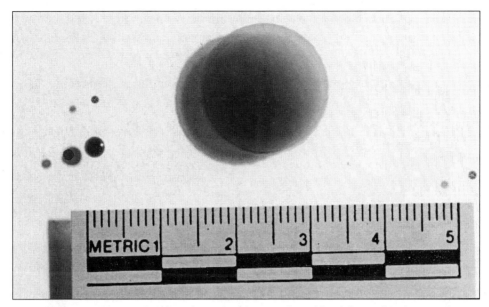

**Illustration 9-6.** Textured surfaces have a tendency to distort blood drops. This photograph shows the blood dropping at 90 degrees and hitting glass.

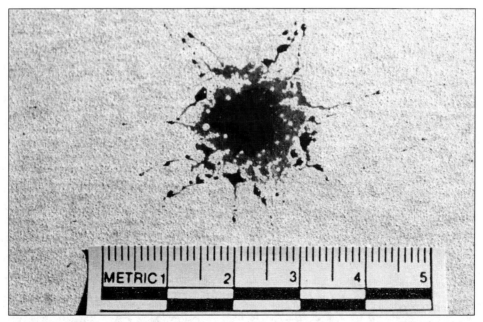

**Illustration 9-7.** A blood drop that fell at 90 degrees onto sandpaper.

(b) **Back spatter**—blood directed back towards the source of force, for example the blood of a victim that spatters the shirt of an assailant who is striking bloodletting blows.

(c) **Forward spatter**—caused by blood that moves in the same direction as the force that caused it.

(d) **High-velocity impact spatter**—caused by a high-velocity force greater than 100 feet per second, most commonly a gun blast. The resultant stain will look like a mist or fine spray of blood.

(e) **Medium-velocity impact spatter**—typically caused by a beating or other similar force and is usually identified by larger drops of blood rather than a mist or spray.

(f) **Low-velocity impact spatter**—the result of a very-low-energy impact on the blood source such as a weak blow. The spatter is usually made up of large drops or collections of them.

(g) **Cast-off stain**—a pattern made by blood projected from a source other than the site of impact, such as a bloody swinging arm or axe.

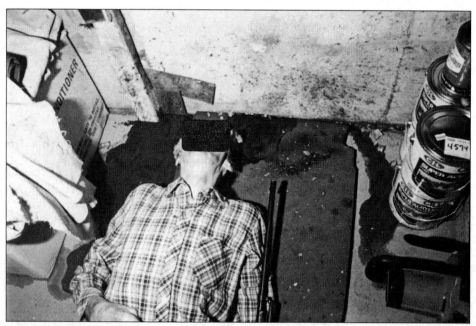

**Illustration 9-8.** High-velocity impact spatter is very common in firearms-related incidents.

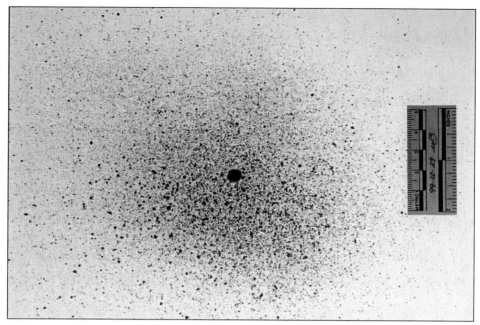

**Illustration 9-9.** High-velocity impact spatter.

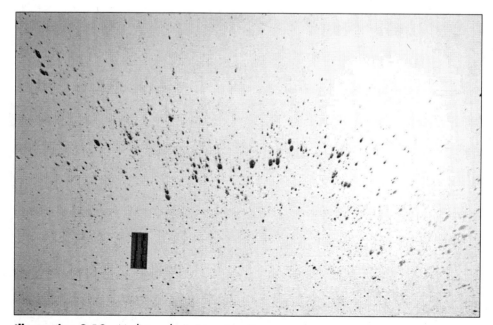

**Illustration 9-10.** Medium-velocity impact spatter.

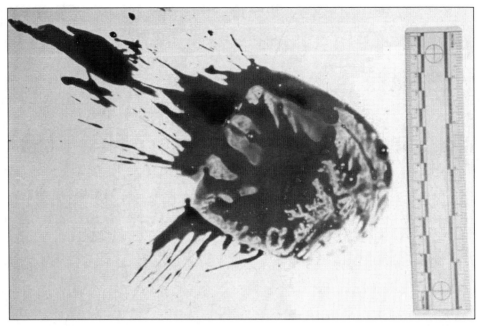

**Illustration 9-11.** Low-velocity impact spatter.

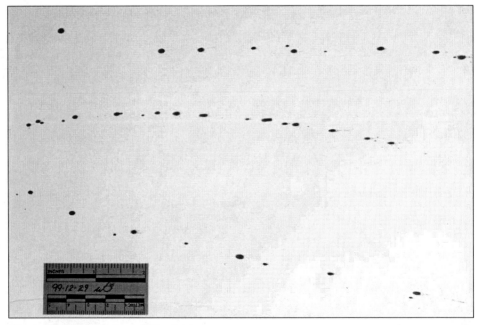

**Illustration 9-12.** Cast-off bloodstains.

***Transfer or Contact Stains*** These are the result of a bloody surface touching an uncontaminated surface. The contact stain will often be the recognizable print of the hand, shoe, or other object that has made it. Transfer stains of various sorts can be useful in determining the identity of a weapon or person, the direction of movement, and the order in which events occurred. Types of transfer stains include:

1. **Contact bleeding**—direct bleeding from a source that is touching the object into which it is bleeding.

2. **Swipe or smear**—a stain made by the transfer of blood to a surface not contaminated with blood. It is usually characterized by feathering at the end of the stain.

3. **Smudge**—a stain so distorted that its origin and history are extremely difficult to identify.

4. **Transfer pattern**—a transfer stain in which a image or partial image can be discerned.

5. **Wipe**—the stain caused by something moving through an already deposited stain, altering the stain's appearance and removing some blood.

**Illustration 9-13.** Contact stain. Suspect footwear leaving a small trace or impression.

**Illustration 9-14.** Swipe. This may be found in the form of impressions made by fingers, palms, or fabric, for example.

## Reconstructing an Incident from Bloodstains

The concepts above are some among the many that investigators can use to gain information and reconstruct events from the appearance of bloodstains. In addition to reading the evidence to determine the velocity of blows and identity of causes, bloodstain pattern interpretation experts can also gain reasonable estimates of the **directionality** (an indication of the direction of travel of blood drops) and, if bloodstain evidence is extensive enough, the approximate **point of origin** of the blood that produced stains.

*The shape of bloodstains depends on the angle of impact—that is, the angle formed between the line of direction of a blood drop and the plane of the surface it hits.* A drop of blood that strikes a smooth surface from an angle of 90 degrees will form a circular stain. In other words, the length and width of the stain will be equal (uneven surfaces, such as concrete, present many angles of contact and therefore change the shape of the stain). *As the angle from which blood drops strike the surface becomes more acute, the stains are increasingly elongated* and assume the shape of teardrops. *The narrow end or tail of the stain always points in the direction in which the blood is travelling when it strikes a surface.*

With two or more stains (from which you can determine directionality), you can also find a **point of convergence**, the point at which lines of direction indicated by bloodstains intersect.

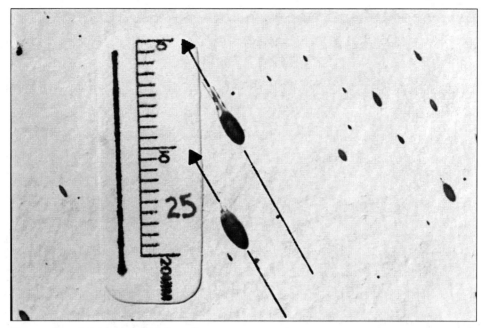

**Illustration 9-15.** Direction of travel.

It is possible to calculate the angles at which a blood drop struck a surface using basic trigonometry. Beginning at the round end of the bloodstain, measure the length and width of the ellipse that begins there, excluding the "tail" of stain and any satellite drops. These measurements will allow you to find the angle of impact, using the following formula:

$$\text{Angle of impact} = \text{Inverse sine of } \frac{\text{Width of stain}}{\text{Length of stain}}$$

For example, if a blood drop measures 3 millimetres by 5 millimetres:

$$\text{Angle of impact} = \text{Inverse sine of } \frac{3}{5}$$

$$= \text{Inverse sine of } 0.6 = 36.8 \text{ degrees}$$

If the stain measures 4 millimetres by 8 millimetres, the ratio of width to length would be $\frac{4}{8}$ or 0.5.

$$\text{Inverse sine of } 0.5 = 30$$
$$\text{Angle of impact} = 30 \text{ degrees}$$

You can use a **sine table** to discover what angle corresponds to a particular width:length ratio. The sine of 30 degrees is 0.5.

**Illustration 9-16.** Sometimes one area of a crime will yield several types of blood spatter evidence.

Having determined directionality, point of convergence, and angle of impact, you can now determine the **three-dimensional flight path of a blood drop**. If you have two or more direction-indicating stains that can be measured, the point at which flight paths converge is the likely point of origin of the blood drops that made the stains. In other words, using the quantities and angles indicated above you can make a reasonable estimate of the distance from the stain height, and the distance from other

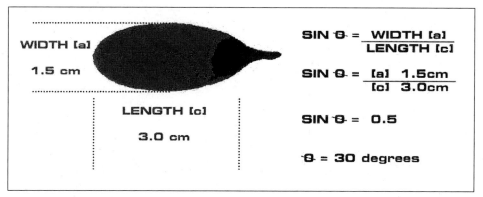

**Illustration 9-17.** Drop measurement.

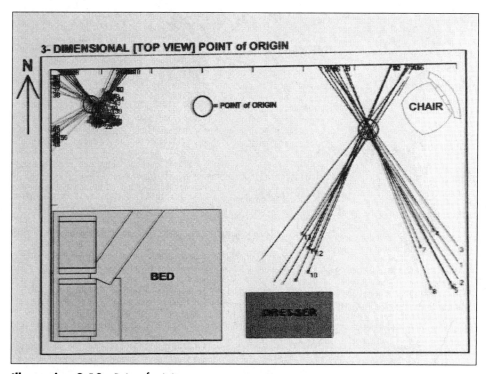

**Illustration 9-18.** Point of origin.

surfaces at which the blood of the stain was generated. This information can be vital to the reconstruction of a crime. The physical movements of victim and accused, the nature and use of weapons, the distance, speed, and location of blows or shots: all can provide explanations to the mystery of a violent incident.

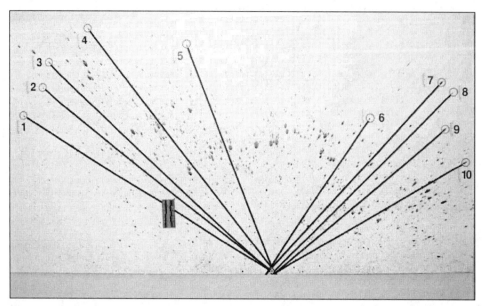

**Illustration 9-19.** Point of convergence.

# Fluid Content Analyses

We have already discussed in several places the analysis of the DNA in various excretions and properties of the human body. In suspected homicides, **toxicologists** are routinely involved in the analysis of fluids, organs, and tissues, usually provided by the pathologist performing the autopsy. They may also render opinions on the possible effect of any foreign substance they discover; this opinion may be an assessment of a drug's effect on behaviour, or it may be a view on whether a toxin could have been fatal. Measures of the amount of carbon monoxide, for example, are accompanied by an estimate of whether it could have been the cause of death. These opinions require considerable expertise, because the levels of various toxic substances the body can withstand are different for every individual.

In cases where the sobriety or drug intake of a person is in question, the toxicologist will perform tests beyond the rudimentary breath analysis procedures by the officer on patrol. Further analysis by specialists in pathology may be necessary when the health of a person is pertinent. For instance, if one person is suspected of intentionally infecting another with a lethal virus, an analysis of blood from the suspect, the victim, or both may be in order.

*C h a p t e r*

# HAIR AND

# FIBRE

# EVIDENCE

*10*

Among the most likely forms of evidence to be left at a crime scene, or to be transferred to a suspect, are hairs and fibres. These are often minute, sometimes scarcely visible, but they can have strong evidential value. They are also among the pieces of physical evidence likely to be missed by a criminal destroying evidence of crime. When processing a crime scene and searching for trace evidence, recall again the Principle of Alteration. Hairs and fibres are often deposited by an unknowing person whose hair naturally falls out or who transfers the fibres of carpets, clothing, car seats, bedclothes to and from the scene. Struggles in homicides, assaults, and sexual contact will leave pulled hair, particularly pubic hair and head hair, as well as fibre evidence. Fibre evidence can also be found at points of entry in break-and-enter cases, particularly where there is broken glass. Male chest hair is often easily detached and can sometimes be found on the clothing of suspects and victims. A few decades ago forensic scientists, while often sure in their own minds about the identity of hair samples, were still limited to inconclusive reports. A specimen could be pronounced exclusionary (i.e., the hair did not come from the suspect). It could also be considered similar to that of a suspect and therefore possibly left by him or her. But hair evidence could at best be used to corroborate other evidence, and serve to build a case. Hair alone was not conclusive. With the refinement of analysis and identification techniques, however, hair and fibre evidence has become increasingly powerful and one hair at a crime scene can help to refute false alibi evidence.

With introduction of DNA analysis, positive identification is now possible. These principles of identification apply to the hair of any animal (although DNA analysis is not normally needed to identify animal hair). In one recent case, the hair of a cat belonging to a sexual assault victim was found on the clothing of a suspect. The suspect's claim that he had never entered the victim's house was easily refuted and he was convicted. *Investigators should be keenly aware that these advances in forensic analysis also apply to their presence at this crime scene. Hair and fibres are easily deposited by careless investigators and can lead to costly contamination.*

# THE STRUCTURE OF HAIR

Hair is generally characteristic of mammals and all hair has a similar structure or **morphology**, with considerable variations. Hair growth begins in the **follicle**, an organ located beneath the surface of the skin. The **root** of the hair, contained in and attached to the follicle, is also sometimes called the **bulb**. The **shaft** of the hair grows out of the root and ends in a tip. The growth of hair occurs as cells, composed of the protein **keratin**, harden and emerge from the follicle. The resultant shaft of hair has three major features: the **cortex**, the **cuticle**, and the **medulla**. This structure is quite durable and can retain evidential value for a long time. The **cuticle**, the outer layer of hardened cells, gives the hair much of its protection and durability. Cuticle cells form scales that overlap, pointing toward the tip of the hair. The patterns of these scales are most useful in distinguishing between human and animal hair, and in identifying different sorts of animal hairs whose cuticles present highly varied patterns.

The **cortex** lies beneath the cuticle and is made up of elongated cells situated in a regular pattern and aligned parallel to the hair shaft. For investigative purposes the most important feature of the cortex is the presence in it of the **pigment granules** that give hair its colour. Microscopic examination of the cortex can yield important information about the placement of pigment granules, their shape, and their colour. A comparison of these features in two samples can help to make a case for a probable match.

The **medulla** is the core or central channel of cells in a hair shaft. When examining medullae, scientists usually deem them **continuous** (a single channel), **interrupted** (like long dashes), or **fragmented** (occurring in irregular lengths and intervals). Head hairs from persons of Mongoloid racial groups will usually contain a continuous medulla; Negroid and Caucasoid head hair will have either no medulla or one that is fragmented. Animal hairs often have significant medullae that are more than half the diameter of hair shafts (in humans the proportion is usually much smaller). For purposes of identification, scientists sometimes calculate a **medullary index** (= Diameter of medulla/Diameter of hair shaft). They can also identify the species of hair origin by the shape of the medulla, which varies from cylindrical in some animals (including humans) to spherical in others, with a variety of distribution patterns.

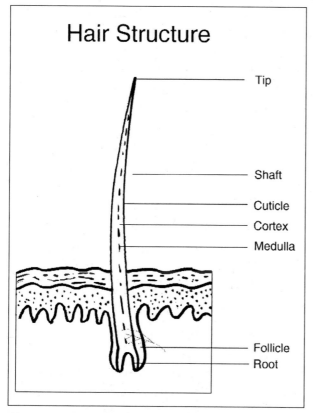

**Illustration 10-1.** Human hair.

# AT THE CRIME SCENE: COLLECTION OF HAIR EVIDENCE

Hair fits almost perfectly the definition of transient trace evidence: it is often small and transient in nature. When processing a crime scene, you must therefore be vigilant for hair evidence in a great variety of places. You may find hair held in the closed hand of a victim, in a watchband, under fingernails, on weapons in violent crimes, on combs and brushes, on bedclothes, on articles of clothing, on hats, and on virtually any surface with which a person has come in contact.

The initial approach to the crime scene should focus on the areas about which you have learned from the perimeter of the scene along the likely path of contamination to the point of entry and continuing along the path of contamination to the focal point(s) of the incident, and then to the point of exit and sometimes beyond. Investigators should attempt to examine the path of contamination visually, entering it as little as possible. You should always be keenly aware that hair fibres are among the types of evidence most easily cross-contaminated by officers. Like all humans, investigators shed many hairs every day (about 80 to 100) and these can cause awkward and expensive damage at the scene. Ideally those processing the scene will be able to wear protective clothing. One Canadian expert recommends a change and packaging for possible evidence of protective clothing after each room has been examined (see Appendix A). In many minor cases, or in the heat of an initial emergency, such precautions are not always practical.

Each crime will dictate what procedure is most practical, but generally you should follow a regular series of steps in the collection of hair evidence. Generally speaking, there are four means of observation and collection of hair evidence and investigators may use any one or combinations of all four:

1. **Visually observed hairs.** An alert officer at a crime scene is constantly on the lookout for hair and other trace evidence, and these visually observed hairs may be collected or marked and photographed.

2. **Tape.** Clear tape can be highly useful in collecting both visible and invisible hairs and fibres. A thorough taping of car upholstery, for example, can be highly productive of evidence not easily recovered by other methods.

3. **Vacuum sweeping.** A thorough coverage of the scene with this method is likely to yield a great deal of evidence. Vacuum sweepers can be used to cover stationary surfaces such as floors, walls, and cars. A special filter attachment is available for forensic purposes, and after vacuuming it can be sealed and marked. It is generally not recommended that you vacuum clothing, bed sheets, bodies, or other moveable objects. Sweepings from distinct areas should be packaged separately.

4. **Forensic light sources.** Laser and other high-intensity light sources, and ultraviolet light, among others, may reveal hairs and fibres otherwise unnoticed. Discrete hairs that you have observed visually can be picked up with rubber-gloved fingers, with tweezers, or with clear tape. Tweezers can damage hairs and must be used with caution. If the hair is on a moveable object such as a pillow, sheet, or garment, seize and package each object separately in its own paper bag. Put loose hairs in a vial or other container such as a round pillbox or glass jar, then seal and mark the container. Make sure to package separately individual hairs or groups of hairs found separately.

## Standard Comparison Samples

For purposes of comparison and identification you should sample extensively the hair of all persons who may have left hair at the scene. You as an investigator may have to contribute samples as well once you have entered a crime scene whose log records your presence.

Hair is removed first by combing with a sterile comb. Each envelope in a sex-crimes kit, for example, has its own sterile comb. Such combs should be used once only, and packaged with the sample. After combing, hairs should be pulled from five different areas of the scalp. The standard is 20 hairs taken from each of the front, centre, back, and both sides of the head, for a comparison or control sample of 100 hairs. Pulled hair will often constitute the most valuable samples, because attached tissue, roots, and follicles are convenient for DNA analysis. Pubic hair should also be combed and then pulled from different areas to make up a collection of 30 to 50 hairs. Combed and pulled hair should be placed in separate containers. If there is interest in any other part of the body, you should take about 30 hairs from each area, such as the leg, arm, chest, or beard, and package samples from each area separately. Investigators should use the same methods for hair collection from dead bodies. While special envelopes are provided in various evidence kits, investigators should be careful in using envelopes for packaging and preservation of hair. Poor-quality commercial envelopes should be avoided, because they may not provide a proper seal and hairs may escape from the corners.

Some veteran investigators enclose evidence in paper using a **druggist fold** or **four-fold** procedure. Place the evidence in the centre of a piece of paper. Fold one end of the paper over by one-third, and do likewise with the other end. Proceed the same way with the sides, folding them on top of the previous folds. To complete the process, tuck the loose ends into one another. This procedure will give you a small rectangular package that contains evidence securely.

If you are required to take **animal hairs**, follow similar procedures and take samples from various areas of the animal. Make sure that you have collected hairs of all the various colours and lengths available.

## HAIR COMPARISON AND ANALYSIS

You now have hairs collected at the crime scene and samples from known subjects. In the laboratory, hair samples properly collected, preserved, and labelled can link a suspect to victim or a crime, refute alibi evidence, or corroborate other evidence. Hair of the victim may have been found on the suspect and vice versa. Crime-scene hair may be found to belong to a suspect, or a suspect may be discovered to be carrying animal hair that is from the crime scene. In the case where there is no known sample, a great deal of information about a suspect can nonetheless be scientifically teased from crime-scene hair samples.

In the laboratory, hair samples are measured and tested for:

(a) length

(b) diameter

(c)  colour and distribution of pigment granules and the presence of dye or bleach

(d)  structure and shape (presence, size, and nature of the medulla)

(e)  change in structure (usually due to disease or deficiency) or damage to structure

(f)  fungal or other infections

From these observations it is then possible to determine:

1. Whether it is human or animal by taking the medullary index and examining hair structure.

2. The species of animal.

3. The body area from which human hair came (scalp, pubis, beard or mustache, other body areas, eyebrow, eyelash, nose, etc.). Usually known from hair structure (e.g., pubic hairs—short and curly, continuous medullae; head hairs—pigment relatively unvaried, diameter relatively uniform along shaft; whiskers—cut or shaved at tips, coarse, triangularly shaped hair).

4. Whether the hair was pulled or fell out (usually pulled hair will bear some tissue from the follicle).

5. Whether the hair has been crushed or burned.

6. How the hair has been treated (dyed, bleached, permed, etc.) and how recently.

7. Colour.

8. Hair length.

9. Likely racial origin. This can be helpful, but it is uncertain because variations and exceptions are frequent. The three major human racial groups can sometimes be identified: Mongoloid—usually continuous medullae; Negroid—sometimes flat or oval in cross-section, kinky, uneven distribution of pigment granules; Caucasoid—even distribution of smaller pigments, usually straight or wavy, round in shape.

10. Sex (from pulled hair roots).

11. The presence of disease or some poisons and damage.

12. DNA (mitochondrial from the shaft alone, nuclear DNA if some tags of flesh are present).

The microscopic examination, analysis, and comparison of hair structure can provide important corroborative evidence and also exclude some suspects from a crime scene. At best, the comparison of questions to known hair samples with DNA analysis allows an investigator to know that the questioned hair and the comparison sample could have come from the same source. Mitochondrial DNA obtained from hair shafts can identify family lines. When DNA analysis is possible, a positive identification can be made.

# FIBRE EVIDENCE

Fibre evidence is deposited and picked up in much the same way that hair is transferred during crimes of violence, break-and-enters, vehicle thefts, and other crimes that include contact between persons or between persons and objects. The bodies of victims and suspects, the path of contamination at crime scenes, tools and weapons, and the clothing, homes, and vehicles of persons involved may yield crucial clues that can aid you in reconstructing a crime and building the weight of physical evidence in a case. As an investigator in an age of mass-production of fabrics, your major problem is the specific identification of the source of fibres. Examining the nature of fibres so as to match them to possible sources, and gradually narrowing down these possibilities, are the sometimes complex tasks of the investigator and the forensic scientist.

The first basic distinction is between **natural** and **synthetic** fibres.

## Natural Fibres

Natural fibres are those that come from an animal or plant. In the case of animal furs and hair, you will notice that the investigator is actually collecting samples that we have just dealt with in our discussion of hair, and the techniques are the same. The fibres from sheep, cattle, camels, lamas, alpacas, and goats are usually called hair. Those from rabbits, wolves, raccoons, beavers, muskrats, mink, lynx, and bears are referred to as fur. Forensic scientists rely mainly on microscopic comparisons of these fibres with control samples.

Plant fibres such as linen and cotton can be easily identified. But if the fibre from a widespread source such as cotton is undyed, its evidential value is limited. A multicoloured, dyed cotton can, however, give the investigator greater hope of identifying a source, as can a mixture of fabrics. Nevertheless, natural fabrics such as hemp, cotton, silk, and linen must be examined for dyes and compared with standard samples. Natural fibres when examined microscopically will often appear to have an irregular pattern. For example, a cotton fibre under a microscope will look like a twisted belt or ribbon. In addition to natural fibres extracted from plants, there are mineral fibres, such as asbestos and fibre glass, that are essentially natural fibres but may have undergone extensive processing and manufacture.

## Synthetic Fibres

Although natural fibres are still widely used and often enjoy resurgent popularity in fashion design, the twentieth century has seen a steady increase in the use of machine-made fibres. **Rayon** (1911) and **nylon** (1939) were the two most significant early developments. Rayon is one of those fibres manufactured from the cellulose taken from wood and other naturally occurring materials. Nylon was the first truly synthetic fibre or polymer, made from synthetic chemicals. **Polymers** are the long-chained molecules that scientists discovered could be developed into strong multipurpose fibres and fabrics. The polymer is unusual in that, unlike most materials, which comprise relatively few atoms, it links together many molecules and therefore up to millions of atoms. Made up as it is of a long chain of repeating molecular units (monomers), the polymer has given scientists an exciting and almost infinite number of possibilities of combining different molecules to make new and useful materials. The synthetic rubbers, plastics, glues, and paints that surround us today are the products of polymer research, and the work goes on.

There are several principal synthetic fibres that appear under a great variety of trade names in Canada, Britain, and the United States. Nylon or rayon, for example, may be called by any of several dozen different trade names. Other synthetic fibres include acetate, acrylic (of which kevlar is best known), modacrylic, olefin, polyester (called terylene in the U.K.), PBI, spandex, sulfar, and vinlon.

## Collection of Fibres

As you might expect, the collection of fibres is similar to that of hair. In most cases crime-scene collection involves very small amounts of material and all suspect fibres should be collected. You should place samples from different areas in clear plastic or paper bags, appropriately strong envelopes, tins, or vials. You can also use tape to collect fibre evidence from a likely area and put it on document collector sheets of clear plastic. Areas like car seats may have to be extensively taped to recover fibres. Garments worn by victims or suspects and other moveable items should be bagged separately. Make sure as well that you are protecting other seized objects that may contain fibre evidence. All containers should be sealed and marked immediately.

## Analysis, Comparison, and Evaluation of Fibres

As with other material fragments, the most straightforward matching is that of a scrap of cloth to its garment or item of origin. In matching fibres, methods used are first visual, then microscopic, and finally other forms of analysis that we shall discuss presently. Keep in mind the matching principle. With each type of examination, the comparison of known fibres to the unknown seized samples either shows differences that exclude the possibility of a match or similarities that encourage extensive tests. Except in the case of the patch torn from a known piece of fabric that can provide a physical match of individual characteristics, the search in fibre comparisons and identification is for class characteristics.

An identification or forensic technician can take the following measures:

1. Visual or microscopic matching for colour, shape, and type of materials.

2. Microscopic matching for the colour and diameter of fibres. Significant differences in colour and diameter exclude the possibility of a match. If there are no such differences, the investigator may continue.

3. Microscopic examination for striations or pitting on the fibre.

4. Microscopic cross-section examination to determine the shape of the fibre. If fibres are considered then to have the same colour and other properties, further testing can reveal the composition of the fabric.

5. Visible-light microphotospectometry to measure and compare the uptake of visible light in fibres. Scientists can also use solvent to extract the dyes from a fibre and then separate them on a chromatography plate for colour comparisons.

6. The chemical composition of the fibre. At the factory, polymers are melted and then extruded through small holes to make fibres. This process lines the molecules up in a regular, crystalline fashion. In the laboratory a microphotospectrometer using infrared light can also distinguish among polymers by observing the patterns in which fibres absorb infrared light. Every type of fibre refracts light distinctively. Fibre evidence, independent of stains (such as blood) that can be individually characterized, is always class evidence and cannot be used alone to make a positive identification. But the more unusual a fibre or fabric, the greater the weight of the matching evidence. A rare combination of fibres and dyes that matches another such fabric can constitute very strong class evidence. A match of two fibres of blue denim, on the other hand, does not. A list of similarities thus increases the likelihood that matching fibres are from the same source and therefore it can considerably add to the weight of evidence. From these tests the lab should be able to tell you:

(a) if it is a natural or synthetic fibre

(b) the type of fibre

(c) colour of fibre

(d) type of textile, rope, etc. of fibre origin

  (e)  if an unknown fibre could have come from a specific textile or garment

  (f)  if two (or more) fibres could have come from the same source

## Textiles

If you have seized textiles, buttons, ropes, or cords, the laboratory can also provide additional useful information not only by fibre analysis but also by:

1. comparing buttons

2. comparing yarn and thread

3. comparing and identifying the weave or construction of fabrics, ropes, and cords

4. examining impressions left by textiles, ropes, and cords

    Hair and fibre evidence, handled correctly, can be important to an investigation and reconstruction of a crime. It can also have considerable weight in court. But a comparison of fibre evidence in itself cannot constitute a positive match. And neither, usually, can hair matches be considered positive, except in the case of DNA testing. Two hair shafts matched for mitochondrial DNA can identify the family of the source. If the shaft bears tissue containing nuclear DNA, a hair/DNA comparison can point directly to an individual suspect.

    Hairs and fibres are thus classic examples of trace evidence. They are often dropped, torn out, or transferred in some other way from person to person and place to place. They can easily go unnoticed, or be the result of contamination. The alert, careful investigator can take advantage of these characteristics, and gain much of evidential value.

# 11

# GLASS, SOIL, AND VEGETATIVE MATTER

Three products of the earth—glass, soil, and vegetative matter—are almost everywhere, and at most crime scenes. The commonness of this type of evidence can limit its usefulness. But together with other evidence, and processed carefully, they can all add important circumstantial weight to a case.

## GLASS

Glass, one of the commonest substances found at crime scenes involving vehicles or buildings, often has a complex story to tell. But investigators must learn to interpret the signs that make up the story. Was the shot through a window fired from outside or inside a building? What sort of weapon was used to smash a mirror? Are the glass shards in a suspect's clothing from the crime scene? If several shots were fired through a pane of glass, in what order were they fired? How and where was the force applied that broke a window? The answers to such questions usually lie in the fragments of glass and in the cracks and holes at a crime scene. Physical matching, fracture analysis, and examinations of the makeup and structure of glass can all provide important evidence.

### Composition

Glass is essentially sand and metal oxides heated to melting point and then cooled into a hard, brittle, and usually clear substance. The main component is sand, and common additives are sodium and lime. There are also special varieties of glass, such as tempered glass (tempered by rapid heating and cooling), and other types made heat-resistant through the addition to sand of other elements or the substitution of sand with other materials. To create a "safety" glass such as that used in vehicle wind-shields, manufacturers usually compress plastic between two sheets of glass, a process called *lamination*. All the characteristics of different types of glass affect the way they will react to force. The behaviour of glass will reflect its content and man-ufacture as well as the forces acting on it.

When observing and collecting glass evidence, remember that your care in col-lection of fragile pieces will help forensic specialists in their later determination of its origin.

## At the Crime Scene: Recognition, Collection, and Preservation

To preserve the evidential value of glass, never forget that it is an excellent medium for other evidence, often a virtually ready-made microscopic slide. It may contain fingerprints, blood, and other fluids, hair, fibres, footprints, paint, tire marks, and tool marks. A clumsy investigator's handling or footprints could destroy a wealth of information. When considering the examination of glass evidence, remember that many of the most important observations that follow can be made by officers in the initial period at the crime scene as well as in the lab to which seized evidence and photographs have been submitted.

When possible and practical, investigators should seize all glass evidence. In approaching a crime scene it is prudent to follow these steps:

1. **Visually inspect the scene for glass evidence.** This will include holes and cracks in glass as well as glass fragments and slivers. The examination should begin at the point of entry, where glass may also indicate the entry method (e.g., glass smashed with a hand, tool, bullet, etc.). Continue carefully along the path of contamination to the focal point and point of exit, all three of which may be indicated by glass evidence. Be extremely careful in proceeding, because the nature and arrangement of glass evidence can be crucial to its analysis and inter-pretation. Many of the observations concerning fracture pattern analysis, weapon type, and force used can be made on this initial examination. Remember to look for fingerprints and other evidence adhering to glass. Examine all fragments both outside and inside.

2. **Photograph glass evidence.** Good photographs should be taken of broken win-dows, from the outside and inside, along with close-ups from the side to show fracture lines and the edges of holes and craters. Photograph the shards on the floor

showing their pattern, and examine closely to see if close-up shots of particular pieces may be necessary.

3. **If you pick up glass fragments, wear gloves and pick up by the edges.** After picking up glass *never put it back into the crime scene—you will alter the crime scene.*

4. **Seize and protectively package all fragments, regardless of size.** Remember when collecting and packaging glass fragments that there may be a possibility of physical matching or reconstruction, and you must protect the edges of each fragment. To avoid cross-contamination and destruction of glass evidence, fragments from each area should be packaged separately, and each fragment separately wrapped. Never toss fragments into a cardboard box or other such container. Wrap each piece separately in cotton batting or facial tissue and pack it firmly in layers of similar material. If you suspect fragments in clothing or other material, handle the item as little as possible, collecting any large, obvious pieces that may fall off easily. Package the garment separately, making sure that wet materials have been allowed to dry before packaging. Whenever possible a complete window, headlight, or other item should be seized and wrapped for later analysis and comparison.

Both at the crime scene and in the laboratory, there are three major areas usually considered in glass evidence examination:

1. fracture pattern analysis

2. characteristics of force applied

3. the nature and identity of the glass

The nature and identity of glass comprise its class characteristics. As soon as glass is fractured or damaged it acquires individual or accidental characteristics.

## Fracture Pattern Analysis

An investigator can learn much from an initial examination of broken glass. In order to interpret glass evidence, it is necessary to understand the way glass breaks and the behaviour of different types of glass under various kinds of force.

### *How Glass Breaks*

Force applied to glass stretches it to its limit of elasticity in the direction the force is travelling. When the limit is exceeded, the glass fractures or cracks in the following patterns:

1. *Fracturing begins on the side opposite to that on which force has acted.* This knowledge alone is crucial to the determination of the nature and direction of force. In addition, glass fractures follow a pattern of radial and concentric cracks.

2. **Radial** *fractures occur first,* radiating outward from the point of impact on the side opposite to the force.

3. *The continued stretching of the glass then causes* **concentric** *fractures,* circles originating on the side to which force is applied. These two types of fractures together form a spiderweb-like pattern around the point of impact.

4. *If a high-velocity projectile such as a bullet strikes the glass the point of impact and centre of the fracture pattern may be a hole. Such forces usually form craters or concave areas on the exit side of the glass.* The glass fragments from the centre will often be minute particles sprayed in the projectile's direction of travel.

5. Force applied to glass may also cause **backward fragmentation**. The compression of glass causes chipping that follows the fracture lines. The resulting chips may fly backward toward the source of force. This is why it is important to look for glass in suspect clothing and footwear.

### Cross-Section of Fractures

Looking at the process of fracturing on the edge of a piece of glass, technicians can also see characteristic patterns of **stress marks**. On the edge of a radial fracture, there are markings that begin on the side opposite to the surface subjected to force. Often called **rib marks** because of their resemblance to a rib cage, they tend to arc downward toward the source of force. It is well to remember what forensic scientist Richard Saferstein calls "**The 3R Rule: Radial cracks form a Right angle on the Reverse side of the force**" (R. Saferstein, *Criminalistics* (1998), page 119). *Rib marks on a concentric fracture, however,*

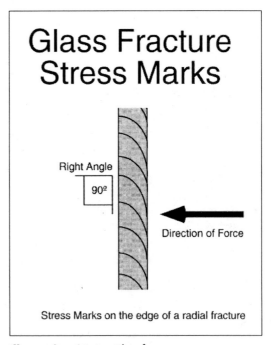

# Glass Fracture Stress Marks

Right Angle

90º

Direction of Force

Stress Marks on the edge of a radial fracture

**Illustration 11-1.** Glass fracture.

*while assuming a similar shape, arc downward in the opposite direction, the direction of travel of force.* In addition to rib marks, investigators often discover **hackle marks** at right angles to rib marks. As is clear from the glass fracturing process, these two types of stress marks, along with cratering, can be used to determine the nature and direction of the force that caused the fracture.

## Sequence of Impacts

It is possible when reconstructing a crime with glass evidence to determine the sequence in which shots were fired or other forces applied. The most useful characteristic of fractures in this determination is the fact that *a fracture will always end at a previous line of fracture.* The sequence of impact can be read as follows:

1. The first bullet will create the distinctive spiderweb pattern we have already observed.

2. Radial fracture lines from subsequent projectiles passing through the same surface now encounter the boundary established by the first fracture pattern, and end

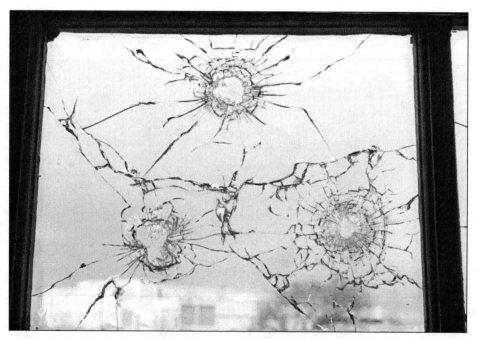

**Illustration 11-2.** Bullet sequence. Sometimes it is difficult to determine the sequence of shots, especially if there are several shots in a small area. It is fairly easy to see the last shot of the three as being the one in the lower right portion of the photograph. Can you identify the order of the first two?

**Illustration 11-3.** An angle shot results in fracturing directed away from the point of impact.

**Illustration 11-4.** Cratering.

there. This is only true, of course, if the points of impact are close enough to affect each other.

In addition to determining the side of the glass on which force was exerted, you may be able to discern that a bullet, for example, was fired from an angle less than perpendicular. The fracture pattern and cratering may be less symmetrical, extending toward the direction of travel of the force or projectile.

## *Physical Matching*

In the simplest case, physical matching involves putting fragments of glass back together like the pieces of a jigsaw puzzle, to determine whether they were once part of the same whole object. For example, you find glass fragments in the pant cuffs of a hit-and-run victim at the hospital. They appear similar to fragments you have found and seized at the accident scene. Later, you find a suspect vehicle with a broken headlight. Removing the headlight, identification technicians are able to fit the fragments you have found at the scene and on the victim into the broken light. This reconstruction of physical evidence becomes a strong circumstantial case.

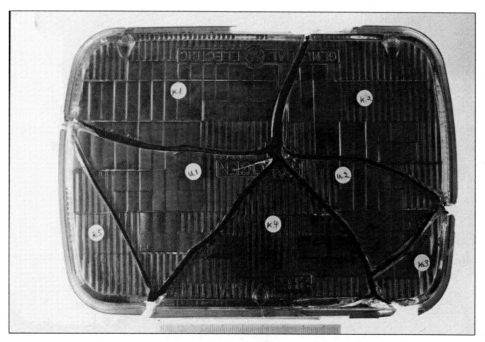

**Illustration 11-5.** Physical matching of glass: headlight reconstruction.

## *Determining Origin, Content, and Manufacture of Glass*

Various tests can determine a number of class characteristics of glass fragments that will allow them to be physically matched to known glass. In addition to matching the shape of fragments, it is also possible to match striations or ream marks created in the manufacturing process. Crime laboratories can also test glass for density, refractive index, and chemical content.

- **General characteristics.** Glass may be examined and measured first of all for some of its most easily observable characteristics, such as colour, curvature, thickness, and surface designs.

- **Density.** The mass per unit of volume or density of glass can be determined by flotation of a fragment in a solution of adjustable density. The density of the solution is adjusted until the fragment is suspended. Fragments of comparison samples can be added to see if their density is the same.

- **Refractive index.** If fragments are found to be of the same density, their refractive indices may then be compared. For this test they can be immersed in a liquid whose refractive index is adjustable by raising or lowering temperature. When the refractive indices of the liquid and the glass fragments are the same, the halo around the edge of the fragments, known as the **Becke line**, disappears. Fragments with similar refractive indices and densities are possible from the same source.

- **Trace elements.** In some cases comparison may require that glass be examined for trace elements such as arsenic, copper, zinc, aluminum, magnesium, etc. Spectrographic analysis can help to determine if the highly variable impurities in glass are the same and further narrow the possibilities of origins.

In summary, it is possible to learn a great deal from submitted glass fragments. Analysis, comparison, and laboratory testing may reveal:

1. that two or more pieces of glass can be physically matched (i.e., fit together as part of a whole) or can be used to reconstruct a whole item

2. whether pieces of glass have the same properties and could have the same origin

3. from which side and angle, and on what trajectory, a projectile penetrated a sheet of glass

4. what type of force or instrument was used to fracture glass

5. the sequences of penetration of multiple holes in glass

6. the use of glass and its distribution

# DUST, SAND, AND SOIL

Unfortunately, investigators, unlike Sherlock Holmes, cannot instantly identify the scene of a crime from the soil on a suspect's boots. Dust, sand, and soil, *common disintegrated surface matter composed of both artificial and natural materials*, are found at most crime scenes. Because they often comprise small particles, they are easily transferred to and from suspects, victims crime scenes, vehicles, and weapons. They can provide a vital link in the reconstruction of a chain of events. The soil on a suspect's shoes, for example, may be compared with samples collected at a crime scene enabling the investigator to begin to exclude or include the alibi evidence of the suspect. Naturally occurring soil or sand can have distinctive properties. Soils in most parts of the developed world are extensively mapped and a soil scientist can often identify the regional origin of a soil by studying its **texture** (proportions of sand, silt, and clay), **colour** (related to the amount and type of organic and mineral matter), and **mineral composition**. In most cases, the investigator is interested in the shallow surface material. But in some instances, such as the excavation of a body or a weapon, you have to dig deeper. Soil naturally occurs in layers or **horizons**, each different in character. For the most part investigators collect material from the top or **A horizon**. While it may have a distinctive local character, the soil investigators collect will often be a heterogeneous sample. That is, it is a mixture of widely different materials, some of which may establish its uniqueness: plant material, seeds, paint chips, sawdust, cement particles, glass and metal fragments, etc. These elements can distinguish a soil from all others of its type and help investigators to match two samples more closely. Scientists can also compare **diatoms** or microscopic organisms which can link or differentiate samples of some soils.

In addition to the various elements that may link two samples, collected soil or dust may also contain traces of other sorts of evidence important to an investigation: blood, semen, hair, fibres, and other traces that may be linked directly to a suspect or a victim.

## Collection

When the area of an incident is known or suspected, investigators should perform a thorough collection of standard crime-scene samples. In the case of soil and dust the nature of specific crime scenes makes a great deal of difference in how you will proceed. Think of the variations yourself. A suspicious death in an outdoor environment will require a different kind of collection from an indoor homicide where the suspect may have entered the premises through a window above a flowerbed bearing unreadable impressions.

## *Standard Samples for Comparison*

Here are some general rules to follow:

1. Photograph collection surfaces before sampling.

2. If possible, collect about a cup of soil from each location. Surface samples should be collected to about 1 centimetre depth. Keep samples completely separate, because soil may vary considerably from place to place. Use clean plastic, glass, or metal containers. Above all avoid cross-contamination.

3. Work outward from the focal point of the incident, taking measurements of collection distance from the focal point. If using a grid search, sample soil from each grid, numbering and labelling samples appropriately. If possible, work along a suspected path of contamination. Collect to a focal point radius of 100 metres.

4. If you suspect notable foreign matter such as blood or hair, carefully take and label a separate sample. If you suspect a lump of dirt has blood on it, for example, seize and package the whole lump.

5. If you encounter an indentation or hole, collect separate samples from various layers, being sure to take samples from the top, bottom, and sides. But remember, *always photograph such areas to take into account possible tool and other impressions.*

6. Take samples from all alibi areas and suspect areas—that is, where the suspect claims to have gone or may have gone.

To what are these standard samples to be compared? It may be that you have deposits on footwear, floors, weapons, tools, bodies, clothing, or other items associated with the suspect or victim. Soil, dust, and sand evidence from these surfaces must also be carefully collected. The method of collection may vary a great deal. The following are some points to consider in soil evidence collection.

## *Collection of Suspect Material*

1. Collect dust and soil only after (a) the area has been photographed and (b) other forms of evidence such as blood, hair, weapons, and fingerprints have been seized.

2. When possible package in paper entire items of clothing, footwear, etc. that may contain soil evidence.

3. Handle items gently when collecting so as not to dislodge soil or dust. Make no attempt to remove soil.

4. Soil and dust from floors and furniture and vehicle interiors can be removed with vacuum sweepers, or in some cases small samples may be removed with tape. Whatever item is used to sweep, soil must be clean to avoid cross-contamination and your gloves, clothing, and sweeping implement also packaged as evidence.

5. Package soil from suspects, victims, and items associated with the investigation separately.

6. Inspect the undercarriage of suspect vehicles for soil deposits that may provide a link to a crime or accident scene. Collect in lumps for the identification of distinctive deposits. Collect deposits of soil from possible scenes of automobile impact or accidents for later comparison.

When comparing unknown to known samples of soil, police services sometimes make use of outside agencies with expertise in soil testing and analysis. Soil scientists, for example, can often texture soils quite accurately and quickly by hand, wetting them and rubbing them between their fingers to determine by touch the content of sand (gritty), silt (silky), and clay (sticky). Soils are dried and visually compared for colour. Low-powered microscopy can then identify and compare the presence of various artificial materials as well as particles of plant and animal origin. With a high-powered microscope, experts can further identify the mineral content of soil and rocks. Every mineral crystal has a distinctive shape, colour, refractive index, and density that can be identified. Such analyses may also be helpful in identifying building materials made from natural minerals.

Many forensic scientists have traditionally used **density gradient tubes**—upright glass tubes containing layers of liquids of different densities—to establish and compare the densities of soils. The liquid with the highest density sinks to the bottom of the tubes while that of the lowest density stays at the top, with a series of layers in between going down in order of ascending density. When soil is inserted into the tubes, its various components stay suspended where the density of the liquid equals that of the soil. Two tubes of the same liquid side by side, to which the same amounts of soil for comparison have been introduced, will show the same density distribution pattern if the known and unknown samples are of common origin.

*The evidential value of soil evidence is highly variable.* It increases in value only insofar as a particular soil can be severely localized and distinguished from other soils. Such a uniqueness requires either that you have encountered a pattern of highly varied local soil types, or that your evidence is distinguished by the presence of some unique debris.

# VEGETATIVE MATTER

Evidence of botanical origin will often be quite common at a crime scene. Properly processed, it can have substantial evidential value. Even in highly urbanized areas, grass clippings, wood splinters, plants, seeds, sawdust, twigs, leaves, and quantities of vegetable foods are often among the evidence transferred to and from crimes, suspects, and victims. Chips from a wooden window frame or doorframe damaged during a forced entry, for example, may be found on a suspect's pant cuffs, pockets, clothing, or tools and later matched to their source by both physical examination and more intensive laboratory analysis. The same is true of sawdust and plants. Splinters from wooden weapons may be found in a wound. As with other forms of evidence, technicians search for class and individual or accidental characteristics that can narrow down the possibilities of origin.

## Collection

(*Remember*: Note and photograph first.)

1.  If you suspect botanical evidence, collect and package all of a suspect's clothing, including headwear and shoes, and submit them to the laboratory. Include ashes, burnt wood, and burnt vegetation.

2.  Collect all visible individual items of vegetative matter and package them separately.

3.  Pick up items with gloved hands if other methods such as tweezers or forceps may damage evidence of potential value for physical matching. Caution medical examiners at auto and medical staff at emergency units to deal likewise with such evidence if possible. Bandages and cleaning materials initially used on wounds may also be appropriately seized and packaged.

4.  Take representative standard control samples, collecting several from the crime scene. Concentrate on materials similar to those found on suspect persons, vehicles, and tools, as well as those in areas of damage.

5.  Air-dry clothing and other materials seized and package them in paper. Damp exhibits are subject to mould.

## Comparison, Analysis, and Identification

Scientists may proceed through many levels in the analysis and comparison of botanical materials. Tests could involve a variety of activities, from fairly straightforward physical matching of splinters or screw holes to a parent body of wood to the analysis of **anthracograms** (carbon pictures) of burnt wood or vegetation.

The wood evidence you collect could be a large weapon such as a baseball bat, minute sawdust particles, or any size or shape in between. Wood is so widely used in construction, tools, weapons, and furniture, and there are so many species and treatments, that competent experts can often make successful comparisons, matching wood to an object, tool used on it, or even tree of origin.

From very small particles a careful microscopic examination can reveal the tree species of origin. Generally wood is divided into hardwood and softwood, hardwood being characterized by greater density. In some cases where microscopic examination does not yield clear results, wood particles or plant material can be burned and an ash picture called a **spodogram** of the distinctive structure formed by minerals will reveal the species.

Scientists can also therefore examine crime-scene specimens of **carbonized** wood and vegetation under a microscope and the anthracogram will be characteristic of a particular species of tree or plant.

Class characteristics of grain, colour, and structure enable identification of species under the microscope, but gross visual comparisons often play an important part in matching individual characteristics, which can then be confirmed by microscopic and other comparisons. The external curvature of the bole or trunk, the matching angles of a cut, and the comparison of annual rings are simple means that can be used to match two pieces of the same tree. Bark patterns, extended cracks, knots, bruising, or decay can also indicate common origins, by helping investigators decide, as in the case of glass and other "jigsaw puzzle" evidence, that the separate pieces under examination were part of a common whole.

Any distinctive treatment or working of wood can make identification more likely. The blades of knives, saws, chisels, planing machines, and other tools can leave individual marks, although horizontally machine-sawn wood is visually impossible to match from saw marks alone. Comparisons of wood grain continuity in this case can often bring success. Once wood has been painted, varnished, or oiled, the substance applied can give valuable clues. If more than one layer has been applied, a sequence of colours provides matching possibilities, and in any case scientists can submit the components of paint and other materials to chemical analysis and spectographic examination to determine whether two substances are consistent with the same source.

Botanical materials such as seeds, plant fragments, leaves, twigs, and pollen can also serve as useful evidence. Investigators may need the services of highly skilled experts in botany, usually from a university, research station, or natural history museum. The pollen grains from the reproductive systems of flowering plants are usually by their very nature structured for easy transfer and will therefore be easily picked up on clothing and footwear. Under a microscope these tiny grains can usually be matched to a particular species of flowering plant, identifying the movements of the carrier and giving other information, such as the time of year when a person was in a particular place.

# PAINT AND PLASTICS

Crime scenes can be littered with substances that we have developed or adopted to beautify and ease our lives: paint, gasoline and oil, plastic bags, dyes, tape, and so on. Like other physical evidence, all may be unknowingly picked up or left at the scene. All have some potential for analysis and comparison by investigators and forensic scientists.

Paint is among the oldest means of decoration and preservation, and painted surfaces are so common that we seldom think of the variety of them all around us. The desire to colour, decorate, and preserve seems to have been a universal instinct throughout human history. This instinct has led people to paint not only images and objects but also to apply cosmetics to their own skin. Pigments from natural sources have been supplemented in modern times by synthetic paints and dyes. As our study of fibres revealed, one of the most fruitful sources of new materials has been the development of polymers, acrylics, and plastics of various sorts. Plastic bags, for example are almost ubiquitous, and acrylics are present in paints, headlight covers, and numerous other durable surfaces and coverings. The range of petrochemical products is vast, but fuels and oils are still among the most commonly used petroleum products.

Consider for a moment any incident involving an automobile. What kinds of evidence could be transferred from an automobile? Paint, plastics, rubber, and oils could all come into play, in addition to metals and glass. Even if we are considering only damage to the front of the vehicle, an accident, assault, or vandalism could include as evidence paint from the body, plastics from a grill, acrylic headlight covers, rubber from tires or hoses, and petroleum and oil from the engines. Fragments or quantities of any of these things present possibilities for matching at least class characteristics and, in some lands, individual or accidental characteristics. But many of these substances can turn up at other sorts of crime scenes and on suspects. Oil transferred from the floor of a burgled garage, cosmetics transferred from a victim to a suspect in sexual assault, or paint gathered on tools used to break and enter. Any of these may tie a suspect to a crime scene.

# PAINT

Paint usually consists of pigments or colour particles and powders held together by a binder that can contain both organic and inorganic substances. The pigments impart colour, and other particles scatter light and make the paint opaque. Binders and extenders enable the paint to be spread smoothly and to dry. Painted surfaces are thus coated with a film that usually hardens when it dries, although some paints will dry to a rubbery texture.

One of the substances traditionally found in paints is lead, and lead oxides are still used in paints that will be subject to weather. Lead compounds are also often found in older paints as yellow and white pigments. Among other materials used for colouring are iron oxide (red), titanium dioxide (white), and chromium (yellow). An interesting pigment variation which forensic scientists encounter in cases of art fraud involves the size of pigments. Modern paints under a microscope will show a small, uniform pigment size. Older paints, for which the pigments were crushed manually, display a great variation in size and shape of pigments. A microscopic examination of pigments in a painting or other supposed "antique" paint can thus reveal whether it is genuinely old or a recent forgery.

Paints of different sorts are manufactured for specific purposes. The paint on the exterior of buildings, for example, is often a latex (or water-based paint) that can contain a variety of binders most often made of vinyl or acrylic. In other cases oil-based paint with binders of polyurethane or alkyds may be used. The coverings least distinguished by pigmentation are clear lacquers, varnishes, and shellac. Among the most widely encountered paint evidence is that from automotive vehicles. These usually comprise a number of layers, sometimes of varying composition. Recent North American vehicles are usually covered with a **topcoat** of acrylic melamine enamel or acrylic lacquer; in some cases, a coat of polyurethane may be applied. **Base coats** of acrylic melamine enamel or melamine polyester are currently the norm. Some recent imported or early-model North American vehicles may also be covered with various sorts of alkyd enamel. The **undercoatings** of automobiles generally come in much greater variety than topcoats, particularly because of the great diversity of pigments and extenders used in them.

# Collection of Paint Evidence

In collecting paint, you may deal with a vast variety of sources and amounts. Your evidence may include things such as motor vehicles from hit-and-run accidents, architectural paint from break-and-enters, or smears or chips of paint acquired by a suspect or victim during a violent crime.

Paint evidence can often be found in minute traces, and investigators must be alert to its possibilities. In one of Canada's Atlantic provinces a few years ago, an RCMP officer of our acquaintance was unsatisfied with the evidence a homicide autopsy was yielding. As he watched the water run into the drain on the autopsy table, he had an idea. He put a clean handkerchief from his pocket into the drain in such a way that it filtered the effluents from the table. The investigator sent the entire handkerchief to the forensic lab where analysis revealed a microscopic paint chip determined to be from an automobile. Further, the lab was able to give the investigator a possible year and make of the vehicle of origin. Investigators traced the vehicle through a mass of automobile registry information. They discovered a car that after several ownerships was resting in a scrap yard. A standard comparison sample from the car matched the paint fragment, and the car was found to contain further forensic evidence of the homicide. All of this evidence could be linked to the last registered owner of the car, who was the prime suspect. He was accused and convicted of murder.

The paint at a crime scene or on a vehicle, weapon, victim, or suspect will often be found as chips or smears. Here are some crucial points to remember in the collection of paint evidence:

1.  If possible you should seize and package the entire item containing paint evidence (e.g., pieces of clothing, tools, bumpers, etc.) and wrap each item separately. You should collect paint samples from all damaged items: doorframes, safes, motor vehicles, etc.

2.  Be sure to collect fragile chips first. (If paint is actually in tool impressions, however, collect samples from areas close to the impression but not in it; otherwise you may be altering impression evidence.)

3.  Collect paint chips with extreme care, so as not to break them. Protect the edges for physical matching. Use tweezers, or if damage is possible use a clean sheet of paper for collection. Do not use tape to collect paint evidence.

4.  Collect and package paint chips separately.

5.  **Packaging.**

    (a) Paint chips should be placed in a piece of paper using the druggist or four-fold procedure described in Chapter 10, and then sealed in an envelope.

Metal containers or plastic ones with snap-on lids may also be used. Avoid plastic bags.

(b) You can package and submit liquid paint samples in paint cans or place them on glass slides.

6. **Standard comparison samples.** In order to provide samples for comparison to suspect evidence, you should:

(a) take samples from all damaged areas

(b) take samples from uncontaminated areas of the same object (vehicle, wall, etc.)

(c) take samples from all colour areas

(d) remove paint samples with a scalpel, a razorblade, or a sharp knife, and package as above. Be sure to scrape down to the unpainted surface of the vehicle or other object so that all layers of paint are represented in your sample. Never use the same instrument to collect paint from more than one source.

(e) package all standards separately, and keep them away from suspect evidence to avoid cross-contamination.

## Analysis and Comparison of Paint Evidence

The most frequent purpose of forensic paint comparisons is the establishment of common origins. Questioned samples or samples of unknown origin are compared with samples of known origin. The ultimate goal is to link a suspect or to eliminate a suspect from the scene of a crime.

In the most straightforward initial paint analyses, forensic specialists search for three matching characteristics that investigators may have already suspected from a visual appraisal:

1. colour

2. texture of paint surface

3. sequence of paint layers and thickness

4. possibility of physically matching fragments

All of these characteristics can be revealed under a comparison microscope. Any trained identification officer should be able to examine microscopically the edges of a paint chip for possible matches to the painted surface from which it may have come, putting together a forensic jigsaw puzzle. Another gross feature that can aid investigation is the pattern of striations on the underside of a paint chip.

These are made by the metal of the vehicle or other surface that has been painted and can also be matched.

Scientists in forensic laboratories often examine sequences of paint layers and the thickness of samples by placing paint chips on edge. They can then microscopically measure thickness and identify the number, colour, and order of layers.

### Colour

While colour and surface textures may seem the most obvious characteristics, the accurate establishment of colour alone can lead the scientist into more complex tests. For comparison of automotive coverings, the RCMP has one of the most complete systems of comparison samples in the world. Their reference panels contain not only topcoats (on which U.S. laboratories tend to concentrate), but also the complete systems of automotive paint layers from a vast range of makes, models, and years.

### Composition

The further examination of paint samples that are considered similar may include a variety of techniques, including, among others, pyrolysis gas chromatography, emission spectroscopy, neutron activation analysis, x-ray diffraction, x-ray spectroscopy, and infrared spectroscopy, to determine the constituent elements of paint. Paints that at first examination appear identical may sometimes be discovered to have distinctive spectra and therefore actually be of different origin.

## PLASTIC BAGS AND WRAPPINGS

Plastic bags, plastic wrappings, and other such objects are in nearly universal use and can often be important evidence. They not only provide surfaces for the accommodation of other evidence (e.g., fingerprints, drug traces, etc.), but also contain characteristics that can establish links between suspect evidence and a common origin. Drug dealers arrested with several plastic bags in their possession, for example, can sometimes be linked to the stash of drugs in a house where the drugs were packaged, through the matching of plastic bags. In addition, the fingerprints on such bags could be used to link accomplices together. There is always of course the possibility of a jigsaw-puzzle type of physical match, whether it be of fragments of plastic in bags or other items, credit cards used in fraud, or wrappings from stolen merchandise. Plastics are usually the polymers we have discussed in the section on synthetic fibres. They currently have so many uses that a list of products containing plastics would include most things human beings use from cars to computers.

## Collection

1.  Take care in handling both rigid and supple plastics to avoid damage and contamination. Remember plastic can be an excellent surface for fingerprints.

2.  Do not compress or fold plastic bags that may be useful for physical matching. Avoid breakage of rigid plastics. Seize and submit all plastics as far as possible in the condition at the time of seizure.

3.  Avoid stretching of plastic, which can destroy its potential for physical matching.

4.  If a roll or box of plastic or plastic bags is discovered, seize the entire roll or box as well as any sealing or cutting equipment.

5.  To package rigid plastics, use heavy plastic bags or metal tins. Supple plastics should be submitted to the lab either in their original container or in sealed metal tins.

6.  Seize and package comparison samples as above.

## Comparison and Analysis

Plastics can be subjected to the same sorts of chemical and physical analyses as other polymers. Before such tests are performed, however, this sort of evidence may yield important information through microscopic examination. Manufacturers' forming and stretching of molten and heated plastics create distinctive patterns of lines that run side by side on the surface of plastic bags and wrappers. Bags or coverings manufactured close together in the same series will often bear lines that can be microscopically matched, as will fragments of the same bag. This can allow investigators to match known to unknown evidence of common origin. To confirm similarities, in some cases scientists will perform the more exhaustive chemical and physical tests possible with any polymer.

# ARSON

The investigator on an arson case may in fact be investigating one or more other crimes. While arson is usually considered to be the malicious intentional burning of property, its effects and motives may indicate more.

Some arsonists may simply be vandals; others, called **pyromaniacs**, burn to satisfy a psychological urge; others may be attacking a specific person or persons; others set fires so that fraudulent insurance claims may be made on a property or building; some arsonists may be intent on murder or on concealing evidence of homicide or other crimes; arson or the threat of arson has also historically been a form of extortion. In short, arson can be a crime against persons or property or both.

The collection and interpretation of physical evidence in an arson case is particularly crucial, as physical evidence will often provide the strongest indications of motivations and hence of suspects. Arson is a particularly perplexing crime: first, because the evidence often consists of things that have been burned; second, because the ostensible victim can, in many cases, also be a prime suspect, especially in cases of the concealment of evidence or insurance fraud.

The arson crime scene is a peculiar place, in which normally recognizable objects, bodies, furniture, fire-starting substances, electrical equipment, and so on have been altered drastically. Potential exhibits are often covered with a film produced by the smoke from burning construction materials and from the combustion of the synthetics, polymers, and other common, everyday substances. What's more, there is almost always a great deal of contamination of the crime scene by others. Firefighters and emergency medical staff, while highly trained and aware of the necessity of protecting evidence, have the duty above all to protect life and property. They move bodies, smash doors and windows, walk through crime scenes, and cover the scene with water and firefighting chemicals. They also "mop up" the scene, breaking open roof, walls, and ceilings and throwing burning objects, such as sofas and mattresses, from buildings. As a result, arson scenes are among the "messiest" an investigator encounters, and few officers are thoroughly trained in arson investigation. At the same time arson is a crime for which the investigator's reconstruction is crucial.

# THE NATURE OF FIRE

The first thing investigators should know is the basic nature of fire. Think of the three forces of nature *earth, wind,* and *fire,* and you essentially have the three elements necessary for the creation of fire. It can be expressed as a formula:

$$Fuel + Heat + Air (oxygen) = Fire$$

Of course, fire is not really an "element," but the manifestation of a chemical reaction called **oxidation**, in which oxygen is combined with other substances with sufficient energy to produce heat and flames. In fire, energy is converted from one form to another and the reaction produces a new arrangement of atoms and therefore different substances. Fire is thus a process of conversion, using and liberating energy to produce something new. Every substance has a certain heat at which it begins to burn, the **ignition temperature**, and every burning substance releases a specific amount of heat known as the **heat of combustion**. The solid fuel does not itself burn. It must first become a gas, whose molecules move and collide quickly enough to sustain fire. In order for fire to begin, the fuel must be at a sufficient temperature known as its **flashpoint**. A source of heat introduced to it raises the fuel to its gaseous state and its ignition temperature.

The investigator is therefore seeking the elements that allowed the fire to start and continue. These elements, the fuel, the sources of air and of heat, and the products of fire, are the physical evidence that enable the reconstruction of an arson.

The investigation of arson can be a very slow process. You, the investigator, must wait until the fire has been extinguished, smoke has been vented out of the building, and the area is safe to enter. In other words, you enter a "cold scene." While you wait, valuable evidence is being destroyed. And although fire may create investigative leads, recognizing and collecting them can be a painstaking process; arson investigations are often among the longest that investigators undertake.

# PRELIMINARY STEPS

But while investigators may have to await the safe entry of a burnt structure, there is often much to be done even while the blaze continues. Remember upon your arrival that every fire is a potential crime and may need to be treated accordingly with the establishment of a **perimeter**, an initial **exterior search**, and all the elements of crowd control, victim safety, and evidence preservation we discussed in Chapter 2.

In quickly inspecting a building exterior, you can immediately begin to look for evidence and suspects. You may be able to detect a possible **point of origin** if the fire has started on an exterior wall, for example; a roughly shaped "V" pattern will often indicate that a fire was ignited at the bottom of the "V." There may also be obvious quantities of fuel and accelerants in the area of the fire. If the fire is burning uncontrollably, you must still continue investigating.

1.  Firefighters should be informed that this is a suspicious fire. It may also be the case that firefighters, first on the scene, recognize the possible crime involved and tell police officers.

2.  Photographic coverage, if at all possible, is invaluable. The burn patterns, the fire and smoke themselves, the colour and travel of smoke, the crowd, adjacent vehicles, and licence plates should all receive as much coverage as possible.

3.  If firefighters are aware of the suspicious nature of the fire, "cleanup," or other activity that may damage to physical evidence, should be delayed as much as possible after the fire has been extinguished.

4.  As soon as the fire is out and a structure is safe to enter, investigators can begin their search as they would the processing of other crime scenes. The area inside the perimeter of the scene should be searched for the signs of forced entry, foot and tire impressions, and the other physical evidence you are now accustomed to seeking at crime scenes.

In a sense, you are systematically examining this scene as you would others, looking for points of entry, paths of contamination, focal points, and points of exit, with the significant addition that the major destructive force is fire. Here are some items that should be of special interest:

*   **Point of entry.** Broken door, windows, locks, tool impressions, and damaged alarm systems can all be indicative of forced or illegal entry. Collect evidence in all such locations.

*   **The interior of a building.** The interior can yield a great deal on first inspection. If you are fortunate, the path of contamination may have been made obvious by the arsonist's trail of fuel or accelerants, to a focal point such as a safe,

desk, or the bed of a homicide victim. Remember, in an arson the important focal point you are looking for may be the point of origin of the fire.

- There are several kinds of evidence specific to arson investigations. Some of these, you will notice, may already have been detected on your approach to a burning fire. Remember that you should constantly be on the lookout for the elements of fire (fuel, sources of air, and sources of heat) and its products or effects.

- **Smoke colour.** Through photographs, your visual observations, or the accounts of witnesses, the description of smoke may provide clues about the nature of the fuel for the fire. Forensic scientists usually expect, for example, that burning vegetative matter will produce white smoke, petroleum products black, alcohol blue, etc.

# POINT OF ORIGIN

Finding the point of origin of a fire is often a difficult process requiring considerable experience. But there are indicators to which you must be alert. For example, fire usually burns upward. The **charred "V" shape** on the exterior or interior of a building may thus indicate, like an arrowhead, the point of origin below or at the bottom of it. Another factor to look for is the intensity of burning, which will often be greater close to the point of origin. Putting these two factors together, because fire burns upward you are looking for a low point that shows evidence of intense burning.

Investigators sometimes find that light bulbs and other objects will become distorted with bulges protruding toward the most intense heat source. **Light bulb distortion** can thus be a valuable aid in discovering point of origin.

The point of origin may also be indicated by the materials or trail of materials used to ignite the fire. Be aware that there may be more than one point of origin in an arson fire; in fact, the existence of multiple points of origin is a strong indicator of arson.

The sources of air such as drafts, winds, open or broken windows, and holes in floors or walls may also affect the point of origin. While a point of origin may appear to be on a lower floor, you may in fact be examining a secondary fire started after the original fire destroyed the upper floor on which it began or even when firefighters destroyed a structure to control a fire.

Points of origin are crucial sites of evidence and you should quickly protect them from possible contamination, as you take notes, sketch, and photograph the scene. Remember, one of the simplest approaches to determining point of origin may be the observations of witnesses to the start of the blaze.

**Illustration 13-1.** A "V" burn pattern may be a good starting point for the investigation of "point of origin" in a fire. This is usually a location where the fire was most intense.

# PHYSICAL EVIDENCE OF ARSON

## Igniters

Substances or devices used to start fires are called **igniters**. The most useful igniter devices are matches, but investigators often search for a wide range of sources of ignition. Arsonists may, for example, start a fire with a candle that burns down slowly and gives them ample time to leave the scene. (A candle will burn about 1.5 inches or 3.75 centimetres per hour, although tapering and other characteristics will vary the rate.) Candles can thus be cut to specific lengths or arranged in various ways to ignite other fuels. Other delayed-ignition devices such as time fuses may be more sophisticated, but their object is the same: to allow the arsonist to escape. The ingenuity of arsonists constantly creates new devices: a burning cigarette with matches wrapped around it, a magnifying glass positioned to use the sun's rays, a shorted light switch, an ordinary stove with its timer set to ignite fuels with a burner, etc.

As with other physical evidence, the investigator searches not only for things that can help reconstruct the actions of the arsonist and the progress of the fire, but also for physical objects that can be traced to sources. For example, investigators could trace a match used in arson to a matchbook in the possession of a suspect.

## Accelerants

If you think of fire as a reaction, it makes more understandable the role of **accelerants**, which are *substances that increase the speed of a fire or other reaction.* In about 80% of arson cases, investigators find gasoline. Fortunately, gasoline is not only easy for arsonists to acquire, but also one of the most easily detected substances. Most investigators can find it by its familiar odour alone. As with igniters, however, the range of accelerants is vast, ranging from paint thinners, alcohols, lighter fluid, and kerosene to a number of other flammable liquids, petroleum products, and substances found in any well-stocked hardware store. The most convenient device is the investigator's nose, which can be sensitive to various accelerants if they are not too heavily disguised by burnt or burning debris. Some arson investigators use dogs, which can sometimes detect odours with a sensitivity greater than that of scientific instruments.

To detect flammable vapours, arson investigators sometimes use portable **catalytic combustion detectors**, or "sniffers," which can measure electrically the heat resistance created by the oxidation of vapours found at arson scenes and identify substances used as accelerants. Most investigators will submit suspect accelerants to the laboratory for analysis.

**Illustration 13-2.** In this case an accelerant was used to make the fire appear to have been started by the stove in the kitchen.

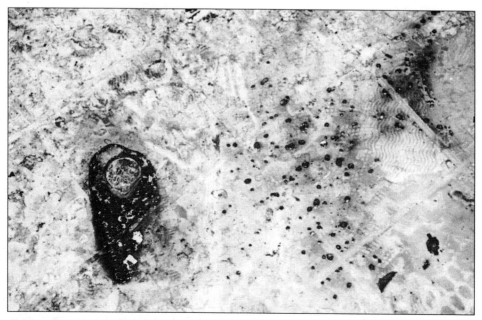

**Illustration 13-3.** Often trails of accelerants remain detectable after the fire has been extinguished.

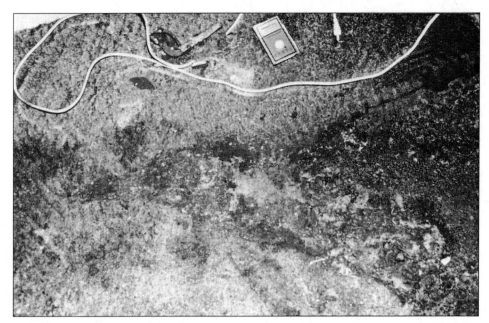

**Illustration 13-4.** Accelerant trail on carpet.

## Some Results of Fire

As you look more closely at the arson scene, it is important to note the characteristics of burned objects and surfaces.

**Crazing**, an irregular cracking pattern that occurs in glass subjected to rapid, intense heat, can be an indicator of accelerant use. When masonry surfaces undergo intense heat, **spalling**—fragmentation of brick or concrete surfaces—may occur. In burnt wood, investigators can measure the **depth of char** or **depth of burning**. This can inform them about fire duration (deeper=longer) and point of origin. They may also observe and record a **line of demarcation between burned and unburned substances**. If a cross-section of wood shows a clear line of demarcation, the fire was probably fast and hot. Looking at the pattern of charred material from a 90-degree angle, above a charred floor, for example, if the charring seems to follow the shape of a pool or a stream, some kind of liquid was likely used to accelerate the fire. A common sign of heat intensity is **alligatoring**, the eruption of blisters or ridges in wood. The hotter and more rapid the fire, the larger and more protruding the alligatoring blisters it produces.

An overall look at the arson scene may also be instructive. Because we know how fire usually behaves, any indications of unusual behaviour can be signs of arson. If fire normally burns upward and toward sources of ventilation, evidence

**Illustration 13-5.** A line of demarcation is visible on the wall just above the heat register.

that it burned otherwise is important. Fire that burns along a **trailer**—a deposit of liquid or other fuels or accelerants—and deviates from its usual patterns may have been started intentionally. If gases were present, they may have caused walls to explode in a distinctive way, with heavier gases causing walls to collapse outward at the bottom, lighter gases more toward the top, and rapid explosions causing walls to cave in.

## Collection and Preservation of Arson Evidence

**Photography** is often crucial to the processing of an arson scene because so many important physical clues such as burn patterns and trailers cannot be easily transported. Photographs or videotapes of a fire as it burns, of the crowd observing it, and of interior and exterior fire damage may later become crucial evidence. Smoke colour, point of origin, evidence of accelerants, igniters, ventilation, and burn patterns should all be included. Remember two things above all: (a) arson evidence is often fragile or volatile, so use extreme care in collection and packaging; (b) valuable evidence can be disguised by smoke or fire, so collect potential evidence even if it appears too damaged to be useful.

Some things to remember in collecting arson debris and associated physical evidence:

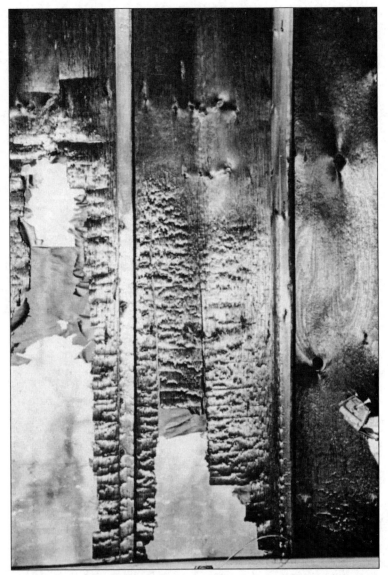

**Illustration 13-6.** Alligatoring on wood is an indicator of intense burning.

1. *Before collecting arson debris and associated physical evidence, the location of all evidence seized should be recorded by note and photograph.*

2. Collect samples of ash, soot, and charred material. If you are dealing with a small fire such as one in an incinerator, furnace, fireplace, burning barrel, or bonfire, collect all ash and burnt matter. If possible seize the entire container (burning barrel, etc.), because forensic laboratories can sometimes recover minute

**Illustrations 13-7(a) and 13-7(b).** Accelerant trail shows the destructive intention of the suspect. Exhibits of accelerant residues seized may be identified by a forensic laboratory.

traces of bones, dental work, and other materials that are resistant to fire. If you are processing a fire-damaged building, concentrate on areas likely to yield valuable evidence, such as possible point(s) of origin; collect several litres of material (if possible) from each.

3. Be sure to search thoroughly the area(s) where you think the fire to have originated, taking samples of all materials and all suspect residues.

4. Collect evidence from surfaces that would normally be expected to hold fingerprints. Smoke and melted materials such as polymers may actually preserve prints. Process and package moveable items as you would other print-bearing materials.

5. Be persistent in attempting to collect prints from likely surfaces. Smoke-damaged surfaces may require many lifts with fingerprint tape before anything is revealed. In some cases fire-melted materials can be lifted or soaked off fingerprints that are still usable.

6. *Warning: If you suspect explosives, call an explosives expert.* Collect all potential timing, ignition, and accelerant devices or substances. These are wide-ranging and may include clockwork systems, electronic apparatus or part of a building's electrical system, magnesium rods (used with detonators to imitate electrical fires), detonators, explosives, matches, candles, cigarettes, sodium metal, flammable liquids, phosphorus, fertilizers, and other flammable or porous materials that may contain accelerant residues (rugs, rags, wood upholstery, etc.).

7. Search for other types of evidence that may be related to arsonists or victims, such as bodily fluids and feces, hair and fibres, buttons, clothing, etc.

8. The clothing of suspects should be seized and packaged to be analyzed for possible accelerant residues.

9. Handle charred or singed documents with extreme care. If possible keep them in any container in which they are found. Otherwise, slide sheets of metal, thin cardboard, or paper under them and place them in an appropriately sized box. While collecting, protect them from gusts of wind or air.

10. **Comparison samples.** Samples of flammable liquids found at or near the scene or in the suspect's possession should be seized in their entirety, as should evidence of fire-starting devices. You should also seize comparison samples of ash and other materials from areas away from the point of origin, and apart from suspected accelerant-containing materials. For instance, if you seize a flooring sample at the point of origin, you should also seize a comparison sample of the

same material from another part of the floor. Comparison samples of documents may be documents from the suspect(s) source of charred documents.

11. **Packaging and storage.** All arson debris should be packaged and sealed in clean, airtight metal tins. In some cases, investigators may use sealed mason jars, but the rubber sealer rings in these may be damaged by some flammable liquids and it is extremely important not to allow volatile residues to escape or be contaminated by degraded sealers. If you find flammable liquids remaining in a container, seize and stopper or seal the entire container, taking care not to damage possible fingerprint evidence. Authorities disagree on packaging recommendations. Some advocate glass bottles with Teflon-lined screw caps. Containers should be about three-quarters full. Sealable paint tins available at paint stores are often most useful. If charred documents are found in a transportable container, they should be kept in it. If not, they should be sealed in boxes of the correct dimensions between layers of soft paper or tissue. Keep seized evidence refrigerated if possible and keep flammable liquid samples well away from fire debris.

# ANALYSIS AND COMPARISON

## Persistence and Prints

It cannot be overemphasized that in the collection and analysis of arson evidence, persistence pays off. Should you find a possible weapon or glass evidence at an arson scene, never assume that smoke, fire, and debris have ruined its evidential value. About 15 years ago, one of the authors of this book conducted an informal experiment. He is a good secretor and decided to test the durability of his own fingerprints. Having made several prints on microscope slides, he placed the slides in the police department incinerator where the janitors burned the trash every night. The slides sat in various parts of the fire all night: on a ledge where smoke and heat were the major influences, and in the centre where the slides would be in contact with direct flames, melting plastics, and other burning materials. The following morning, he began to examine the slides for fingerprints. On the smoke-damaged slides he began to try lifting with fingerprint tape, using one piece of tape after another. With the fourteenth lift, he began to see the fingerprint and with the fifteenth and sixteenth pieces of tape he began to get clear, readable prints. The prints that had been in the fire and covered with burning material were also productive. In some cases, the prints were readable after the melted material had been pried or even soaked and washed off the slide.

*Beware:* The forensic analyst or investigator attempting this process is gambling. Because there is no way of knowing where prints are situated on a smoke-damaged item, you run the risk of lifting only a part of a print at the end of all your labours. If you perform this task carefully, however, there is still the possibility of taping the area likely to contain the rest of the print and subsequently putting together a more complete print. (*Note:* For court evidence, any damage resulting from these lifts would need to be accounted for as the matching principle requires.)

One thing that scientists examining arson debris are particularly trying to find and identify is evidence of **accelerant residues**. When they receive the investigator's submission of unknown liquids, various kinds of charred materials, and comparison samples, forensic scientists and technicians begin systematically to try to detect and isolate the residues in question. If successful in concentrating or isolating accelerant residues, they then attempt to identify them.

The concentration of accelerant residues may involve a number of techniques. Materials may be subjected to steam distillation and analyzed in liquid form. Scientists can also use solvent extraction. Solvents are added to the debris, the mixture is shaken, and accelerants are dissolved from the charred material. The solvent can then be evaporated to leave a concentration of residues for analysis. A more straightforward technique involves the collection of accelerant residues that collect in the "head space" above the debris in sample containers. In "head space" techniques the container may be at room temperature or it can be heated to force the residues out of the debris more quickly and completely. The vapours are then extracted with a syringe and analyzed. Because the sample size in this technique is limited to the size of the syringe used, researchers have developed a vapour concentration technique. Charcoal is placed in a container containing fire debris, or in a tube leading from such a container. When the container is heated, vaporized accelerants are absorbed by the charcoal. The accelerant is then collected from the charcoal by washing with solvent (usually carbon disulfide) or by desorption with heat, and is subjected to analysis.

Gas chromatography is generally considered the most useful means of identifying accelerant residue types and origin. Most turn out to be gasoline or kerosene, but chromatography can identify the full range of accelerants. What's more, scientists can sometimes identify the specific "signature" on the resulting graph that allows them to suggest the origin of an accelerant. They compare the graph to one from a comparison sample taken from the likely source of the gasoline or other accelerant. If the irregularities that separate a particular accelerant from all others of its type are present for both the suspect substance and the known sample, there is a possible match indicating a common source. This process can be particularly important when accelerant residues found in the clothing or possession of a suspect seem to match those found at an arson scene.

In some cases scientists may go further, combining mass spectroscopy (G-MS) or infrared spectroscopy with gas chromatograph analysis (GC-IR) to ensure the accurate identification of accelerant signatures. Scientists have also developed techniques of identifying the olfactronic signatures (basically evidence of the distinctive odours) of a full range of things, from accelerants and explosives to drugs and even human beings. The implications of research into the characteristics and effects of smells are vast; their immediate importance to the forensic analyst is that they offer yet another means of matching a known to an unknown substance.

## Death by Fire?

Accelerants, although very important, are only one of the types of evidence recovered from arson scenes. Much of the other evidence collected will be analyzed in ways with which we have become familiar: hairs and fibres, cloth, wood, tools, glass, tool marks, firearms, documents, blood, and so on. For example, there are many questions scientists and investigators must answer about a charred human corpse discovered at an arson or fire scene.

A person whose body is found at a fire site did not necessarily die there; or if the person did die there, he or she may not have died as a result of fire or smoke. Was the death a result of accident, suicide, or homicide? Autopsy evidence can provide answers to these questions. Blood samples seized at autopsy can be tested for carbon monoxide levels. If these levels are extremely elevated, the victim probably died from smoke inhalation. Such determinations are not certain, because different individuals can tolerate different levels of carbon monoxide (perhaps as low as 35% saturation); the toxicity of carbon monoxide can also depend on other factors such as the speed of carbon monoxide intoxication, and the presence of other depressants in the blood.

Depending on how badly burned a body is, the investigator may be able to observe some visual signs of death by fire or smoke, although these must be later confirmed by pathologists. A common error is often made by inexperienced investigators who first see a burnt body. The corpse usually appears in a contorted position as if exposed to extreme pain. This "pugilistic attitude" is deceptive; all burnt bodies experience a contraction of the muscles under extreme heat and the investigator's perception of a person writhing in agony is often a false one. The skin may give the impression of wounds that are actually heat cracks, and broken bodies will also be a result of heat. Nonetheless, no officer ever forgets the first burnt corpse encountered. It is a terrifying sight. Other characteristics, however, can be genuine indicators of death by smoke and fire. Smoke stains may be apparent around the nostrils, indicating that the victim was breathing during the fire; the pathologist will usually find additional evidence of smoke inhalation in the air passages, the nose, and

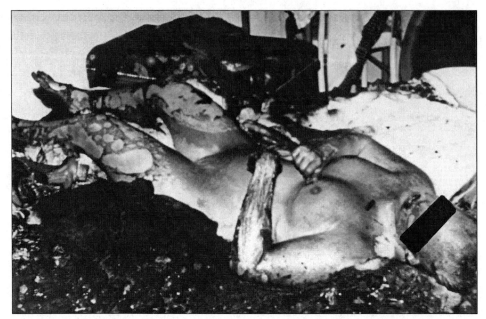

**Illustration 13-8.** Death by fire leaves the investigator a complex scene. Fire may cause the body to settle in a "pugilistic" attitude that it actually assumed after death.

the lungs. Slight reddening and blistering of the skin may also be taken as signs of life during fire.

# EXPLOSIONS AND EXPLOSIVES

The forensic investigation of bombings and other explosions is usually a highly specialized activity, undertaken by well-trained explosives experts and bomb squads. No investigator, no matter how highly trained in other aspects of forensic science, should ever attempt to disarm a suspected explosive device. However, some may be called upon to process a scene where an explosion occurred or is thought to have occurred, and others may be unfortunate enough to encounter explosive devices. In all cases this is an area of investigation in which you must exercise extreme care, especially to make sure that all persons are well away from danger.

The range of explosive devices is considerable. Although we are accustomed to the TV and film depiction of highly sophisticated bombs, many devices are easily made with commonly available and inexpensive components. The Internet has been a great help to would-be bombers who wish to develop their own distinctive bombs. New combinations of explosives and detonation devices are constantly appearing; there are, however, several common types: **dynamite** and **blasting caps** stolen from construction sites; **pipe bombs** made from pipes, caps, and smokeless powder; **fertilizer** mixed with **diesel fuel** and detonated; **fuses** wrapped around the exhaust manifolds of cars; combinations of chlorine, sugar, and water; and a bottle, dry ice, and water.

Explosives are usually classified as "low" or "high":

- **Low explosives**, such as those homemade bombs described above, often contain mixtures that are stable, and will not actually explode unless confined to a container when ignited. Most "low explosive" bombs consist of an oxidizing agent and some sort of fuel.

- **High explosives** are those that will explode whether or not sealed in a container. Some high explosives, such as **dynamite** and **TNT**, are called **non-initiating** or **secondary**, because they are not particularly sensitive to friction, heat, or shocks. They require primers or blasting caps.

  **Primary or initiating high explosives** are those that are highly sensitive to shocks, friction, or heat. Consequently, explosives for commercial use tend to be non-initiating, being safer to transport and use. For military uses, and in some terrorist operations, a very common explosive is **C4** (also known as **ROX** or **cyclotrimethylenetrinitramine**), a non-initiating high explosive frequently produced as **plastic explosive** or **plastique**. Plastique is a pliable plasticine-like substance that can be molded. A blasting cap or a safety fuse is needed to detonate it.

**Blasting caps** are themselves explosive devices, and must be handled with great care. They are the most frequently used types of **detonators** (i.e., devices used to set off explosives). Usually an electrical charge or a burning safety fuse sets off the blasting cap, which in turn detonates the explosive. A car bomb, for instance, can therefore be wired to the ignition of the vehicle. The electrical charge released by turning on the ignition ignites the blasting cap and hence the explosives.

## Collection and Analysis of Explosives Evidence

The scene of an explosion requires an extremely thorough search. If done correctly, however, it is usually a rewarding search, because explosives leave residues and fragmentary evidence at the scene. Proper collection is therefore absolutely crucial; it is almost always left to experts, but other investigators may be required to assist. While we present here some general guidelines concerning the collection of explosives evidence, officers encountering explosion scenes should always seek the assistance and advice of the nearest forensic laboratory or accredited explosives expert. This is doubly the case where you suspect the presence of undetonated explosive devices.

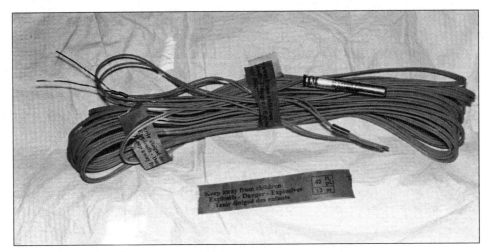

**Illustration 13-9.** Blasting caps.

**Illustration 13-10.** Explosives such as this Vibrogel® are best seized with the aid of properly trained personnel. The average officer does not have the expertise to deal with explosives.

1. *Photograph, sketch, and note as with an arson scene.*

2. A systematic search should begin with the crater(s) made by the explosion(s). Seize all loose dirt and debris from the crater or hole and package it.

3. You should also seize any porous or nonporous materials around the crater. These are likely to have accumulated residues of explosives. Be especially vigilant in collecting from scorched or blackened surfaces. Remember that explosive residues may be at a considerable distance from the centre of the explosion, depending on its size, and a thorough search must often encompass a vast area. Don't forget to search high areas such as trees, roofs, ledges, sills, etc. that may contain debris hurled by a violent explosion. If possible, you should seize entire

items likely to contain explosive residues: floor tiles, wood, etc. Do not attempt to scrape them, but package object and residues together.

4. In many cases, explosive residues are still dangerous. Nitroglycerine residues, for example, are sensitive to shock; they must be neutralized by experts. Be on the alert for any suspected explosive materials in bottles or as pools of liquid, stains, material in cracks, etc.

5. Some of the evidence, which might be a long distance from the centre of the explosion (especially one detonated by someone who did not wish to be killed by it), may include: detonators, fuses, wires, containers of explosives, batteries, clocks, timers, and tools used in crimping wires or assembling explosive devices.

6. You should also be collecting all the types of evidence available at crime scenes: tool marks, footprints, tire tracks, hairs and fibres, bloodstains, fingerprints, safe insulation, etc.

7. As with arson investigations you should seize, package, and submit the clothing of suspects that may contain explosive residues. The suspect's vehicle, residence, workshop, etc. must also be searched and any suspect items seized. Suspects themselves may also bear traces of explosive residue and debris, if they are apprehended soon after the explosion. In this case samples can be taken from the suspect's hands with an acetone-moistened swab and later tested for explosives.

8. Package all explosives evidence in sealed containers. Consult explosives experts for the packaging and transportation of any volatile or explosive materials.

*Note:* Because in arson and explosion investigations there is often a large contingent of officers, it is particularly important to maintain an evidence log and to detail the name of the collector, date, time, and location for each piece of evidence collected.

As with accelerant residues and other arson evidence, scientists have found gas chromatography, mass spectrometry, and the analysis of odours to be invaluable in the detection and identification of explosives. Because of the immediate threat involved with explosives and the vast extent of some bomb scenes, the processes of detection and identification must often be undertaken at the scene so that explosions can be prevented as well as analyzed after the fact.

In Canada, scientists have developed a portable instrument called the **trace atmospheric gas analyzer** or **TAGA**. It uses both the chemical ionization of odour molecules and mass spectrometry to test samples of air for chemical content. It can detect minute amounts of explosive in air samples from airplanes, suitcases, and other places where explosions have occurred or may be likely to occur. American investigators also make use of portable, high-speed gas chromatographers which can identify the components of vapour containing explosive residues.

Laboratory work on explosive debris usually involves an initial microscopic examination to detect explosives particles. Debris is then usually washed to dissolve any explosive residues, and the resulting solution concentrated. The concentrate can then be analyzed by various processes of chromatography and mass spectrometry to reveal the "signatures" of explosive components.

# DOCUMENTS

We are surrounded by documents, from credit card slips to videotapes. As new means of recording, copying, and distributing information appear, the variety of documents grows. This growth in the so-called "information age" means that growing expertise is also required to collect and analyze documents.

Virtually any means by which information is recorded and any marking capable of being understood by a person can be considered a **document**. We naturally think of handwriting evidence, and the authenticity of wills, contracts, accounting ledgers, suicide notes, and other such material when considering questioned documents. But to take in the entire field of documents as defined in law, we must go much further. *Not only written and printed materials, but also credit cards, computer disks and hard drives, sound recordings, photographs, charts, graphs, maps, videotapes, videodisks, and any other recording or storage device for information must be included.*

Any crime may involve document evidence, although there are some in which documents are central, such as **fraud**, **forgery**, **false pretenses**, **threatening** or **obscene letters**, **industrial** or **other espionage**, and **crimes involving contracts**, **deeds**, or **wills**. Discovering the authenticity or alteration of such documents is often a crucial element of the investigation. In other cases, such as armed robberies in which notes are used or videotapes recorded, suicides in which notes are left, or homicides made to look like suicides, document examination may also play a major part. In other words, documents may be the tools of crime in a forgery or the evidence of crime in a homicide. To the investigator used to dealing with more obvious examples of violence or theft, documents may seem relatively harmless, but they can destroy or harm a person just as much as the weapons of other crimes.

The examiner of documents in the twenty-first century is no longer simply concerned with pen and ink or even with mechanically printed documents. The advent of a whole new range of information sources has expanded the expertise such an investigator requires. A few years ago Robert M. Hill, an officer in the southwestern United States, investigated a particularly difficult case. A woman was suing a corporation for sexual harassment, using diary notations she claimed to have made in 1993 and 1994, while the harassment was allegedly occurring. From a badly damaged label on the diary, the ingenious officer was able to find the Internet address of the company that had sold her the diary. Through further research on the URL of the company, Hill discovered that the website of the company had not been established until the spring of 1995 and therefore the woman could not have made her diary notations until later in 1995 when the diary was first marketed. The lawsuit was quickly dropped. Detective Hill had proved equal to the forensic demands of several types of documents in a dawning new age of document examination. (*Journal of Forensic Identification*, 49(2)(March-April 1999), 114–116.)

Document examination, like many other forensic professions, is a highly specialized field whose practitioners must develop keen judgement for differences and similarities of detail and keep abreast of a rapidly developing information technology. No matter what technologies are involved, however, document examination is still a means to the investigator's familiar end: identification. What was the source of a document or of alterations to a document? Can a document be linked to a suspect? The principles of matching and comparison in this case demand a different sort of skill and knowledge.

The knowledge required to deal with evidence under the simple title of questioned documents is complex. The investigator must be interested in the entire range of materials and processes by which questioned documents are created. The multitude of ways in which an individual may be linked to a criminal act through document analysis can generally fall under two categories:

1. The **form and content of information** in the document—handwriting, hand printing, printed documents, spreadsheets, financial accounts, electronic digital databases, video images, recorded sounds, etc.

2. The **methods and materials used to store information**—papers, inks, toners, writing instruments, typewriters, printers, copying machines, computers, fax machines, computer hard drives and disks, answering machines, rubber stamps, and others.

In other words, documents analysts may find themselves studying the manufactured composition and origins of paper or ink as well as the nature of the markings they produce. As you can imagine from the list above, such investigations can lead to a whole series of diverse forensic inquiries. The recognition, collection, and analysis of such evidence requires that the investigator be ready to encounter a great range of circumstances.

# COMPUTER CRIME

The development of computers has introduced a whole new range of crimes and new methods of committing old crimes. Computers may be the object of theft themselves, or they may be used to steal information, goods, or money, to defraud, to violate copyright, to vandalize or charge records, to obtain information for blackmail, to launder or transfer money, to harass, intimidate, and threaten, or to distribute pornography. The nature of computers and computer networks requires a new sort of forensic expertise. Investigators and scientists are now being trained in the seizure, recovery, and analysis of computer crime evidence.

"Electronic crimes" are now directly responsible for immense losses, far surpassing those caused by other "white collar" crimes and offences such as robbery. While computer "hacking" may often seem a harmless juvenile activity, it can result in enormous damage, expense, and personal anguish. One virus from an ingenious "cyber punk" or "techno-vandal" can destroy entire systems of information or perhaps even lead to deaths with the destruction of safety, transportation, or communications systems. Investigators should be aware, however, that the majority of electronic crimes are committed by "insiders" to a company or system, and therefore the staff of corporations or organizations to which the damage was done are often the initial suspects.

Remember, the investigation of computer crime may require special expertise, but it is fundamentally a crime to be investigated like any other. The need for skill and care in the seizure and analysis of this sort of documentary evidence does not alter the fact that you are still in many cases handling transient evidence that you hope will lead you to the source of the offence.

# COLLECTION OF DOCUMENT EVIDENCE

Methods will vary widely depending on the nature of the crime and the crime scene. Some general guidelines, however, are useful. In the case of paper documents:

1. Investigators should submit all written or printed documents and writing instruments: paper, typewriters, rubber stamps, ink and pens, etc.

2. If for some reason you cannot submit original documents, submit photographs or photocopies.

3. *Remember that documents provide an excellent surface for fingerprints or other trace evidence.* Paper absorbs the perspiration and oils exuded from the skin and can therefore be a source of clear, durable prints. Some authorities advise the use of forceps to avoid contamination. Prints on documents should be processed using the least destructive methods possible, such as iodine fuming.

4. If you find writings on a wall, desktop, body, or other surface that may difficult to submit, consult a forensic laboratory for assistance at the scene. If such assistance is not possible, photograph the writings with both close-up and longer-range shots, including a scale ruler, and submit photographs. In some cases after photographing, you may be able to seize a portion of a wall or other surface for submission.

5. Documents should never be altered, marked, folded, or creased. If documents are torn, never attempt to repair them. Pieces torn out of a document may be crucial to later physical matching. Do not unfold documents that are found folded.

6. Documents should be immediately placed in transparent envelopes which may later also serve as part of packaging for laboratory submission. Do not mark envelopes with documents inside them because you may make impressions through the envelopes. Collect and store documents flat. Never staple them.

7. Do not use plastic folders for photocopied documents. The static electricity created may affect some of the powders used in the copying process. Use paper envelopes instead.

8. If it is necessary to mark documents, do so carefully using a corner or the back of the documents in as little space as possible.

9. If documents are wet with blood or other liquids, allow them to dry, taking appropriate measures to avoid possible DNA contamination.

10. For laboratory submission, place the document folders or envelopes between sheets of cardboard and tape the boards together. Place them in a box of the appropriate size. (For collection of charred documents, see Chapter 13.)

11. Be sure to mark the submission appropriately if the document is to be examined for fingerprints.

# Comparison Samples

You should submit all possible materials that could link the document to anything or any person involved in its preparation and collect as many samples as possible to assist in lab analysis.

## *Collected and Requested Writings*

In gathering materials for handwriting comparison, investigators generally make use of two types of samples, **collected** and **requested** writings.

*Collected Writings*  Also called **informal exemplars**, these are writings that the suspect has done unaware of their possible use as comparison samples. They may be any writings that the person has done in the normal course of daily affairs: notes, letters, business transactions, and others.

The investigator must be thorough in checking all possible sources of such writings, such as **prior statements to police** and **other criminal justice documents, tax returns, wills, driver's licence** or **passport applications, land registry, personal diaries, notebooks, church registries,** any **government records, rental agreements, personal correspondence,** and **other documents obtained from acquaintances or relatives**. There are many possible sources, and the main requirement is that the authorship of any writings must be proven to the satisfaction of a court. The proof of authorship may necessitate a witness to the execution of the comparison sample itself, to an admission of authorship by the suspect, or to the suspect's writing in some other context. To be certain, investigators should always consult the most recent version of the **Canada Evidence Act**, being careful to watch for amendments.

Collected writings can have several advantages over those requested. They are more likely to represent the natural, undisguised writing of a suspect. The penmanship, spelling, grammar, and usual vocabulary of the suspect are often more evident in collected writings. It is also possible, if a crime has only been discovered after some time has elapsed, to obtain collected writings that occurred near or at the time of the offence.

In order to obtain samples of the greatest evidential value:

1. Try to collect writings that were executed with the same types of instruments and media as the questioned writings.

2. Remember: The closer to the date of questioned writings the sample was written, the greater its value. (A person's handwriting may change with age, education, or illness).

3. The source of collected writings should, as much as possible, be similar to the source of questioned writings. In other words, in a case of questioned invoices, another invoice should be found—or most commonly, in the case of a questioned cheque, another cheque written by the suspect.

***Requested Writings***   These, sometimes referred to as **formal exemplars**, are done at the request of an investigator or a third party. Obtaining requested writings that will be of investigative value to laboratory analysts and of evidential value in court is a complex matter, and several major points must be emphasized.

1. The investigators should always be present to witness any requested writings as they are being written.

2. Every attempt should be made to duplicate the conditions under which the questioned documents were written, and to ensure that the suspect is writing naturally.

   (a) Be sure the style of writings is comparable. If the questioned document was printed in block letters, the requested writing should be done in the same style.

   (b) The materials used should be similar to those of the questioned document: that is, the size and type of paper or surface (lined or plain, foolscap, small notepaper, etc.), the writing instruments (ballpoint, fountain pen, pencil, etc.).

   (c) Ideally, you should dictate the exact contents of the questioned document. Otherwise, the texts selected should be chosen for their similarity to those of the questioned document and for their ability to encourage a complete sample of the suspect's writing habits. If you are using a common sample document, be sure to dictate dates that are the same as those on the questioned document. For a commonly used sample, see the "Canada Letter" in Illustration 14-1, which is designed to elicit the full range of letters in both upper- and lowercase. To capture the style of questioned phrases, you can change the wording of any such document, slipping in expressions, words, or sentences from the questioned document. Use a common or standard document if the use of the questioned text would damage your investigation.

   (d) Dictate the document or documents you have prepared, making every effort to encourage spontaneous, natural writing. Some investigators find that varying the speed of dictation, interrupting the suspect with questions, comments, new paper, and other distractions help to produce a more representative sample of the suspect's writing style and habits.

   (e) When suspects are writing, you should not assist them with the text itself in any way. Do not allow them to see the text from which you are dictating. Remove each sample from a suspect before beginning the next one. Never

1953 51st Ave. West
Toronto, ON

Aug. 27, 2000

Mr. & Mrs. W.E. James

c/o Gold Medal Hospital X-Ray Department

Lincoln Road

Postal Zone "B"

New York, NY

Dear Vera and Eric:

We are enjoying a quiet and lazy Canadian holiday. Following a visit with Dr. Harry Young at Erie Beach from the 18th to the 20th of July we journeyed to Sarnia and London. After six days in that zone we went on to Niagara Falls via St. Thomas for a change of scenery. There we met John Oliver and Ken Guest, both of whom are presently working for Upper Canada Insurance Co. Last time I saw Ken was in 1993, I believe. Do you remember him? He has deserted the x-ray field to become a salesman.

Quite recently we heard from Murray Robertson who has gone "down under." He is flying now for United Airlines Ltd., Flight No. 600, I think, out of New Zealand. Incidentally, Murray sold us his car for eight hundred dollars cash and seventeen monthly instalments of twenty-five dollars and fifty cents. (Total price $1241.50.) His interest rate was $6^1/2\%$.

Remind George that I haven't heard from Jean or him for 7 or 8 months. Presently we are at 6465 Queen St., Toronto M4T 1J9. Our mail could be forwarded here for the next 2 or 3 weeks, if you wouldn't mind.

Very truly yours,

Bob

**Illustration 14-1.** The "Canada Letter."

help the suspect with any aspect of the text such as punctuation, grammar, spelling, etc.

3.  When taking a suspect's statement, try to ensure that the suspect writes out the statement. If the suspect refuses, ask for a signature on the document. Failing such a signature, you will need to seek other specimens from documents such as those listed above.

4.  If you suspect forgery of a document, comparison standards vary, but you should try to obtain:

    (a) the victim's signature—5 to 10 samples, along with any particular victim signatures that could have been used by the suspect for copying

    (b) the victim's name written by the suspect—15 to 20 samples, written in your presence on separate sheets

    (c) samples of reasonable length (e.g., the "Canada Letter")

    (d) all other signatures or writings of the suspect found

## Paper Collection

Do not overlook the importance of paper itself as evidence. Establishing the age and type of paper can provide vital clues to the authenticity or source of questioned documents.

1.  Paper collection is particularly important for comparison standards. You should collect not only the paper of the documents themselves but also other papers that may be used for standards of comparison.

2.  Handle paper evidence as little as possible. It should be kept clean and dry and never creased or fold (unless that is its original state).

3.  Paper that is wet should be allowed to dry at room temperature before packaging.

4.  Keep sheets of paper in the same order that you find them in. Cutter marks on paper edges can reveal the sequence of sheets in a bundle by physical matching. Submit watermarks of all paper samples. Watermark features can tell you date of manufacture. (More on watermarks below.)

5.  If you must mark paper evidence, keep your descriptors (time, date, place, and initials) close to an edge or corner of the paper. Any additional notes should be on the envelope or container in which the evidence is packaged. Package paper evidence as you would other documents described above.

For processing of charred documents, see Chapter 13.

## Inks

The wide variety of inks available may be useful in establishing the origin of documents. You should submit to the laboratory all suspect inks, cartridges, ribbons, and ink-containing instruments that may be relevant to your case. Protect them from breakage and spillage in suitable containers.

# WRITING AND PRINTING INSTRUMENTS

The range of writing instruments, both traditional and recent, is great and ever-increasing. While some, such as laser printers, increase the possibility of anonymity for the suspect, the collection of any device used in making documents could be of crucial importance in linking a document to a suspect.

In addition to manual instruments such as pens and pencils, you should collect evidence of any other device which may have been used in document preparation.

## Computer Seizures

Computers and computer evidence should always be handled insofar as possible by an expert authorized to seize them. In case you ever have to perform such a seizure yourself, here are some basic guidelines.

1. Photograph everything with overall, medium-range, and close-up shots. Be sure to include:

    (a) close-ups of the screen if it is turned on

    (b) shots of the arrangement of all computer cables and connections

    (c) shots from all sides of other equipment and documents surrounding the computer as well as overall shots showing the precise location of the computer in the room

    (d) subsequent shots of any items you have labelled

2. *Do not touch the keyboard.*

3. When removing a computer *do not use the on/off switch*. Simply unplug it.

4. Be sure to identify and label all cables or wires and the ports or outlets to which they are connected for subsequent reassembly.

5. Do not allow a suspect to touch the computer. Even if suspects seem genuine and offer to help or instruct you in shutting down, never allow them to shut the computer down or touch the keyboard. They may be destroying evidence.

6. Any toggle switches should be taped to remain in the position in which you found them.

7. Seize everything that may possibly be of evidential value: notebooks, clipboards, disks, printouts, manuals, and any other equipment or paper including "sticky" or pinned notes and the contents of garbage cans. Use your imagination. Be sure, for example, to inspect the undersides of desks, tables, etc. where notes may have attached or written containing passwords and other valuable information.

8. Be alert for any magnetic fields, which can erase or damage electronic information. Radio transmitters and radio waves in general, motors, speakers, and storage in plastic can all alter computer disks. Seized disks should always be packaged in paper or anti-static cardboard disk envelopes. Do not write on the outside of a disk. Disks that are in the drive should be removed. A blank disk may be inserted for transport.

## Printing and Reproduction Devices

1. These include typewriters, printing equipment, copy machines, paper-cutting devices, chequewriters, computers and their printers, offset plates, plate burners, flats, embossing machines and encoders for credit and other cards, photographic equipment and photographic materials, and paste-up materials and other graphic art devices. It should be noted that many of these instruments may also themselves be analyzed as documents.

2. Exercise extreme care in approaching electronic and other writing and reproduction devices. Particularly with computers, it is best if possible to have an expert on hand to avoid losing evidence when unplugging, turning them off or on, restarting, etc. *Do not adjust or operate the equipment before submission.*

3. Remember the range of other evidence such as fingerprints, DNA, hair and fibre, etc. which may adhere to printing and reproduction devices.

4. Be sure to collect all garbage from printers, paper-cutters, and other devices. If dealing with wastepaper baskets and other small garbage containers, remove entire containers. Collect pertinent evidence from dumpsters and other large containers.

5. If possible, submit to the laboratory the entire piece of equipment. If you cannot submit the equipment, seize and submit the parts of the equipment that make the actual printed impressions, such as ribbons, print wheels, etc., from typewriters and word processors.

6. When a printing device cannot be submitted, you should always take standards of comparison:

   (a) *Computer printers.* For printers with ribbons, change the ribbon and submit the original. In addition to the original ribbon or printing elements, you should perform tests with all fonts and interchangeable elements, using the text of questioned documents. Ideally you should make at least five specimens of the questioned document text. You should also collect as many samples as possible of printed matter from files thought to have been made by the same printer on or near the date of the questioned document. Laser-printed copies should be packaged in paper to avoid the problem of toner sticking to plastic and document folders.

   (b) *Typewriters.* When machines cannot be submitted, seize original ribbons and elements. Make samples of both direct carbon and new ribbon impressions, using at least 20 lines of the questioned document text.

   (c) *Chequewriters.* (1) Make 10 to 20 impressions of the exact amount of the questioned cheque. (2) Make 10 to 20 impressions of each symbol on the chequewriter.

   (d) *Photocopiers.* Remember to package all photocopied and laser-printed documents in paper rather than plastic; otherwise the toner may stick to a plastic surface. To make comparison samples:

      (i) Do not adjust the photocopier in any way; especially avoid cleaning the platen glass (the glass surface on which documents are placed for copying).

      (ii) First of all, close the lid of the machine with no document on the platen and make at least ten copies. Then make another ten copies of a clean sheet of blank paper on the platen. Repeat the process with a clean sheet of graph paper. You should submit all of the articles used in this test.

      (iii) Check to see if there is a record of any repairs or adjustments to the machine.

# DOCUMENT EXAMINATION, ANALYSIS, AND COMPARISON

As you can see from the extensive instructions on evidence collection, the range of materials included in document evidence can be vast. Consequently, the types of examinations and comparisons to which experts submit documents and the media and equipment used in their preparation are also numerous. Nonetheless, forensic examiners are trying to answer some basic questions common to all investigations when examining documents: Who, what, when, where, why, and how? Each of these questions about document evidence may help you to determine the answers to others. Finding out how a document was made may well lead you to the discovery of who wrote it. Knowing when a document was made can immediately help you in the question of how it was made, and so on. A laser-printed document in French, for example, could not have been produced on an alleged date of 1962 by a person who knows only English. A document using up-to-date slang may be an indication of both the date of the document and the age of its author.

A document examiner must therefore be familiar with many kinds of knowledge or in some cases be able to call upon other experts to solve specific problems. The most common uses for document examiners are those that involve handwriting. Generally, we learn to write at school from the same or similar models of script. These models define the class characteristics of handwriting. As we acquire the habit of writing, our script accumulates unique combinations of features or individual characteristics that a handwriting expert can use to identify a particular person's writing. Even though a person may not write in exactly the same way every time, certain habits will repeat themselves in every example written naturally without any attempt to disguise. Large and numerous exemplars or requested writings stand the best chance of giving the forensic analyst a good sample to work on.

The two most important tools in the laboratory are the eyes and the microscope. Document examiners compare questioned documents with requested and collected writings in every way possible: the slant of writing, letter shapes and sizes, distinctive disconnections and connections between letters, pen pressure, smoothness, the strokes with which words and letters are begun and ended, and the height of certain letters relative to that of others. Here the matching principle is important: examiners look for similarities that may indicate questioned and comparison documents may have been written by the same hand, and for important differences that indicate different writers.

Even when an examiner is fairly certain and highly skilled, the analysis of handwriting is not an exact science and the results of analysis are expert **opinions**, not absolute certainties. They are nonetheless important opinions which can be helpful in answering fundamental questions, such as, "Who wrote this document?" or "Is the signature on this cheque genuine?" In cases of forgery in which a suspect has tried to imitate the victim's signature, it may often be possible to answer the second question, but impossible, on the basis of handwriting alone, to answer the first; in other words, the signature on a cheque or letter may be an obvious forgery, awkwardly or shakily written, but it is difficult to say who committed the forgery. A skilled, experienced document examiner has acquired a very subtle science, however, and can often see significant similarities between writings that initially appear quite different but

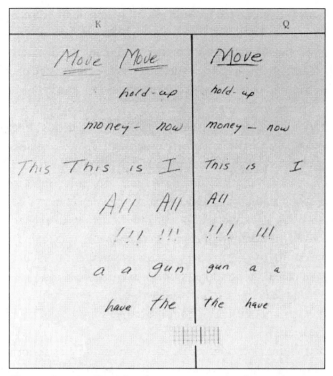

**Illustration 14-2.** A handwriting comparison showing known sample "**K**," compared to questioned sample "**Q**," prepared for court presentation.

contain enough similarities to maintain the suspicion of a particular writer. The examiner considers the effects of illness, hand injuries, intoxicants, and even deliberate handwriting disguise, and may decide that someone should not be eliminated as a possible suspect.

**Dates** are often crucial to cases involving questioned documents, and examiners will often try to determine the authenticity of a date or the authenticity of a signature relative to a date. Was the document dated by a different hand? Did the machinery or ink or watermarked paper used to produce a printed document exist on the questioned date? Was the alleged signer dead or ill when the document was actually signed? These are questions that may be answered by the comparisons of questioned documents with requested or collected writings. In other cases, examiners may require other techniques, such as the chemical analysis of ink or the closer scientific examination of paper.

**Paper** is still a common medium for documents, and it can provide the examiner with many clues about the origin and authenticity of documents. Paper is a Chinese invention now usually made from wood, although the finest-quality papers are still often made, as they have been for over 500 years, from linen or cotton rags. Paper manufacturers separate cellulose fibre in wood mechanically or chemically and pour the fibres suspended in liquid over a screen.

When this pulpy mass is dried and pressed, it contains the distinctive pattern of the process called the **watermark**. The pattern may also be imprinted chemically after manufacture, or paper may be specially watermarked by particular or companies that buy from a paper manufacturer. Watermarks are useful in identifying the origin of paper. Along with characteristics such as staple or binder-ring holes that do not match those of other pages, or different inks, watermarks may also allow investigators to detect pages that have been fraudulently put into a larger document.

Some papers may also be made suitable or glossy for colour photographs by the addition of clay. When examining paper, scientists can detect pieces of rubber from erasers or remnants of ink from an erased signature. Attempts to alter documents can also change detectably the pattern of fibres on the paper's surface, leaving evidence of alteration. The composition of papers can allow scientists to identify the source and sometimes the date of paper. In addition to having these distinctive characteristics, paper can be a medium for other evidence such as fingerprints. In some cases scientists can recover enough DNA from the saliva on a licked envelope flap to make an identification.

Modern papermaking and printing have evolved into complex processes in an effort to defeat forgers, while forgers often make use of new technology to commit their crimes. Authorities are continually involved in a contest with counterfeiters to make banknotes difficult to reproduce illegally. Canadian authorities now manufacture some bills with metal tags that vary distinctively in colour when examined. When producing important documents such as cheques and passports, many countries rely on paper manufactured especially for those purposes and that is not readily available to or producible by forgers. But a major problem rests in the fact that forgers nonetheless can now make use of highly sophisticated printers and copiers whose products can often pass quick inspection by a busy retail clerk.

**Inks** vary considerably in their composition although the basic carbon black or soot originally used to make them is still frequently in use today. The inks of different manufacturers have distinctive chemical "signatures" that can be analyzed in the laboratory. Scientists use thin-layer chromatography to separate an ink's components in solvent into its unique fingerprint. They also sometimes apply ultraviolet light to see if some components will fluoresce. These tests can be used to identify the origins of an ink and to detect the addition of words or numbers that fraudulently alter a document.

The production of printed documents on machines has enormously complicated and sometimes frustrated the task of examining questioned documents. **Typewriters**, while widespread and relatively inexpensive, are possible to identify as the sources of documents because of the class characteristics of various makes of machines

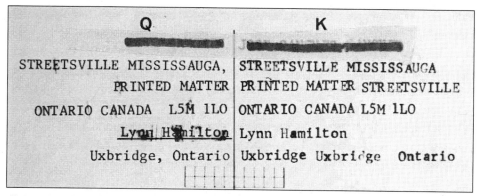

**Illustration 14-3.** Typewriter comparison of known to questioned sample.

and minute individual or accidental characteristics acquired during manufacture or use. A typewritten document contains characteristic differences in letters that can be microscopically compared to a sample made by a suspect machine. By examining the alignment of typewritten letters, one can see if additions have been made later. Forensic examiners can also investigate the date of manufacture of a typewriter to see if in fact it existed on the date of a questioned document it produced.

But typewriters are now in limited use, and most offices and individuals produce printed documents with computer-linked **printers**. These printers can produce an entire range of printing fonts in almost uniform fashion. Documents produced by the **dot matrix printers** that succeeded typewriters sometimes contain distinctive patterns that may be linked to specific machines. The pins that produce the letters may acquire individual characteristics that can be identified and matched to a document, but such defects are relatively rare. In any case, many dot matrix machines have been replaced by newer types of printers. **Inkjet** machines essentially spray the ink on paper; in rare instances, the distinctive splattering at the edges of letters can help examiners with aid of microscopy to find the printer at the origin of a document.

Documents made by **photocopiers** and **laser printers** are usually difficult to link to individual machines. It is also extremely hard for examiners to distinguish photocopied documents from those produced by laser printers, because laser printing and photocopying employ much the same process to fix ink to paper. Both use a **toner** that is usually a combination of carbon black and plastic, and both create an electrostatic pattern and then fuse toner to paper. While these processes usually result in documents with few distinctive identifying characteristics, there is usually more hope of matching in the case of some photocopiers, particularly those that are poorly maintained and in frequent use. You have noticed in the "collection" section of this chapter the instructions for investigators seizing photocopier evidence. The samples they take on clean blank paper and on graph paper can help forensic experts locate distinctive marks produced by a dirty platen glass or a scratched or dirty drum. These damaged or ill-maintained parts may leave distinctive lines or marks on copies that can be identified and matched to questioned documents.

Because much information is now electronically stored, **hard drives** and **disks** must be considered documents. Like paper documents, they must also be seized at a crime scene and later analyzed and connected to their authors. The laboratory detection of computer-related crimes—an electronic "break-and-enter" into a computer system by a hacker, a theft of money, information, telephone time, or software, or threats and harassment—still has the same goal as other investigations: to identify the evidence of the offence and the offender. And like all forensic specialists and other investigators, examiners must be able to account for the continuity or chain of evidence and to reconstruct in court the steps taken to analyze the evidence.

A trail of electronic impulses may at times be more difficult to follow, however, and only those expert in the use of computers and computer software can follow it. The recovery, translation, and analysis of computer files has come to require increasing sophistication on the part of police services. For this particular type of forensic examination, examiners carefully assemble the computer hardware and software needed. They then attempt to copy the material they are to examine, avoiding use of the original seized computers, disks, or hard drives. Using a full range of utility programs, they examine the data and print all files recovered, taking careful note of every step they have taken.

# THE INVESTIGATOR AS WITNESS: PRESENTATION OF EVIDENCE IN COURT

The ultimate end of a police investigation is a successful prosecution of the offender. While the majority of accused persons plead guilty to either the original charge or some lesser offence, many will plead not guilty and the matter will proceed to trial. It is at this point that you will take on another of the various roles of a police officer: the witness.

## THE ROLE OF THE WITNESS

In the Canadian legal system, the investigating officer is not a party to the trial. What that means is that, unlike in a lawsuit, for example, where the parties are the plaintiff, or the party suing, and the defendant, *a police officer is a witness like any other*. A police officer as witness is under the same obligation as any other witness testifying under oath, namely, *to tell the truth*.

While it may seem obvious, the importance of telling the truth when testifying cannot be overstressed. The success or failure of the entire system of justice depends upon the various players in the system performing their roles with integrity. If there is a perception that a police officer is not telling the truth under oath, not only may there be an injustice in the case at hand, but public confidence in the entire criminal law process will be undermined. It is not an overstatement to say that *it is a far more serious matter for a peace officer to lie under oath than for a civilian witness to do so*. Lying when testifying, or **perjury**, is a serious criminal offence, carrying with it a penalty of 14 years in most cases, and life imprisonment in the case of perjury at the trial of a capital offence.

# ORGANIZATION

As stated above, part of a police officer's job is to testify as a witness. Therefore, testifying at a trial should be approached with the same professionalism as any other aspect of your job.

Essential to testifying in a professional manner is being organized. Being organized means having a thorough grasp of all the relevant material you will be asked about. This may be as simple as reviewing your notes before court, or as complicated as reviewing and examining hundreds of complex documents. Whatever the particular case is about, or the amount of material involved, there is no excuse for a police officer as a professional witness to be unprepared.

Being prepared in the context of testifying means two things: first, having a detailed knowledge of the material or exhibits you are discussing or introducing; second, being able to access those materials easily when you are on the stand. A small amount of preparation before court will eliminate embarrassing or time-wasting delays and uncertainty. Your credibility in court, in the eyes of a judge or jury, will be adversely affected if you come across as unprofessional.

# COMMON DIFFICULTIES

Again, the most important thing to do when testifying is to tell the truth. However, even the honest witness can experience some difficulties testifying. The following are some examples of common problems witnesses face, and some suggestions on how to deal with them.

## Objectivity

As stated earlier, a police officer is not a party to the action or case. Therefore, in a strictly legal sense, the officer has no stake in whether a conviction is obtained. However, because a police officer has been so involved in the investigation, and may have put hours of work into it, it is easy for the officer to come across on the witness stand as being **biased** against the accused. This perception of bias can affect the degree to which a jury or judge accepts the officer's evidence: the judge or jury may feel the officer is too involved to testify objectively.

It is vitally important to remain objective when testifying. The purpose of a trial is for the trier of fact, whether a judge or a jury, to reach a conclusion about what really occurred. They reach this conclusion by listening to all the evidence. A single witness or police officer may not know everything that happened. That is why it is important for all witnesses, including investigators, to give the evidence they are able to contribute fairly and objectively.

## Uncertainty

Very often, witnesses will be asked questions to which they are unsure of the answers. This is to be expected, as different people will focus on different things when an event occurs, especially when it occurs quickly.

There is a tendency on the part of witnesses, however, to try to answer every question. This is simply human nature: people want to be helpful, and when they are asked something, they want to be of assistance, and they may guess the answer as a result.

The problem with this tendency, however, is that when the witness is wrong it can make that witness look wrong, or worse, it can make the witness look like a liar. In order to avoid giving this impression, *the best advice is simply to admit when you are not sure about something.* You should do this not only because you will come across as a better witness, but because sometimes "I am not sure" is the truthful answer, and your job as a witness is to tell the truth. It doesn't matter that you don't remember a particular event: another witness may well be called to fill in any gaps you leave in the story.

Similarly, if you are certain of something, say so.

## Arguments

Often a question asked by a lawyer to a witness will seem rude or argumentative. It may be something in the lawyer's tone, or in the nature of the question itself. Whatever the reason, it is very easy to find yourself arguing with a lawyer or answering rudely. This is a potentially ruinous mistake for two reasons.

First, rules of evidence govern what is a proper or improper question. If the court allows the lawyer to ask a question, however rudely, it means the court wants to hear the answer. If you snap at the questioner, or argue, or appear facetious, you are not being rude to a (deserving) lawyer: you are failing to answer a question the court wants an answer to.

Second, the lawyer may want you to argue with him or her. This may be to prevent you from giving the court the information it wants (as above), or to put you off-balance. It may also be to make you look biased against the accused. *Whatever the reason, it doesn't matter if you "win" the argument.* By getting into it, you have lost.

## Understanding the Question

All lawyers, whether prosecutors or defence counsel, often think of a question on their feet. That is, not all questions are prepared. Therefore, as in all verbal communication, the meaning of a question can be unclear.

Don't try to guess what the lawyer meant by the question. You may end up only appearing evasive if you get it wrong. Simply advise the lawyer you didn't understand the question. The court can then ask the lawyer to either repeat the question or rephrase it.

## Conclusion

Being a witness is one of the most important roles you will be called upon to perform as a police officer. It is an important part of your job, and should be approached in an organized, professional manner. Most importantly, however, you must always be completely truthful when testifying.

# RULES OF EVIDENCE

After the evidence has been gathered, the final stage of the investigation is to have it presented in court. At this point, the **law of evidence** comes into play.

The rules of evidence comprise an enormous amount of law. While there are specific statutes dealing with the admissibility of evidence, for the most part the law of evidence is found in the common law, or past cases ruled on by judges. Numerous textbooks have attempted to summarize the law of evidence, and many aspects of the law of evidence are the subject of debate: that is, many legal issues involving the admissibility of certain types of evidence are unresolved.

Therefore, in a brief overview such as this, it would be impossible to do more than simply touch upon some of the dominant themes in the admissibility of evidence in criminal trials. But it may still be of assistance to an investigator to be aware of some of the general rules of evidence in Canadian law.

## Relevance and Prejudice

The traditional rule in common law is that evidence will be admissible at trial where it is relevant to a matter at issue, and where its probative value outweighs its prejudicial effect.

Relevance in this context is more or less meant in its usual way: *a thing is* **relevant** *to a matter when it tends to either prove or disprove a fact in issue.* For example, fingerprints of an accused person found on a weapon are relevant in that they tend to show that person held the weapon, which may be an issue at the trial. Similarly, someone else's fingerprints on the same weapon are relevant in that they might suggest someone other than the accused may have held the weapon at the time in question.

Once the particular piece of evidence has been shown to be relevant, the court then must determine whether the **probative value** of the evidence outweighs any potentially prejudicial effect it may have. What this means is the court must decide whether the degree to which the piece of evidence might prove something in issue (the probative value) is somehow negated or outweighed by some potentially unfair inference it might give rise to in the mind of the trier of fact (**prejudicial effect**).

"Prejudicial" in this context does not simply mean negative or against the interests of the accused. After all, what could be more "prejudicial" to a person on trial than ten eyewitnesses pointing at him saying "He did it?" Rather, *prejudicial in this context refers to improper or unfair assumptions or inferences that a judge or jury might consider in determining the guilt of the accused.*

For example, subject to certain exceptions such as rules about similar fact evidence and criminal records on cross-examination (there are always exceptions in law), generally speaking the prosecution cannot introduce evidence of an accused person's prior bad character. The reason for this general rule is that while it may be relevant (a convincing case could be made for the proposition that bad people are more likely to do bad things), the courts are concerned a jury or trier of fact might simply assume that accused persons committed crimes because of that prior bad conduct. Worse still, the triers of fact might seek to punish the accused for those prior bad incidents by convicting them in the present case, for which there may otherwise be little evidence linking them to the crime. In that way, the prejudicial effect of introducing those prior bad behaviours outweighs whatever (arguable) probative value they may have.

## Admissibility vs. Weight

It is important to distinguish between the **admissibility** of evidence and its **weight**. The fact that evidence is admissible to prove something does not mean that it will prove that thing. The trier of fact, which is either a jury or the judge when the judge is sitting without a jury, is allowed to attach whatever weight it sees fit to the evidence. For example, the testimony of a witness who claims to have seen something would be admissible if it is relevant and not unduly prejudicial. However, the trier of fact may attach little weight to the evidence: perhaps the witness has poor eyesight. Similarly, a trier of fact may have problems with the credibility of the witness: that is, the jury may not believe him or her.

## Other Rules of Evidence

Of course, there are many more rules regarding specific types of evidence than simply the general ones about relevance, probative value, and prejudice. Those rules involve the specific admissibility of such things as documents, hearsay, confessions, etc. Those rules are to be found in specific statutes, such as the Canada Evidence Act and the Criminal Code of Canada, and in cases or the common law. Obviously, it would be impossible to discuss them in the context of this section of the text. However, there is one area of the law of evidence that should be addressed: the law regarding the admissibility of evidence obtained as a result of the violation of an accused person's rights.

# TRADITIONAL VIEWS OF ILLEGALLY OBTAINED EVIDENCE

With the general exceptions of statements or confessions made by accused persons, courts did not concern themselves traditionally with the manner in which evidence was obtained. In other words, the way in which particular pieces of evidence were obtained by investigators, whether lawfully or unlawfully, did not affect their admissibility in evidence.

The reason for this lack of remedy for accused persons was that there was no law or rule excluding illegally obtained evidence. The only issue was whether that evidence complied with the general law of admissibility. If a law was broken by an investigator, that could be dealt with subsequently, either criminally, in a civil case, or through the police disciplinary procedures.

This view was the rule in Canadian law until the enactment of the **Constitution Act of 1982**. The view that a breach of this law or of the rights of an accused could not lead to the exclusion of evidence (again, other than confessions) came to Canadian law via English common law.

The difficulty with admitting evidence no matter how it was obtained was that it seemed there was no consequence to the state for violating a citizen's rights: in the end, the evidence went in anyway. And to many people, this created a perception of unfairness in the criminal trial process.

## The American Experience

One approach to dealing with the perceived harshness of the traditional admissibility of illegally or wrongfully obtained evidence can be found in the United States. There are many exceptions to the following rule in American law that cannot be dealt with here, but generally speaking American courts have held that evidence obtained or derived from a breach of an accused person's rights will not be admissible at trial. This approach can be seen as exactly opposite to the British (and Canadian, prior to 1982) view of the issue.

The advantage to this approach is that the perceived unfairness in the British common law model as between an accused person and the state is eliminated: if the state or its agents in some way violate an individual's constitutional rights, the evidence obtained as a result is excluded from the trial.

The disadvantage to that approach is that, again bearing in mind there are certain exceptions, any evidence will be excluded however minor the breach of the accused person's rights. That is, no matter how small or inadvertent the breach, essential, probative, and relevant evidence will be excluded. Hence the entry into our language of the notion of "getting off on a technicality": the (arguably) noble or proper goal of preventing the violation of persons' rights can result in evidence being excluded for (arguably) trivial breaches.

## The Charter of Rights and Freedoms

In drafting the Charter of Rights and Freedoms (see Appendix C), its Canadian authors had to address the debate between the traditional Anglo-Canadian rule regarding unlawfully obtained evidence and the strictly exclusionary rule in the United States. Rather than choose one or the other, the drafters of the Charter chose a (some might say typically Canadian) middle route. Under the Charter, evidence obtained as the result of the violation of a right or freedom contained in it can be excluded pursuant to the Charter's section 24(2):

> Where ... a court concludes that evidence was obtained in a manner that infringed or denied any rights or freedoms guaranteed by this Charter, the evidence shall be excluded if it is established that, having regard to all the circumstances, the admission of it in the proceedings would bring the administration of justice into disrepute.

In other words, while evidence obtained as a result of a violation of an accused person's rights may lead to that evidence being excluded, it will only be excluded where it is established that admitting that evidence at trial would bring the administration of justice into disrepute.

Therefore, in Canada, the onus is firstly on an accused to establish that one of his or her Charter rights have been violated in some way. At that point, the court considers whether the admission of that evidence would bring the administration of justice into disrepute.

Of course, it is in that determination that the legal "battle" takes place. While every case is in its own way unique, and it is difficult to generalize in a brief summary such as this, some guidance for an investigator can be found in the Supreme Court of

Canada's decision in *Regina v. Collins* [1987] 1 S.C.R. 265, 56 C.R. (3a) 193, 33 C.C.C. (3d) 1 (S.C.C.). In that case, the court set out a three-stage approach to determine how admission of evidence would affect the administration. The Supreme Court held that a trial judge should consider (1) how admitting the evidence would **affect the fairness of the trial** and (2) the **seriousness of the violation of the right or rights** in question.

As to the first factor, the effect on the fairness of the trial, generally speaking *what the court considers here is the source of the evidence*. That is, was the evidence obtained as the result of the breach **conscriptive evidence**—evidence provided by the accused against himself? If so, *such evidence will more likely be excluded as opposed to real physical evidence*, as it offends notions of the right against self-incrimination. In other words, it is more "unfair" to conscript an accused as effectively a witness against him- or herself at trial. Examples of conscriptive evidence are statements by the accused and breath samples. Again, conscriptive evidence will likely be excluded if it is obtained in violation of a Charter right.

The second factor a court considers is the seriousness of the breach of the Charter right. *A more serious breach is more likely to lead to the exclusion of evidence than a minor one.* In this way, the Charter attempts to address the concerns raised by the American approach of automatic exclusion. Nonetheless, the courts take all Charter breaches seriously, and only the most trivial breaches generally will be saved by this consideration.

Finally, the courts consider the effect exclusion will have on the perception of the administration of justice. While this consideration is similar to considering the seriousness of the offence in that it would suggest inclusion of evidence obtained through a trivial breach, there is also a suggestion that the seriousness of the offence may be a factor supporting inclusion versus exclusion. However, it must always be remembered that the repute or disrepute of the administration of justice is in the eyes of the courts, not public opinion or the eyes of the law enforcement community. It is submitted that it would be very rare for a piece of evidence otherwise considered to make a proceeding unfair or obtained via a serious breach to be "saved" by resort to this part of the *Collins* test.

*In fact, since the decision in* Collins, *the courts have generally tended to exclude rather than include evidence. Therefore, it is probably best for an investigator to proceed from the assumption that evidence obtained as the result of a Charter breach will be excluded at trial.*

## Unreasonable Search or Seizure

Section 8 of the Canadian Charter of Rights and Freedoms states:

Everyone has the right to be secure against unreasonable search or seizure.

This section enshrines a **constitutional right to privacy for individuals**. Section 8 protects this right to privacy by preventing the state from searching and seizing people and their property. *Individuals are protected against unreasonable search and seizure anywhere that each individual has a reasonable expectation of privacy.* The protection includes both the physical person of the individual and places. The principle that section 8 protects individuals where they have a reasonable expectation of privacy is found in the Supreme Court of Canada's decision in the case *Hunter v. Southam Inc.* [1984] 41 C.R. (3d) 97 (S.C.C.). That case further states that **a search, without a warrant, of a place where a person has such a reasonable expectation of privacy is *prima facie* unreasonable**. (*Prima facie* means self-evident, without need of proof or argument.) That is, the court will assume a violation of section 8 where there is warrantless search of a protected place.

It is impossible in this brief description to discuss in detail all the factors the courts consider to determine whether a privacy right extends to a given place, but they include such ones as the **use or purpose of the place**, the **ease or restrictions of access** to it, and **ownership or possession** of the place. The decision about any given place or kind of place must be made by the judge in each individual case. *In the past, the courts have found a right to privacy not only with respect to people's bodies and homes, but also to their offices, motor vehicles, and other places.*

There are, of course, exceptions to the rule requiring warrants, such as **searches for weapons incidental to arrest** and **cases where a warrantless search is necessary to preserve evidence**. Nonetheless, those cases are rare exceptions, and wherever possible, prior judicial authorization of a search or seizure in the form of a search warrant must be obtained to prevent a breach of section 8. As stated above, the breach of an individual's Charter rights can have a serious effect on your investigation.

## Conclusion

Any violation of an individual's rights as guaranteed by the Charter of Rights and Freedoms can have a devastating impact on an investigation. As discussed above, a Charter violation at one point or in one aspect of an investigation has the potential to render inadmissible evidence obtained elsewhere in the investigation. *It is therefore vitally important, perhaps more than ever before in Canadian criminal law, that procedures with respect to obtaining evidence be followed throughout the course of an investigation.* While the law is always changing, a grasp of both the rights of accused persons and the implications of those rights in the evidence-gathering process is essential to present-day investigators.

# MAJOR CRIME SCENE PROTOCOLS: JUDICIAL INSTRUCTIONS TO POLICE

On June 26th, 1996, the Lieutenant Governor in Council directed that a Public Inquiry be held to investigate the circumstances involved in the wrongful conviction of Mr. Guy Paul Morin. The Honourable Fred Kaufman, Q.C., a former judge of the Quebec Court of Appeal, was appointed as Commissioner of this board. The Order in Council directed the Commission to inquire into the conduct of the investigation into the death of Christine Jessop, the conduct of the Centre of Forensic Sciences in relation to the maintenance, security, and preservation of forensic evidence, and into the criminal proceedings involving the charge that Guy Paul Morin murdered Christine Jessop. Furthermore, the Commission was also directed to make such recommendations as it considers advisable relating to the administration of criminal justice in Ontario. The mandate of the Commission was threefold: investigative, advisory, and educational.

The hearings began on February 10th, 1997 and continued for 146 days. The Commission utilized the testimony of one hundred and twenty witnesses as well as the transcripts of evidence from both trials and documents filed with the Ontario Court of Appeal. The fruition of this inquiry was 119 individual recommendations for change, of which 33 recommendations are directly concerned with the collection, maintenance, security, and preservation of forensic evidence. The final three recommendations, i.e., #117, 118, and 119, focus on the acceptance and implementation of this report by the Government of Ontario. Once legislated into law these recommendations will have a major effect on the practical application of crime scene examination, and the presentation of forensic evidence in court. In addition to these recommendations, the degree of sensitivity of the most recent DNA technologies demand the forensic investigator to adopt additional strategies to avoid the possibility of cross-contamination.

This precis will address Mr. Justice Kaufman's concerns and introduce a number of protocols which will result in the reduction of possible cross-contamination. The Commission's recommendations, relevant to forensic evidence, will be presented as they have been in the April 1998 report. The protocols for forensic crime scene examiners will be detailed at the conclusion of the Commission's recommendations.

## Recommendation 2: Admissibility of hair comparison evidence

Trial judges should undertake a more critical analysis of the admissibility of hair comparison evidence as circumstantial evidence of guilt. Evidence that shows only that an accused cannot be excluded as the donor of an unknown hair (or only that an accused may or may not have been the donor) is unlikely to have sufficient probative value to justify its reception at a criminal trial as circumstantial evidence of guilt.

## Recommendation 3: Admissibility of fibre comparison evidence

Evidence of forensic fibre comparisons may or may not have sufficient probative value to justify its reception at a criminal trial as circumstantial evidence of the accused's guilt. However, the limitations upon the inferences to be reliably drawn from forensic fibre comparisons needs be better appreciated by judges, police, Crown and defence counsel. This requires better education of all parties, improved communication of forensic evidence and its limitations in and out of court, in written reports and orally.

## Recommendation 5: Trial judge's instructions on science

Where hair and fibre comparison evidence or other scientific evidence is tendered as evidence of guilt, the trial judge would be well advised to instruct the jury not to be overwhelmed by an aura of scientific authority or infallibility associated with the evidence and to clearly articulate for the jury the limitations upon the findings made by the experts. In the context of scientific evidence, it is of particular importance that the trial judge ensure that counsel, when addressing the jury, do not misuse the evidence, but present it to the Court with no more or no less than its legitimate force and effect.

## Recommendation 6: Forensic opinions to be acted upon only when in writing

(a) No police officer or Crown counsel should take action affecting an accused or a potential accused based upon representations made by a forensic scientist which are not recorded in writing, unless it is impracticable to await a written record. Where a written record is not obtained prior to such action, it should be obtained as soon thereafter as is practicable.

(b) The Crown Policy Manual and the Durham Regional Police Service operations manual should be amended to reflect this approach. The Ministry of the Solicitor General should facilitate the creation of a similar policy for all Ontario police forces.

(c) Where a written record is only obtained after such action, and it reveals that the authorities acted upon a misapprehension of the available forensic evidence, police and prosecutors should be mindful of their obligation to take corrective action, depending upon the original action taken. Corrective action would, for example, include the immediate disclosure of the written record to the defence and, if requested, to the Court, where the forensic evidence has been misrepresented (even inadvertently) in Court. It would also include the re-assessment of any actions done in reliance upon misapprehended evidence.

## Recommendation 7: Written policy for forensic reports

The Centre of Forensic Sciences should establish a written policy on the form and content of reports issued by its analysts. The Centre should draw upon the work done by forensic agencies elsewhere and the input of other stakeholders in the administration of criminal justice who will be receiving and acting upon these reports. In addition to other essential components, these reports must contain the conclusions drawn from the forensic testing and the limitations placed upon those conclusions.

## Recommendation 8: The use of appropriate forensic language

The Centre of Forensic Sciences should endeavour to establish a policy for the use of certain uniform language which is not potentially misleading and which enhances understanding. This policy should draw upon the work done by forensic agencies or working groups elsewhere and the input of other stakeholders in the administration of criminal justice. This policy should be made public.

# Recommendation 9: Specific language to be avoided by forensic scientists

More specifically, certain language is demonstrably misleading in the context of certain forensic disciplines. The terms "match" and "consistent with" used in the context of forensic hair and fibre comparisons are examples of potentially misleading language. CFS employees should be instructed to avoid demonstrably misleading language.

# Recommendation 10: Specific language to be adopted

Certain language enhances understanding and more clearly reflects the limitations upon scientific findings. For example, some scientists state that an item "may or may not" have originated from a particular person or object. This language is preferable to a statement that an item "could have" originated from that person or object, not only because the limitations are clearer, but also because the same conclusion is expressed in more neutral terms.

# Recommendation 11: The scientific method

The "scientific method" means that scientists are to work to vigorously challenge or disprove a hypothesis, rather than to prove one. Forensic scientists at the Centre should be instructed to adopt this approach, particularly in connection with a hypotheses that a suspect or accused is forensically linked to the crime.

# Recommendation 12: Policy respecting correction of misinterpreted forensic evidence

A forensic scientist may leave the witness stand concerned that his or her evidence is being misinterpreted or that a misperception has been left about the conclusions which can be drawn or the limitations upon those conclusions. An obligation should be placed on the expert to ensure that these concerns are communicated as soon as possible to Crown or defence council. Where communicated to Crown counsel, an immediate disclosure obligation is triggered. The Crown Policy Manual and the Centre's policies should be amended to reflect these obligations. The Centre's employees should be trained to adhere to this policy.

## Recommendation 14: Policy respecting documentation of work performed

(a) The Centre of Forensic Sciences should establish written policies regulating the content of records kept by analysts and technicians of the work done at the Centre. At the least, these policies must ensure that the records identify the precise work done, when it was done by whom it was done and the identity of any others who assisted, or were present as observers when the work was performed. The policy should also regulate the retention period and location of these records. All records referable to the work done on a criminal case must be located within the file(s) respecting that criminal case (or their location clearly noted in that file).

(b) The Centre of Forensic Sciences should ensure that all employees are trained to comply with the recording policies.

## Recommendation 15: Documentation of contamination

(a) Where in-house contamination is discovered or suspected by the Centre of Forensic Sciences, the contamination should be fully investigated in a timely manner. The contamination and its investigation should be fully documented. A copy of such documentation should be placed in any case file to which the contamination may relate. The matter should immediately be brought to the attention of the Director, the Quality Assurance Unit and the relevant Crown counsel. The Centre's written policies should reflect these requirements.

(b) The Centre of Forensic Sciences should ensure that its employees are regularly trained to comply with the policies reflected in this recommendation.

## Recommendation 16: Documentation of lost evidence

Where original evidence in the possession of the Centre of Forensic Sciences is lost, the loss should be fully investigated in a timely manner. The loss and its investigation should be fully documented. A copy of such documentation should be placed in any case file to which the original evidence relates. The matter should immediately be brought to the attention of the Director, the Quality Assurance Unit and the relevant Crown counsel. The Centre's written policies should reflect these requirements. In this context, original evidence extends to work notes, communication logs or other material which is subject to disclosure.

# Recommendation 20: Quality assurance unit

(a) The recent establishment of a quality assurance unit by the Centre is to be commended. The unit's staffing and mandate should be reflected in written policies. Dedicated funds should be allocated to the quality assurance unit, adequate to implement this recommendation. The unit's budget should be insulated from erosion for operational use elsewhere.

(c) The unit should include a training offer, responsible for internal and external training.

(d) The unit should include a standards officer, responsible for writing, or overseeing the writing of policies

# Recommendation 24: Monitoring of courtroom testimony

The Centre of Forensic Sciences should more regularly monitor the courtroom testimony given by its employees. Monitoring should, where practicable, be done through personal attendance by peers or supervisors. Monitoring should exceed the minimum accreditation requirements. All scientists, regardless of seniority, should be monitored. Any concerns should be promptly taken up with the testing scientist.

The monitoring scientist should be instructed that any observed overstatement or misstatement of evidence triggers an immediate obligation to advise the appropriate trail counsel.

# Recommendation 25: Training of Centre of Forensic Sciences employees

The Centre of Forensic Sciences' training program should be broadened to include, in addition to mentoring components, formalized, ongoing programs to educate staff on a full range of issues: scientific methodology, continuity, note keeping, scientific developments, testimonial matters, independence and impartiality, report writing, the use of language, the scope and limitations upon findings, and ethics. This can only come with the appropriate allocation of funding dedicated to training.

# Recommendation 26: Proficiency testing

The Centre of Forensic Sciences should increase proficiency testing of its scientists. Efforts should be made to increase the use of blind and external proficiency testing for analysts. Proficiency testing should evaluate not only technical skills, but interpretive skills.

## Recommendation 29: Post-conviction retention of original evidence

The Ministries of the Attorney General and the Solicitor General, in consultation with the defence bar and other stakeholders in the administration of criminal justice, should establish protocols for the post-conviction retention of original evidence in criminal cases.

## Recommendation 72: Skills, training and resources

(a) Rank and file officers need to be educated and trained on a continuing basis on a wide range of investigative skills. Their educators need themselves to be fully trained in these skills and in their communication to others. Financial resources need be available, secure from erosion for operational purposes, to ensure that training for all Ontario police forces is state-of-art.

## Recommendation 91: Minimum standards for police

(a) The Ministry of the Solicitor General should consider setting minimum provincial standards respecting the initial and ongoing training of police officers on a full range of subjects, relevant to the issues identified at this Inquiry.

(b) The Ministry of the Solicitor General should consider setting minimum provincial standards for conduct of criminal investigations, relevant to the issues identified at this Inquiry.

## Recommendation 93: Body site searches

When conducting searches at a body site, police investigators should be mindful of the lessons learned at this Inquiry. Such lessons include the desirability of:

(a) a grid search;

(b) preservation of the scene against inclement weather;

(c) adequate lighting;

(d) coordinated search parties, with documented search areas;

(e) a search plan and search coordinator;

(f) full documentation of items found and retained, together with precise location and continuity;

(g) adequate videotaping and photographing of scene;

(h) adequate indexing of exhibits and photographs;

(i) adequate facilities and methods for transportation of the remains;

(j) decontamination suits in some instances;

(k) resources to avoid cross-contamination of different sites. This may require that different officers collect evidence at different sites, where a forensic connection between the sites may be investigated.

# PROTOCOLS

The majority of these recommendations specifically cite the Centre of Forensic Sciences as the agency responsible for the maintenance, security, and preservation of forensic evidence. However, this agency can only analyze the forensic evidence it receives from police investigators. If this material has been contaminated at its source the results of any subsequent CFS analysis will be flawed.

The elimination of cross-contamination, as well as the possible perception of cross-contamination, should be the impetus for implementing a number of protocols relating to crime scene management. Adherence to the following protocols will address Mr. Justice concerns and establish the Toronto Police Service as one of the world's most proactive agencies with respect to the collection and handling of forensic evidence.

## Protocol 1: Multiple Site Examinations

The investigator(s) involved in the examination of one crime scene will not attend a second crime scene, nor have contact with any suspect. A second investigator, having no prior contact with the first crime scene, will attend the second site or interview room. Where this is not practicable, the original investigator(s) may attend a second site or interview room with a suspect upon completion of following directions:

1. the investigator(s) must don a new "officer protection suit," including complete hair and footwear protection.

2. the investigator(s) have the opportunity to bathe/shower and change their clothes, including footwear, worn at the original site.

## Protocol 2: Officer Protection Suits

These garments will be worn by crime scene investigators for each major crime scene. Where one building may contain more than one crime scene, e.g., a house with victims in more than one room, the investigator will change his/her officer protection suit prior to exiting each room and don a new officer protection suit prior to entering the second scene. The officer protection suits will not be discarded, but rather packaged and identified as an exhibit. These suits will be designated with the next sequential exhibit number.

## Protocol 3: Latex Gloves

The investigator will utilize latex gloves during the collection of all forensic evidence. One pair of latex gloves should be worn for one forensic sample. In the case where specific biological samples are collected from a scene the latex gloves will be retained and designated as an exhibit, e.g., if a bloodstain sample is collected from a wall it may be designated as Exhibit #500, the adjacent control sample may be designated as Exhibit #500A, and the latex gloves used to collect this evidence may be designated as Exhibit #500B.

## Protocol 4: Evidence Storage Areas

The investigator will be responsible for cleaning the evidence locker/drying room with an ammonia based cleaning solution and disposable cloth upon the completion of storage of evidence. Once the area has been cleaned, the investigator will line the floor with a fresh piece of Kraft paper to act as a drop cloth. The previous drop cloth, used by the current investigator, will be retained and designated as an exhibit with the next sequential exhibit number. A plastic envelope will be affixed to the exterior of the lockers/drying rooms which will contain a list to record the investigator's name and date of cleaning.

Exhibits seized from a crime scene will not be stored in the same locker/drying room as any exhibits seized from a suspect or accused person regardless of whether or not the exhibits have been securely packaged.

## Protocol 5: Documentation of Work Performed

A written policy should be implemented to outline the content of work performed by an investigator as it relates to the forensic evidence. The investigator would provide a list of processes used on individual exhibits. This list would also identify when this work was completed, by whom it was done, and the identity of any others who assisted, or were present as observers when the work was done. A copy of this report will be inserted into the case file and be made available for disclosure.

# Protocol 6: Documentation of Contamination

Where in-house contamination is discovered or suspected by Forensic Identification Services, the contamination will be fully investigated in a timely manner. The contamination and its investigation should be fully documented. A copy of such documentation should be placed in any case file to which the contamination may relate. The matter should immediately be brought to the attention of the F.I.S. Director, the Quality Assurance Unit and the relevant Crown council.

For the purposes of this protocol "in-house contamination" includes the alteration, deliberate or otherwise, of a crime scene or any evidence by members of this police service or any member of the public.

# Protocol 7: Documentation of Lost Evidence

Where original evidence in the possession of Forensic Identification Services is lost, the loss should be fully investigated in a timely manner. The loss and its investigation should be fully documented. A copy of such documentation should be placed in any case file to which the original evidence relates. The matter should immediately be brought to the attention of the Director, the Quality Assurance Unit, and the relevant Crown counsel.

# Protocol 8: Quality Assurance Unit

This internal unit will oversee the ethical quality of investigative practices and the handling of physical evidence within F.I.S. The Quality Assurance Unit will set policy and minimum requirements for forensic investigators.

(a) The unit should include a training officer, responsible for internal and external training.

(b) The unit should include a standards officer, responsible for writing, or overseeing the writing of policies.

# Protocol 9: Monitoring of Courtroom Testimony

Forensic Identification Services should more regularly monitor the courtroom testimony given by its members. Monitoring should, where practicable, be done through personal attendance by peers or supervisors. All forensic investigators, regardless of seniority, should be monitored. Any concerns should be promptly taken up with the forensic investigator. The monitoring investigator should be instructed that any observed overstatement or misstatement of evidence triggers an immediate obligation to advise the appropriate trial counsel.

## Protocol 10: The Scientific Method

The "scientific method" means that forensic investigators are to work to vigorously challenge or disprove a hypothesis, rather than to prove one. Forensic investigators, employed by a police service, must retain their impartiality throughout an investigation. Professionalism and impartiality dictates that all evidence, whether inculpatory or exculpatory, be documented, collected, examined, and disclosed in an efficient manner.

In the case of interpretive evidence, such as bloodstain patterns, the analyst must employ the scientific method through experimentation. These experiments must test the Crown's hypothesis as well as that of the suspect or accused.

## Protocol 11: Proficiency Testing

Forensic Identification Services should establish a minimum standard for its forensic investigators and implement a proficiency test paradigm. The curriculum should include crime scene management and cross-contamination avoidance methods. This testing should be administered by the Quality Assurance Unit at regular intervals, not less than once per annum.

## Protocol 12: Body Site Searches

When conducting searches at a body site forensic investigators will:

(a) Establish a grid search of the site at ground level. If excavation becomes necessary, retain ground level grid pattern in concert with stratigraphic profile;

(b) Preserve the scene against inclement weather;

(c) Ensure adequate lighting is used;

(d) Co-ordinate search parties with documented search areas;

(e) Establish a search plan and appoint one investigator as a search co-ordinator. This officer will be responsible for co-ordinating a final search for evidence at the site. This measure will be independent of the first search;

(f) Ensure full documentation of items found and retained (including adequate videotaping and photography), together with precise location and continuity;

(g) Utilize adequate indexing of exhibits and photographs;

(h) Utilize adequate facilities and methods for transportation of the remains;

(i) Employ the previous protocols as they relate to cross-contamination.

# IDENTIFICATION OF CRIMINALS ACT

1.1 This Act is binding on Her Majesty in right of Canada or a province. 1992, c. 47, s. 73.

## IDENTIFICATION OF CRIMINALS

### Fingerprints and photographs

2. (1) The following persons may be fingerprinted or photographed or subjected to such other measurements, processes and operations having the object of identifying persons as are approved by order of the Governor in Council:

    (a) any person who is in lawful custody charged with or convicted of

        (i) an indictable offence, other than an offence that is designated as a contravention under the Contraventions Act in respect of which the Attorney General, within the meaning of that Act, has made an election under section 50 of that Act, or

        (ii) an offence under the Official Secrets Act;

    (b) any person who has been apprehended under the Extradition Act or the Fugitive Offenders Act; or

    (c) any person alleged to have committed an indictable offence, other than an offence that is designated as a contravention under the Contraventions Act in respect of which the Attorney General, within the meaning of that Act, has made an election under section 50 of that Act, who is required pursuant to subsection 501(3) or 509(5) of the Criminal Code to appear for the purposes of this Act by an appearance notice, promise to appear, recognizance or summons.

## Use of force

(2) Such force may be used as is necessary to the effectual carrying out and application of the measurements, processes and operations described under subsection (1).

## Publication

(3) The results of the measurements, processes and operations to which a person has been subjected pursuant to subsection (1) may be published for the purpose of affording information to officers and others engaged in the execution or administration of the law.

R.S., 1985, c. I-1, s. 2; 1992, c. 47, s. 74; 1996, c. 7, s. 39.

## No liability for acting under Act

3. No liability, civil or criminal, for anything lawfully done under this Act shall be incurred by any person

(a) having custody of a person described in subsection 2(1);

(b) acting in the aid or under the direction of a person having such custody; or

(c) concerned in the publication of results under subsection 2(3).

R.S., 1985, c. I-1, s. 3; 1992, c. 47, s. 75.

# DESTRUCTION OF FINGERPRINTS AND PHOTOGRAPHS

4. Where a person charged with an offence that is designated as a contravention under the Contraventions Act is fingerprinted or photographed and the Attorney General, within the meaning of that Act, makes an election under section 50 of that Act, the fingerprints or photographs shall be destroyed.

1992, c. 47, s. 76; 1996, c. 7, s. 40.

# CANADIAN CHARTER OF RIGHTS AND FREEDOMS

*Schedule B*
**Constitution Act, 1982 (79)**
Enacted as Schedule B to the Canada Act 1982 (U.K.) 1982, c. 11, which came into force on April 17, 1982

# PART I
# Canadian Charter of Rights and Freedoms

Whereas Canada is founded upon principles that recognize the supremacy of God and the rule of law:

## GUARANTEE OF RIGHTS AND FREEDOMS

### Rights and freedoms in Canada

1. The Canadian Charter of Rights and Freedoms guarantees the rights and freedoms set out in it subject only to such reasonable limits prescribed by law as can be demonstrably justified in a free and democratic society.

## FUNDAMENTAL FREEDOMS

2. Everyone has the following fundamental freedoms:
    (a) freedom of conscience and religion;
    (b) freedom of thought, belief, opinion and expression, including freedom of the press and other media of communication;
    (c) freedom of peaceful assembly; and
    (d) freedom of association.

## DEMOCRATIC RIGHTS

### Democratic rights of citizens

3. Every citizen of Canada has the right to vote in an election of members of the House of Commons or of a legislative assembly and to be qualified for membership therein.

### Maximum duration of legislative bodies

4. (1) No House of Commons and no legislative assembly shall continue for longer than five years from the date fixed for the return of the writs of a general election of its members.

## Continuation in special circumstances

(2) In time of real or apprehended war, invasion or insurrection, a House of Commons may be continued by Parliament and a legislative assembly may be continued by the legislature beyond five years if such continuation is not opposed by the votes of more than one-third of the members of the House of Commons or the legislative assembly, as the case may be.

## Annual sitting of legislative bodies

5. There shall be a sitting of Parliament and of each legislature at least once every twelve months

# MOBILITY RIGHTS

## Mobility of citizens

6. (1) Every citizen of Canada has the right to enter, remain in and leave Canada.

## Rights to move and gain livelihood

(2) Every citizen of Canada and every person who has the status of a permanent resident of Canada has the right

   (a) to move to and take up residence in any province; and

   (b) to pursue the gaining of a livelihood in any province.

## Limitation

(3) The rights specified in subsection (2) are subject to

   (a) any laws or practices of general application in force in a province other than those that discriminate among persons primarily on the basis of province of present or previous residence; and

   (b) any laws providing for reasonable residency requirements as a qualification for the receipt of publicly provided social services.

## Affirmative action programs

(4) Subsections (2) and (3) do not preclude any law, program or activity that has as its object the amelioration in a province of conditions of individuals

in that province who are socially or economically disadvantaged if the rate of employment in that province is below the rate of employment in Canada.

# LEGAL RIGHTS

## Life, liberty and security of person

7. Everyone has the right to life, liberty and security of the person and the right not to be deprived thereof except in accordance with the principles of fundamental justice.

## Search or seizure

8. Everyone has the right to be secure against unreasonable search or seizure.

## Detention or imprisonment

9. Everyone has the right not to be arbitrarily detained or imprisoned.

## Arrest or detention

10. Everyone has the right on arrest or detention

   (a) to be informed promptly of the reasons therefor;

   (b) to retain and instruct counsel without delay and to be informed of that right; and

   (c) to have the validity of the detention determined by way of habeas corpus and to be released if the detention is not lawful.

## Proceedings in criminal and penal matters

11. Any person charged with an offence has the right

   (a) to be informed without unreasonable delay of the specific offence;

   (b) to be tried within a reasonable time;

   (c) not to be compelled to be a witness in proceedings against that person in respect of the offence;

   (d) to be presumed innocent until proven guilty according to law in a fair and public hearing by an independent and impartial tribunal;

   (e) not to be denied reasonable bail without just cause;

(f) except in the case of an offence under military law tried before a military tribunal, to the benefit of trial by jury where the maximum punishment for the offence is imprisonment for five years or a more severe punishment;

(g) not to be found guilty on account of any act or omission unless, at the time of the act or omission, it constituted an offence under Canadian or international law or was criminal according to the general principles of law recognized by the community of nations;

(h) if finally acquitted of the offence, not to be tried for it again and, if finally found guilty and punished for the offence, not to be tried or punished for it again; and

(i) if found guilty of the offence and if the punishment for the offence has been varied between the time of commission and the time of sentencing, to the benefit of the lesser punishment.

## Treatment or punishment

12. Everyone has the right not to be subjected to any cruel and unusual treatment or punishment.

## Self-crimination

13. A witness who testifies in any proceedings has the right not to have any incriminating evidence so given used to incriminate that witness in any other proceedings, except in a prosecution for perjury or for the giving of contradictory evidence.

## Interpreter

14. A party or witness in any proceedings who does not understand or speak the language in which the proceedings are conducted or who is deaf has the right to the assistance of an interpreter.

# EQUALITY RIGHTS

## Equality before and under law and equal protection and benefit of law

15. (1) Every individual is equal before and under the law and has the right to the equal protection and equal benefit of the law without discrimination and, in

particular, without discrimination based on race, national or ethnic origin, colour, religion, sex, age or mental or physical disability.

## Affirmative action programs

(2) Subsection (1) does not preclude any law, program or activity that has as its object the amelioration of conditions of disadvantaged individuals or groups including those that are disadvantaged because of race, national or ethnic origin, colour, religion, sex, age or mental or physical disability.

# OFFICIAL LANGUAGES

## Official languages of Canada

16. (1) English and French are the official languages of Canada and have equality of status and equal rights and privileges as to their use in all institutions of the Parliament and government of Canada.

## Official languages of New Brunswick

(2) English and French are the official languages of New Brunswick and have equality of status and equal rights and privileges as to their use in all institutions of the legislature and government of New Brunswick.

## Advancement of status and use

(3) Nothing in this Charter limits the authority of Parliament or a legislature to advance the equality of status or use of English and French.

## English and French linguistic communities in New Brunswick

16.1. (1) The English linguistic community and the French linguistic community in New Brunswick have equality of status and equal rights and privileges, including the right to distinct educational institutions and such distinct cultural institutions as are necessary for the preservation and promotion of those communities.

# Role of the legislature and government of New Brunswick

(2) The role of the legislature and government of New Brunswick to preserve and promote the status, rights and privileges referred to in subsection (1) is affirmed.

# Proceedings of Parliament

17. (1) Everyone has the right to use English or French in any debates and other proceedings of Parliament.

# Proceedings of New Brunswick legislature

(2) Everyone has the right to use English or French in any debates and other proceedings of the legislature of New Brunswick.

# Parliamentary statutes and records

18. (1) The statutes, records and journals of Parliament shall be printed and published in English and French and both language versions are equally authoritative.

# New Brunswick statutes and records

(2) The statutes, records and journals of the legislature of New Brunswick shall be printed and published in English and French and both language versions are equally authoritative.

# Proceedings in courts established by Parliament

19. (1) Either English or French may be used by any person in, or in any pleading in or process issuing from, any court established by Parliament.

# Proceedings in New Brunswick courts

(2) Either English or French may be used by any person in, or in any pleading in or process issuing from, any court of New Brunswick.

## Communications by public with federal institutions

20. (1) Any member of the public in Canada has the right to communicate with, and to receive available services from, any head or central office of an institution of the Parliament or government of Canada in English or French, and has the same right with respect to any other office of any such institution where

(a) there is a significant demand for communications with and services from that office in such language; or

(b) due to the nature of the office, it is reasonable that communications with and services from that office be available in both English and French.

## Communications by public with New Brunswick institutions

(2) Any member of the public in New Brunswick has the right to communicate with, and to receive available services from, any office of an institution of the legislature or government of New Brunswick in English or French.

## Continuation of existing constitutional provisions

21. Nothing in sections 16 to 20 abrogates or derogates from any right, privilege or obligation with respect to the English and French languages, or either of them, that exists or is continued by virtue of any other provision of the Constitution of Canada.

## Rights and privileges preserved

22. Nothing in sections 16 to 20 abrogates or derogates from any legal or customary right or privilege acquired or enjoyed either before or after the coming into force of this Charter with respect to any language that is not English or French.

# MINORITY LANGUAGE EDUCATIONAL RIGHTS

## Language of instruction

23. (1) Citizens of Canada

(a) whose first language learned and still understood is that of the English or French linguistic minority population of the province in which they reside, or

(b) who have received their primary school instruction in Canada in English or French and reside in a province where the language in which they received that instruction is the language of the English or French linguistic minority population of the province, have the right to have their children receive primary and secondary school instruction in that language in that province.

## Continuity of language instruction

(2) Citizens of Canada of whom any child has received or is receiving primary or secondary school instruction in English or French in Canada, have the right to have all their children receive primary and secondary school instruction in the same language.

## Application where numbers warrant

(3) The right of citizens of Canada under subsections (1) and (2) to have their children receive primary and secondary school instruction in the language of the English or French linguistic minority population of a province

(a) applies wherever in the province the number of children of citizens who have such a right is sufficient to warrant the provision to them out of public funds of minority language instruction; and

(b) includes, where the number of those children so warrants, the right to have them receive that instruction in minority language educational facilities provided out of public funds.

# ENFORCEMENT

## Enforcement of guaranteed rights and freedoms

24. (1) Anyone whose rights or freedoms, as guaranteed by this Charter, have been infringed or denied may apply to a court of competent jurisdiction to obtain such remedy as the court considers appropriate and just in the circumstances.

## Exclusion of evidence bringing administration of justice into disrepute

(2) Where, in proceedings under subsection (1), a court concludes that evidence was obtained in a manner that infringed or denied any rights or freedoms guaranteed by this Charter, the evidence shall be excluded if it is established that, having regard to all the circumstances, the admission of it in the proceedings would bring the administration of justice into disrepute.

# GENERAL

## Aboriginal rights and freedoms not affected by Charter

25. The guarantee in this Charter of certain rights and freedoms shall not be construed so as to abrogate or derogate from any aboriginal, treaty or other rights or freedoms that pertain to the aboriginal peoples of Canada including

(a) any rights or freedoms that have been recognized by the Royal Proclamation of October 7, 1763; and

(b) any rights or freedoms that now exist by way of land claims agreements or may be so acquired.

## Other rights and freedoms not affected by Charter

26. The guarantee in this Charter of certain rights and freedoms shall not be construed as denying the existence of any other rights or freedoms that exist in Canada.

## Multicultural heritage

27. This Charter shall be interpreted in a manner consistent with the preservation and enhancement of the multicultural heritage of Canadians.

## Rights guaranteed equally to both sexes

28. Notwithstanding anything in this Charter, the rights and freedoms referred to in it are guaranteed equally to male and female persons.

## Rights respecting certain schools preserved

29. Nothing in this Charter abrogates or derogates from any rights or privileges guaranteed by or under the Constitution of Canada in respect of denominational, separate or dissentient schools.

## Application to territories and territorial authorities

30. A reference in this Charter to a Province or to the legislative assembly or legislature of a province shall be deemed to include a reference to the Yukon Territory and the Northwest Territories, or to the appropriate legislative authority thereof, as the case may be.

## Legislative powers not extended

31. Nothing in this Charter extends the legislative powers of any body or authority.

# APPLICATION OF CHARTER

## Application

32. (1) This Charter applies

    (a) to the Parliament and government of Canada in respect of all matters within the authority of Parliament including all matters relating to the Yukon Territory and Northwest Territories; and

    (b) to the legislature and government of each province in respect of all matters within the authority of the legislature of each province.

## Exception

(2) Notwithstanding subsection (1), section 15 shall not have effect until three years after this section comes into force.

## Exception where express declaration

33. (1) Parliament or the legislature of a province may expressly declare in an Act of Parliament or of the legislature, as the case may be, that the Act or a provision thereof shall operate notwithstanding a provision included in section 2 or sections 7 to 15 of this Charter.

## Operation of exception

(2) An Act or a provision of an Act in respect of which a declaration made under this section is in effect shall have such operation as it would have but for the provision of this Charter referred to in the declaration.

## Five-year limitation

(3) A declaration made under subsection (1) shall cease to have effect five years after it comes into force or on such earlier date as may be specified in the declaration.

## Re-enactment

(4) Parliament or the legislature of a province may re-enact a declaration made under subsection (1).

## Five-year limitation

(5) Subsection (3) applies in respect of a re-enactment made under subsection (4).

# CITATION

34. This Part may be cited as the Canadian Charter of Rights and Freedoms.

# RESEARCH SOURCES AND FURTHER READING

*Note:* The most succinct and detailed guides to the handling of physical evidence are the bulletins issued by the RCMP Forensic Identification Research and Review Section, and a completely updated RCMP *Laboratory Service Manual*, both of which are absolute necessities for those specializing in forensic identification. The *Manual* contains sections on the collection, packaging, and analysis of all types of physical evidence, and the bulletins provide updates on procedures and processes. For quick general reference, consult: *Crime Scene Techniques*, compiled by the Canadian Police College Forensic Training Unit with the collaboration of the Forensic Identification Research and Review Section and the Centre of Forensic Science, Toronto, Ontario; and the most recent edition of *Investigator's Guide to Forensic Evidence*, produced by the Royal Canadian Mounted Police Public Affairs and Information Directorate, Minister of Supply and Services, Canada.

Anderson, Gail S., John J. Gaudet, and A. Brian Yamashita, "A Practical Exercise in Forensic Entomology," *RCMP Gazette*, 58(9): 1996, 3–6.

Arcaro, Gino, *Criminal Investigation: Forming Reasonable Grounds*, Port Colborne, Ontario: Jordan Publications, Inc., 1994.

Archer, Katrina, "3D Craniofacial Reconstruction," Master's thesis, August 1998, University of British Columbia, accessed April 25, 2000 <http://katrina.ganache.org/thesis.html>.

Ashbaugh, D. R., "Poroscopy," *Identification News*, November 1982.

Baldwin, Hayden W., "Basic Equipment for Crime Scene Investigators," 1999, unpublished.

Batey, G., J. Copeland, D. Donnelly, C. Hill, P. Laturnus, C. McDiarmid, K. Miller, A. Misner, A. Tario, and A. Yamashita, "Metal Deposition for Latent Print Development," *Journal of Forensic Identification*, 48(2) (March-April 1998): 165–180.

Bellefeuille, Julie, Kathy Bowen, Della Wilkinson, and Brian Yamashita, "Crime Scene Protocols for DNA Evidence," *Bulletin No. 45 (April 1999)*. Ottawa: RCMP Forensic Identification Research and Review Section and the Centre of Forensic Science.

Bennett, Wayne W., and Karen M. Hess, *Criminal Investigation,* 5th ed. Belmont, California: Wadsworth Publishing Company, 1998.

Bolhouse, Roger J., and L.A. Nause, "Tires and Computers," *Royal Canadian Mounted Police Gazette*, 52(1) (1990): 1–11.

Brant, Merrill, "Determining the Distance of Gunshot Wounds to the Head by Appearance and Physical Evidence," *Journal of Forensic Identification*, 48(2) (March-April 1998): 33–46.

Canadian Firearms Centre Web site, accessed June 21, 2000 <http://www.cfc-ccaf.gc.ca/>.

"Canadian Firearms Registry (CFR)," Royal Canadian Mounted Police Web site, accessed June 21, 2000 <http://www.rcmp-grc.gc.ca/html/cfr.htm>.

Canadian Police College Web site, February 10, 2000, accessed June 21, 2000 <http://www.cpc.gc.ca/>.

Canadian Police College, *Crime Scene Techniques.* Compiled by Canadian Police College Forensic Training Unit with the collaboration of the Forensic Identification Research and Review Section and the Centre of Forensic Science, Toronto, Ontario.

Carter, David L., "Computer Crime Categories: How Techno-Criminals Operate," *FBI Law Enforcement Bulletin*, July 1995: 21–25.

Cheeseman, Rob, "Direct Sensitivity Comparison of the Fluorescein and Luminol Bloodstain Enhancement Techniques," *Journal of Forensic Identification*, 49(3) (May-June 1999): 246–256.

"Crime Scene & Forensic Links," Gloucester County, New Jersey—Prosecutor's Office Web site, May 12, 2000, accessed June 20, 2000 <http://www.co.gloucester.nj.us/pros/crime.htm>.

"Criminal Code," Consolidated Statutes of Canada, Department of Justice Web site, August 31, 1999, accessed June 26, 2000 <http://canada.justice.gc.ca/cgi-bin/folioisa.dll/estats.nfo/query=*/doc/ (t34070}?>.

Deangelis, Francis Joseph, *Criminalistics for the Investigator.* New York: Macmillan Publishing Co., Inc., 1980.

DeMont, Philip, and Jill Vardy, "Leaving Them Hanging: Law Enforcement Software," *Financial Post*, 91(20) (May 17 1997): 16.

DePresca, John, "Handling Crime Scene Evidence," *Law and Order,* August 1997: 75–79.

Deutscher, David, and Heather Leonoff, *Identification Evidence*. Scarborough, Ont.: Thomson Professional Publishing, 1991.

Dukelow, Daphne A., and Betsy Nuse, *The Dictionary of Canadian Law*, 2nd ed. Scarborough, Ont.: Carswell, 1995.

Eckert, William G. (ed.), *Introduction to Forensic Sciences,* 2nd ed. Boca Raton, Florida: CRC Press, Inc., 1997.

Farley, M. A., and James Harrington, *Forensic DNA Technology*. Chelsea, Michigan: Lewis Publishers, Inc., 1991.

Fischer, John F., "Forensic Light Sources and Their Application to Tire and Shoe Examination." Unpublished manuscript. Orlando, Florida: Orange County Sheriff's Office.

Fisher, Barry A. J., *Techniques of Crime Scene Investigation,* 5th ed. Boca Raton, Florida: CRC Press, Inc., 1992.

"Forensic Document Examination: Scientific Tools for Detecting Fraud," American Society of Questioned Document Examiners [handwriting experts] Home Page, June 19, 2000, accessed June 20, 2000 <http://www.asqde.org/hart6.htm>.

Fryatt, Arthur, "Detecting Toxic Contaminants Within Human Hair," *RCMP Gazette*, 58(7&8) (1996): 18–19.

Garrison, Dean H., "Protecting the Crime Scene," *FBI Law Enforcement Bulletin*, September 1994.

Geberth, Vernon J., "The Signature Aspect in Criminal Investigation," *Law and Order*, November 1995: 45–49.

Geberth, Vernon J., *Practical Homicide Investigation: Tactics, Procedures, and Forensic Techniques*, 3rd ed. Boca Raton, Florida: CRC Press, Inc., 1996.

Glattstein, Baruch, Lior Nedivi, and Joseph Almog, "Detection of Firearms Imprints on Hands by the Ferrotrace Spray: Profiles of Some Common Weapons," *Journal of Forensic Identification*, 48(3) (May-June 1998): 257–272.

Griffiths, Anthony J. F., Jeffrey H. Miller, David T. Suzuki, Richard Lewontin, and William M. Gelbart, *An Introduction to Genetic Analysis,* 6th ed. New York: W. H. Freeman and Company, 1996.

Harris, Grant T., and Marnie E. Rice, "A Typology of Mentally Disordered Firesetters," *Journal of Interpersonal Violence*, 11 (September 1996): 351–363.

Hill, Robert M., "Document Dating via the Internet," *Journal of Forensic Identification*, 49(2) (March-April 1999): 114–116.

Jackson, Donna M., *The Bone Detectives: How Forensic Anthropologists Solve Crimes and Uncover Mysteries of the Dead*. Toronto, Ontario: Little, Brown and Company, 1996.

James, Stuart H., and William G. Eckert, *Interpretation of Bloodstain Evidence,* 2nd ed. Boca Raton, Florida: CRC Press, 1999.

Juby, T. C., "Forensic Identification of Snowmobile Tracks," *Bulletin No. 42 (November 1994).* Ottawa, RCMP Forensic Identification Research and Review Section and the Centre of Forensic Science.

Kaye, Brian H., *Science and the Detective.* New York: VCH, 1995.

Kirby, Lorne T., *DNA Fingerprinting: An Introduction.* New York: W. H. Freeman and Company, 1992.

Kramer, Robert, "Crime Scene Searches," *All Officers Bulletin.* Cedar Falls, Iowa: Police Division, November 1998.

"Laws of Canada," Department of Justice Canada Web site, March 17, 2000, accessed June 20, 2000 <http://canada.justice.gc.ca/loireg/index_en.html>.

Leadbetter, Martin J., "Use of Automated Fingerprint Identification Systems to Process, Search and Identify Palm Prints and Latent Palm Marks," *Journal of Forensic Identification*, 49(1) (January-February 1999): 18–36.

"Links for Chapter 4: The Police," A Web Resource for Students and Instructors Using *Canadian Criminal Justice: A Primer* by Alison Hatch Cunningham and Curt Taylor Griffiths (1997), September 30, 1999, accessed June 20, 2000 <http://www.cjprimer.com/links4.htm>.

MacDonell, Herbert Leon, *Bloodstain Patterns,* rev. ed. Corning, New York: Laboratory of Forensic Science, 1997.

Mann, Robert W., and Douglas H. Ubelaker, "The Forensic Anthropologist," *FBI Law Enforcement Bulletin*, July 1990.

McKenna, Paul F., *Foundations of Policing in Canada.* Scarborough, Ontario: Prentice-Hall Canada Inc., 1998.

Miller, Kevin, "Blood Reagents—Their Use and Their Effect on DNA," *Bulletin No. 42 (November 1, 1998).* Ottawa: RCMP Forensic Identification Research and Review Section and the Centre of Forensic Science.

Morin, Sgt. Paul, *RCMP Fingerprint Manual*, unpublished Canadian Police College manual.

"Oil Analysis Methodology," United States Coast Guard, Research & Development Center—Marine Safety Laboratory Web site, May 30, 2000, accessed June 20, 2000 <http://www.rdc.uscg.mil/mslpages/method.html>.

Pascua, Corazon S., and E. Roland Menzel, "Fluorescence Detection of Latent Fingerprints: Direct Entry to AFIS," *Journal of Forensic Identification*, 49(1) (January-February 1999): 11–17.

Pilant, Louis, "Equipping a Forensics Lab," *The Police Chief*, September 1992: 37–47.

Rathbun, Ted A., and Jane E. Buikstra, *Human Identification: Case Studies in Forensic Anthropology.* Springfield, Illinois: Charles C. Thomas, 1984.

RCMP Forensic Laboratory Services Directorate Web site, accessed June 21, 2000 <http://www.rcmp-grc.gc.ca/html/labs.htm>.

"RCMP Web Index," Royal Canadian Mounted Police Web site, accessed June 20, 2000 <http://www.rcmp-grc.gc.ca/html/tableof.htm>.

Royal Canadian Mounted Police Web site, accessed June 20, 2000 <http://www.rcmp-grc.gc.ca/html/rcmp2.htm>.

Royal Canadian Mounted Police, *Investigator's Guide to Forensic Evidence*, 2nd ed. Royal Canadian Mounted Police Public Affairs and Information Directorate, Minister of Supply and Services, Canada, 1995.

Saferstein, Richard (ed.), *Forensic Science Handbook,* 3 vols. Englewood Cliffs, New Jersey: Regents/Prentice Hall, 1993.

Saferstein, Richard, *Criminalistics: An Introduction to Forensic Science,* 6th ed. Upper Saddle River, New Jersey: Prentice Hall, 1998.

Salhany, Roger E., *A Basic Guide to Evidence in Criminal Cases,* 3rd ed. Scarborough, Ontario: Carswell, 1994.

Schiro, George, "Protecting the Crime Scene," University of California, Riverside Police Department Web site, accessed April 25, 2000 <http://police2.ucr.edu/evidenc1.htm>.

Skinner, M., and Richard A. Lazenby, *Found! Human Remains: A Field Study for the Recovery of the Recent Human Skeleton.* Burnaby, British Columbia: Archeology Press, Simon Fraser University, 1983.

Taylor, R.M.S., *Variation in Morphology of Teeth: Anthropologic and Forensic Aspects.* Springfield, Illinois: Charles C. Thomas.

Wallace, Harvey, *Victimology: Legal, Psychological, and Social Perspectives.* Needham Heights, Massachusetts: Allyn and Bacon, 1998.

Weston, Paul B., and Kenneth M. Wells, *Criminal Investigation: Basic Perspectives,* 7th ed. Upper Saddle River, New Jersey: Prentice Hall, 1997.

Wilkinson, Della, "Common Chemical Techniques Used for Latent Fingerprint Detection," *Bulletin No. 40 (October 1997).* Ottawa, RCMP Forensic Identification Research and Review Section and the Centre of Forensic Science.

Wolff, Doreen, Robert Kennedy, Earl Lounsbury, Gus MacMaster, Ken Olthuis, David Sweet, Al Tutt, and Brian Yamashita, "Dental Casting Materials for the Recovery of Toolmark Impressions," *Bulletin No. 43 (November 1998).* Ottawa, RCMP Forensic Identification Research and Review Section and the Centre of Forensic Science.

Zeno Geradts, Zeno's Forensic Site: Information on Forensic Science, June 12, 2000, accessed June 21, 2000 <http://forensic.to/forensic.html>.

Zonderman, Jon, *Beyond the Crime Lab: The New Science of Investigation.* New York: John Wiley and Sons, 1990.

# Index

Striations, 149
Strip search pattern, 38
Sulfur casts, 110
Summary conviction offence, 74
Suspect
  avoid path of, 10
  examining residence for evidence, 71, 72
  handling at crime scene, 12

**T**
Teeth marks, 134–39
Test impression, 24
  fingerprint powder and adhesive lifter, 112
  toner powder, 112
  cooking oils and magnetic powder, 111–12
  dust, 113
  footprints, 110–13
  inked, 111
  tires, 120–21
Testifying in court
  arguments, 255
  biases, 254
  common difficulties, 254–56
  organization, 254
  role of witness, 253–54
  uncertainty, 255
  understanding questions, 256
Testimonial evidence, defined, 13
Tests
  blood identification, 165
Textiles, 196
Three-dimensional impressions, 100
  casting, 107–10
  test impressions, 110
3R Rule, 200
Time of death, estimating, 54
  forensic pathologists, 59–61
Tire impressions, 13, 115–28
  class characteristics, 115
  comparing, 121, 123
  crime-scene, 119–20
  direction of travel, determining, 123–24
  measurement of, 124–26
  research data available, 126
  vehicle searches, 124–26
Tire treads, 116–17
  arc width, 116
  blades, 116
  elements, 116
  grooves, 116
  noise treatment, 117, 121
  ribs, 116
  sipes, 116
  stud holes, 116
  tread wear indicators, 116
  wearbars, 116

Tires, composition of, 115–17
  beads, 115
  carcass, 115
  liner, 115
  plies, 115
  shoulder, 115
  sidewalls, 115, 117
  tread, 115, 116
Tire wear, characteristics, 119
  abrasions, 119
  camber wear, 119
  chunk-outs, 119
  cupping, 119
  cuts, 119
  incorrect inflation, 119
  skid depth, 119
  stoneholding, 119
  tears, 119
  toe-in, toe-out, 119
  tread measure, 119
Tool impressions, 128–32
  casting, 129–30
Tool mark
  compression marks, 128
  defined, 128
  evidence, seizing, 129
  matching problems, 128
  scraping marks, 128
  shearing, 128
Tool testing, 130–31
  ACE problems, 131–32
Toxicologist, 61
Toxicology, 61–62
Trace metal detection, 161–62
Trace Metal Detection Technique, 162
Tracs Searches database, 126
Trace atmospheric gas analyzer (TAGA), 235
Trace evidence, defined, 13
Transient evidence, defined, 13–14
Triangulation sketches, 41
Twain, Mark, 5
Two-dimensional impressions, 100
  enhancement, 102–103
  invisible impressions, 103
  lifting, 103
  footwear, developing, 102
  visible, 102–103
Typewriters, 250–51

**U**
Ultraviolet light, 69
United States, 4
Unreasonable search or seizure, 260–61
Urine, 174